DIVERSITY IN HIGHER EDUCATION   VOLUME 4

BEYOND SMALL NUMBERS: VOICES OF AFRICAN AMERICAN PhD CHEMISTS

BY

WILLIE PEARSON, Jr.

Georgia Technical Institute, Atlanta, USA

D1068343

2005

ELSEVIER
JAI

Amsterdam – Boston – Heidelberg – London – New York – Oxford
Paris – San Diego – San Francisco – Singapore – Sydney – Tokyo

ELSEVIER B.V.
Radarweg 29
P.O. Box 211
1000 AE Amsterdam
The Netherlands

ELSEVIER Inc.
525 B Street, Suite 1900
San Diego
CA 92101-4495
USA

ELSEVIER Ltd
The Boulevard, Langford
Lane, Kidlington
Oxford OX5 1GB
UK

ELSEVIER Ltd
84 Theobalds Road
London
WC1X 8RR
UK

First edition 2005

British Library Cataloguing in Publication Data
A catalogue record is available from the British Library.

ISBN: 0-7623-0562-2
ISSN: 1479-3644 (Series)   MAR   2008

⊗ The paper used in this publication meets the requirements of ANSI/NISO Z39.48-1992 (Permanence of Paper). Printed in The Netherlands.

BEYOND SMALL NUMBERS: VOICES OF AFRICAN AMERICAN PhD CHEMISTS

DIVERSITY IN HIGHER EDUCATION

Series Editor: Henry T. Frierson

TO

Cheryl and the men and women who entrusted me to give voice to their biographies.

CONTENTS

viii

ABOUT THE AUTHOR

The author is Professor of Sociology and Chair, School of History, Technology, and Society, Georgia Institute of Technology. Dr. Pearson is the author of six books and monographs and numerous chapters. He has published numerous articles in referee journals. Among his books and monographs related to the topic discussed here are: *Black Scientists White Society and Colorless Science: A study of Universalism in American Science; African Americans, Education and American Science* (Co-Edited with H. K. Bechtel); *Who Will Do Sciences? Educating the Next Generation* (Co-edited with Alan Fechter); *The Role and Activities of American Graduate Schools in Recruiting, Enrolling, and Retaining United States Black and Hispanic Students* (with Gail Thomas and Beatriz C. Clewell) and *Scientists and Engineers for the New Millennium* (Co-edited with Daryl Chubin).

LIST OF FIGURES

LIST OF TABLES

FOREWORD

I am pleased to have been asked by Dr. Willie Pearson, Jr., to write the foreword to *Beyond Small Numbers: Voices of African American Ph.D. Chemists*. The field of chemistry has held particular appeal to African Americans since the early twentieth century. The lives of the first African American doctoral chemists provide a backdrop on the African American experience of the time. Dr. Pearson has interviewed a notable number of African American Ph.D. holders and gained considerable insight into the factors that shaped their professional experiences.

To assist the reader in understanding careers of African American doctoral degree holders in chemistry, Dr. Pearson has separated the interviewees into groups based on when the Ph.D. was awarded. The delineation of the groupings was dictated by periods of significant change in legislation affecting African Americans. From my vantage point as a "Cohort II" member (see text), it is my belief that the most important legislation that led to a significant increase in the number of African American Ph.D. chemists made possible access to better educational opportunity and employment alternatives. These were the civil rights laws that promoted affirmative action. Before affirmative action, there were very few opportunities for an African American doctorate holder in chemistry as contrasted to the range of alternatives available to white counterparts.

The basis for choice and type of college at the undergraduate level, i.e., historically black college or university or predominantly white college or university, reasons for attending graduate school, and sector of employment following the doctorate are cohort dependent and say much about opportunities for African Americans during the various cohort periods. The importance of historically black colleges and universities for the early cohorts is described. Historically black colleges and universities have served not only as places for education, but as places of employment for those individuals seeking teaching opportunities. The absence of opportunity in predominantly white colleges and universities for the early cohorts and the small number even today of African Americans holding tenured positions in these institutions is a major concern especially in view of the comparatively large number of African Americans who have earned Ph.D.s in the past decade.

The professional experiences of the subject group in historically black colleges and universities and predominantly white colleges and universities were found to differ notably owing to the availability of resources leading to, for example, lighter teaching loads in the major research predominantly white colleges and universities as contrasted to historically black colleges and universities requirements. The predominantly white colleges and universities professional experience carried its own burden for some that included feelings of isolation, and lack of collegial support that led, in some instances, to the decision to leave academe.

Some of the individuals in later cohorts who had the option of choosing industrial and government employment also encountered difficulties of not being valued and recognized for their contributions. This is reflected in descriptions of not easily remedied employment dissatisfaction.

As an aside, I found it interesting as an indicator of the variation in the subject group that many of my experiences were atypical for the chemists interviewed. I was born in the Midwest – most were born in the South. I attended a predominantly white university as an undergraduate – most attended a historically black college or university, and I worked in all sectors of the economy – academia, industry, and government – most remained in one sector for their careers. Like many of those interviewed, however, I was encouraged by my parents to attend college and decided on chemistry as a career direction based on my enthusiasm for the subject. I experienced many of the challenges described in the book in a number of environments in which on occasion, similar to others, I was the only African American. The experiences described call attention to the instances of support that some found and, in some instances, the lack of support in other circumstances that appear to have their origin in race.

Dr. Pearson has written a compelling volume on the careers of African American doctorate holders in chemistry. He provides documentation that makes possible a critical assessment of the circumstances that governed the experiences of those African Americans who obtained the Ph.D. in chemistry since the beginning of the twentieth century. The information he gathered goes beyond simply statistics to indepth interviews that yield information not previously available in demographic studies of Black scientists. From such data, Dr. Pearson is able to provide new insight on factors that influenced the choice of chemistry as a career. He includes discussion of the variability of these factors as they impacted the lives of the individuals interviewed for this volume.

Dr. Pearson has made a major contribution to the understanding of the issues that have confronted Ph.D. African Americans in chemistry that I feel certain will have value for persons in other disciplines. There are key findings and resultant policy implications that arise from his analysis. For example, clearly identified is the importance of early education in mathematics and science, which calls attention to the need for excellence in teaching these subjects at the elementary school level. Another aspect that emerges is the impact of mentoring by a teacher or some other individual. The significant benefit is the reinforcement in the young person's mind that he/she is good at chemistry and therefore that it could be a field for further study or even one's life work. There are also policy implications that Dr. Pearson presents that have value for all sectors of employment in chemistry and other areas where technical capability at the highest level is needed. This volume should be required reading for decision-makers in industry, government, academe, and the science organizations. It also has significant historical value.

William A. Lester, Jr.

PREFACE

Writing in the late 1930s, eminent historian Carter G. Woodson (1939) opined that historians rarely mentioned scientific and technical achievements except those in Asia or Europe. He asserted that the Chinese were recognized for inventing printing, gunpowder, and the mariner's compass, but the general public is not informed that Africans discovered and refined iron. Woodson pointed out that seldom is the public informed that the Benin and other Africans learned to cast artistic bronze figures from clay molds built over wax forms or that the San People knew enough chemistry to poison their arrows to kill game without spoiling the flesh of the animal.

Despite more than a century's presence among Ph.D. scientists, there have been few empirical studies that focus on the career experiences of African American Ph.D. scientists (Pearson, 1985; Williams, 1981; Young & Young, 1974). Even less is known about African American Ph.D. chemists (Ferguson, 1949; Geiser, 1935; *Industrial Trends*, 1949; Pearson, 1996; Young & Young, 1976). Besides general biographic accounts of the careers of a few well-known African American chemists (Haber, 1970; Klein, 1971), little is known about the majority of African Americans who earned their doctorates in chemistry after 1916 (Downing, 1938, 1939; Greene, 1946; Hawkins, 1982; Julian, 1969; Massie, 1982; Meier, 1982; Rawls, 1991). This book seeks to contribute to the literature on this segment of the American scientific community by providing insight into the factors that affect the careers of African American Ph.D. chemists.

This book is organized in seven major chapters. The first chapter addresses the historical presence of African Americans in the chemistry community. The second chapter discusses the demographic characteristics of the responding chemists. The third focuses on the interviewees' educational experiences. The fourth chapter discusses workforce-related issues. The fifth chapter discusses professional activities, while the sixth chapter focuses on racial attitudes. The final chapter discusses the implications of the findings for policy and research.

Completion of this book required the able assistance of many individuals whose contributions were of immense importance. In particular, I am indebted to the late Lloyd M. Cooke who first kindled my interest in the careers of African Americans who earned their doctorates in chemistry before the 1954 Brown decision.

I am grateful to the 44 men and women who consented to share their stories. Their experiences provide critical insight into efforts to understand the effects of race on scientific careers. I owe a great deal of gratitude to a number of individuals who have read various drafts of the manuscript, provided biographical, bibliographical and tabular materials, and expert advice. Among these are: Joan Burrelli and Susan T. Hill, Science Resources Statistics Division, National Science Foundation; Terry Russell, Association of Institutional Research; Daryl Chubin, AAAS; Beatriz C. Clewell, Urban Institute; Eleanor Babco, Commission on Professions on Scientific and Technology; Alison Williams, Princeton University; Sharon Haynie, Dupont; Henry Blount, Mathematics and Physical Sciences Directorate, National Science Foundation; and Marge Cavanaugh, Office of the Director, National Science Foundation.

A special mention of appreciation is due to former National Science Foundation Program Officers: Ronald Overmann and Edward Hackett (Science, Technology and Society) and current National Science Foundation Program Director, Larry E. Suter, Division of Research, Evaluation and Communication. To Henry Frierson, Jr., the series editor, I am especially indebted for his encouragement, support, and expert critiques throughout the completion of the book.

A vital part of this project involved undergraduate students. A number of former Wake Forest University undergraduate students made substantial contributions to the project. Among the students who contributed many hours of research, clerical, and technical assistance are: Jennifer Grishkin, Emily Hoban, Craig Ness, Tenika Rudisell, Omari Simmons, LaMaya Covington and Charles Goodman. At Georgia Tech, LaDonna Bowen, Denise Corum, Steven Henderson, Prakash Kumar and Nyema Mitchell played roles in reviewing and/or typing the manuscript. This publication was supported, in part, by grants from the National Science Foundation (SRB 9222547 and a supplemental award from REC/EHR). The project benefited enormously from the administrative assistance of Claudia Colhoun who transcribed the taped interviews and typed the drafts of the manuscript. Finally, I thank Cheryl B. Leggon for providing encouragement and a supportive environment throughout the duration of the project. I, of course, take full responsibility for any deficiencies in the final product.

Willie Pearson, Jr.

THE AFRICAN AMERICAN PRESENCE IN THE AMERICAN CHEMISTRY COMMUNITY: A BRIEF HISTORY

The American ghetto and the American brand of apartheid made the African American with genuine scientific talent and scientific yearnings probably the most poignantly tragic intellectual schizophrenic of the first half of the twentieth century. The inviolate seclusion of the laboratory was never vouchsafed to him, even for a few hours a day. The problems of the ghetto trespass mercilessly upon his "scientific privacy." He was expected, strangely enough by his colleagues of both races, to be a humanist by becoming involved in social problems, which no one expected of his white fellow scientists (Julian, 1969).

PRE-WORLD WAR I

Regardless of race or ethnicity, few scientists have made breakthrough discoveries (Cole & Cole, 1973; Zuckerman, 1977). Science is developed through the day-to-day activities of hundreds of hardworking and mostly little known men and women. African Americans in this group have a far lower profile than Whites. Their achievements have been underplayed, neglected, or ignored (Manning, 1983).

Around the turn of the twentieth century, a small cadre of African American scientists who received Ph.D.s from major research universities began to enter scientific fields. This group represents the first cohort of African Americans to pursue science at the research level. With the possible exception of George Washington Carver, most published in the leading scientific journals, and generally, their professional careers unfolded mainly at historically black colleges and universities. One of the few known exceptions was Julian Lewis, a pathologist who held a post at the University of Chicago, prior to World War II (Manning, 1983; Pearson, 1985).

1

WORLD WAR I

With the advent of World War I in the summer of 1914, the United States (U.S.) chemists and the chemical industry were propelled into the public arena. At the time, the Germans dominated the chemical industry. However, shipments of chemicals from Germany to the U.S. were thwarted by the British blockade. Consequently, several American Chemical Society (ACS) chapters called on U.S. chemical companies to expand production into dyestuffs, pharmaceuticals, and other organic chemicals. The war effort led to expansions in the steel and petroleum industries which stimulated growth in the production of coal-tar chemicals and petrochemicals that the chemical industry could convert to dyes, drugs, and other products. This lessened the dependence on Germany. The increased demand for explosives called for increased supplies of toluene, phenol and nitric acid (Skolnik & Reese, 1976).

By April 1915, Germany introduced gas warfare. In 1917, the Secretary of the Interior charged the Bureau of Mines with working on gas problems, and the Bureau engaged the Chemistry Committee of the National Research Council (NRC) to help initiate the work. The NRC Committee along with others in academe and the chemical industry constituted what ultimately became the Chemical Warfare Service of the U.S. Army. The gases and protective equipment were produced at Edgewood Arsenal in Maryland and New York City, respectively (Skolnik & Reese, 1976).

It was in the midst of this early expansion in the chemical industry that America produced its first known African American Ph.D. recipient. In 1916, St. Elmo Brady was awarded the doctorate in chemistry from the University of Illinois. Brady's career serves to illuminate early African American chemists' struggles to participate in American science. Born in Louisville, Kentucky, Brady was educated at predominantly black Fisk University (Nashville, Tennessee), where he received his A. B. degree in 1908. Five years later, he enrolled in the chemistry program at the University of Illinois, earning a Master's degree in 1914. By the time Brady earned his doctorate, he had published three abstracts (with C. G. Derrick) in *Science*, co-authored papers in the Journal of Engineering Chemistry, and presented papers at annual meetings of the American Chemical Society (*Crisis*, 1916; see also *The Morehouse Journal of Science*, 1928). Brady earned his doctorate during a period of violent acts of racism towards African Americans. Lynching and race riots were not uncommon.

In a treatise of Brady's career, Julian (1969) opines that Brady was blissfully ignorant of his future as an African American and a Ph.D. chemist. According to Julian, Brady's first postdoctoral appointment was Head of the Science Division at Tuskegee Institute. Julian indicates that at Tuskegee, Brady did not have colleagues with whom he could discuss his research ideas. Because of Jim Crow laws, he did not have access to the libraries and equipment of the better financed white colleges and universities in Alabama. Moreover, Tuskegee did not have the resources to provide adequate support for Brady's laboratory or library. Julian asserts that Brady had to purchase his own scientific journals. While acknowledging that Brady was needed at Tuskegee to educate the next generation of African Americans in science, Julian further contends that racial discrimination destroyed the possibility for Brady to be employed in an institution commensurate with his scientific education. Julian argues that had a major white university employed Brady, it would have done much to recruit African Americans to chemistry. However, Julian believes that Brady's doctoral professors lacked the vision and courage to secure an appropriate academic appointment for him. Julian further contends that Brady's advisors may have been unaware of the slow death of Brady's research creativity at the segregated and under-funded Tuskegee Institute. Julian opined that Brady's most talented students readily discerned his plight and chose careers in medicine, rather than chemistry.

From being only a small inorganic chemical industry at the turn of the century and far outstripped by Germany's organic chemistry industry through World War I, the U.S. chemical industry must now be reckoned among the great industrial forces of our times. By World War II, it had grown so strong that it was ready to challenge the Germans (Fortune, 1950).

The war brought a vast expansion of chemical plants in such special lines as explosives, synthetic rubber, and fixed nitrogen. However, the industry's role was largely to supply the managerial talent to build and operate some $3 billion in government war plants. Of particular note was the creation of a $1-billion synthetic-rubber industry. This was astonishing because it was accomplished in only two years. The industry also supplied much of the indispensable talent for building or operating another $1 billion worth of atomic-energy plants. Additionally, the industry increased its plant production. Within four years, the net result was an economic contribution of approximately $20 billion in basic chemicals, intermediates, dyes, solvents, drugs, resins, plastics, coatings, fibers, filaments, and the hundreds of other chemical products that now permeate industry. Most of this output resulted from devoting full capacity to purposes of supporting the war (Fortune, 1950).

During the decade of 1920–1929, no Americans were honored in chemistry, physiology, or medicine, but the Nobel prize in physics went to Robert Milliken in 1923 and to Arthur Compton (with the Englishman Charles Wilson) in 1927. Thereafter, U.S. scientists would receive about one of every three Nobel prizes in physiology, chemistry and medicine combined. The vitality of U.S. science was also found in the production of Ph.D.'s in chemistry from 1921 to 1930. During this decade, applied chemical research was directed more toward the modern practice of synthesizing new compounds and materials deliberately to fill industrial and consumer needs, as opposed to the previous focus on improving and lowering the cost of existing chemicals (Skolnik & Reese, 1976).

According to the historian Kenneth R. Manning (1993), nineteenth-century science not only defined race but actively promoted racism in America. He chronicled the role of science in creating, substantiating, promoting, and disseminating certain negative stereotypes of African Americans and how these views shaped Whites' perceptions of African Americans as well as African Americans' self perception. Manning examines how African American scientists related their work to their own self consciousness as African Americans, and their attempts to resolve the inevitable conflicts and tensions. As an enterprise, science was portrayed as unemotional and objective. As it related to the nature and potential of African Americans, science was almost universally damning. In a speech delivered at the 1913 annual meeting of the American Association for the Advancement of Science (AAAS) in Atlanta and published later in *Science* magazine, James McKeen Cattell, owner and editor of *Science* magazine, is reported to have said: "There is not a single mulatto who has done credible scientific work" (Cattell, 1914, p. 159). The notion that people of African descent were incapable of contributing significantly to science was easily perpetuated in the predominately white world of science, especially in the early twentieth century. Moreover, the scientific contributions of many African American went unrecognized. The social and psychological consequences were particularly pernicious during that period (Manning, 1993, p. 318).

Manning posits that although the theoretical basis for racial inferiority may have had its origins in theology, the onus for buttressing slavery and the peonage of a race was shared equally by science and religion. He opines that prominent nineteenth century naturalists such as George Cuvier, Charles Lyell, and Charles Darwin believed, in varying degrees, that African Americans were inferior to Whites. For example, Darwin and Lyell perceived African Americans as an intermediate species between simians and Caucasians, while Agassiz considered African Americans to be a separate species because of "their black faces with their thick lips and grimacing teeth" (Manning, 1993, p. 320). James Hunt's so-called scientific evidence purportedly showed that weight of a mulatto's brain weighed was intermediate between that of a pure black and a white – the latter, of course, being the heaviest (Manning, 1993). However, Cattell (1914, pp. 158–159) asserts that "mulattoes are by their physical heredity midway between the whites and the negroes, with parentage probably superior to the average in both races, but their social position is that of the negroes, and their performance corresponds with their environment rather than their heredity." This type of thinking, even among the scientific elite, was not atypical (see Gould, 1981).

The Eugenics Movement of the early twentieth century sought to breed "better" human beings by encouraging the reproduction of people with "good" genes and discouraging the reproduction of those with "bad" genes. The movement advocated the coercive sterilization of African Americans, because they were considered diseased and oversexed. Arguably, such ideas promoted, in part, racial fear among many whites and self-antipathy among many African Americans. Although these ideas persisted, the Eugenics Movement faded from the mainstream of American science following its adoption as a key social policy by the Nazis in the 1930s. In the 1960s and 1970s, however, Arthur Jensen, Richard Herrnstein, and William Shockley fostered considerable angst in the scientific community by attributing the difference in IQ scores between African Americans and Whites to genetic differences between the two groups (Gould, 1981; Manning, 1993).

African Americans were a relative rarity in basic science in the U.S. So rare, in fact, that many Whites considered them as encroachers who were out of their depth (Manning, 1993). During the early 1900s and for sometime thereafter, African American scientists practiced their science in an environment where they were under constant disparagement in both the scientific and larger communities. J. E. Wodsedalek (1916) is reported to have argued that chromosomal differences exist between the black and white races. He drew a specious analogy that "the Negro is fully as far removed from the white man as is the ass from the horse, where a great difference in the number of chromosomes apparently exists" (p. 13). He adds that "unfortunately the mulatto is fertile" (p. 13). Ernest E. Just, like Carver, appears to have failed to register a protest. Apparently, Just never commented – either favorably or disparagingly – on the work of eugenicists, like Wodsedalek. White scientists, such as Jacques Loeb, were able to express their outrage at Wodsedalek's remarks because the consequences for them were negligible. Such a response from Just may have resulted in professional suicide. Nevertheless, Just held firm to the principle that the term "Negro scientist" was vacuous and meaningless – except when intended (Manning, 1983). Around World War I, there was an explosion of scientific writings with a strong racialistic bias, rationalizing the growing feeling in America against African Americans (Myrdal, 1944). However, some black scientists did register protests (e.g. the physicist Elmer Imes and the chemist Percy Julian). The work of some African American scientists, William Augustus Hinton (1883–1959), for example, impinged on racial issues in oblique ways. A Harvard graduate and contemporary of Just, Hinton spent a great deal of his career outside of academia. He began his career as a pathologist and was subsequently appointed director of the Wasserman Laboratory, Massachusetts Department of Public Health. During the course of his career, Hinton made several major contributions to serology. In 1936, Hinton published *Syphilis and Its Treatment* which became a classic. His work on syphilis was in an area that medical authorities had always defined as being of special consequence to the black population (Manning, 1983; Schomberg Center, 1999).

Clearly, one of the earliest and most widely known African Americans in chemistry is George Washington Carver (1860–1943) who spent most of his career at Alabama's predominantly black Tuskegee Institute (now Tuskegee University). Many Americans' perceptions of a black scientist is probably George Washington Carver. Portrayals of Carver often focus on his humility, diligence, and manual dexterity. These characteristics were appealing to Whites because they were non-threatening and in many ways reinforced the stereotypes of African Americans. Perhaps for many white scientists, Carver "knew his place" and accepted it. Jenkins (1984) asserts that Carver never spoke out publicly on racial issues despite being subjected to demeaning and sometimes life-threatening experiences.

Carver is probably best known for his ability to convert plant products into a wealth of useful consumer products. For example, he is credited with producing around 165 different commodities from the sweet potato and some 135 compounds from peanut oil. Carver's success with products from these plants, as well as other scientific contributions has been cited as having played a key role in industrial development of the South (Atkins, 1949; Branson, 1955; Ferguson, 1949). Carver also created an "Agricultural Experimental Station" that focused on discoveries that would benefit the society's most needy (Jenkins, 1984).

There seems to be considerable agreement that Carver's scientific achievements (modest as they may have been in the eyes of white scientists) and recognition probably did more than many scholarly papers to stimulate interest in scientific work among African Americans. His contributions to science and the economic development of the South were considered by many (especially non-scientists) to be significant accomplishments. However, some students of science see Carver's contributions very differently. For example, many scholars tend to describe Carver's work as inventive, rather than scientifically creative; product-oriented, rather than pressing to new theoretical heights. Because it appears that he did not publish his research in scholarly journals, it is difficult to assess Carver's scholarly output in science. The late eminent physicist and educator, Herman Branson (1952, 1955), cautioned African Americans not to inflate their contributions to science. Historian Barry Mackintosh (1978, p. 507) questions the significance of Carver's scientific accomplishments. He argues, for example, that the "uses for soils and plants he developed or advocated were not of pioneering importance in science, nor were they widely adopted." Mackintosh asserts that Carver's contribution to science is difficult to measure or authenticate because "Carver left no formulas or other records of his processes beyond one patent for a cosmetic utilizing peanuts" (p. 510). He attributes the myth of Carver's "larger than life" image primarily to journalists, publicists, popular biographers and a few professional historians. Mackintosh claims that Carver's modest contributions to science served the "psychological and sociological purposes of both African Americans and whites." According to Macintosh, Carver's deferential manner to whites and strict accommodationist perspective on race relations appealed to whites, while he served as clear evidence debunking the notion that African Americans were incapable of the sort of abstract thinking necessary in science appealed to African Americans.

Branson (1955) was unable to document that Carver ever published in any scientific peer review journal. However, he did point out that there were African American contemparies of Carver who were making significant and documented contributions to science. A few African Americans (e.g. Ernest E. Just and Charles H. Turner) did conduct research at major laboratories, such as the Marine Biological Laboratory (MBL) at Woods Hole, Massachusetts. However, they often were confronted by the prevailing racial attitudes of the time. Specifically, Just and his family were subjected to racist incidents in both the scientific and non-scientific communities (Manning, 1983).

Branson identified biologists Charles H. Turner (1867–1923) and Ernest E. Just (1883–1941) as conducting cutting-edge research and publishing the results in the top scientific journals. Entomologist Turner (Ph.D. Chicago, 1907) specialized in the behavior and social organization of bees and ants. Despite having his career limited to racially segregated teaching environments, Turner is credited with publishing at least 49 articles in major peer reviewed journals. Additionally, he has the eponymous recognition – Turner's Circling – a behavior of bees.

Cell biologist Ernest E. Just (Ph.D. Chicago, 1916) published a number of significant papers in peer reviewed journals. He was considered one of the most eminent scientists of his time (Julian, 1969). Just was elected to a high level position in his primary scientific society. He was awarded a "star" in *American Men of Science* (now American *Men and Women in Science*) for his significant contributions to science. Like Turner, Just spent much of his career in a racially segregated academic setting – Howard University. In grappling with this problem, some black scientists focused on the positive and submerged the negative. Ernest E. Just believed that science had much to offer the black community. In his view, African Americans could benefit from science's "objective" approach as opposed to their typically emotional and intuitive outlook. They could gain insights into themselves – and into all the social forces that shaped and influenced their lives – if only they would lay out the facts and dissect them clinically, in microscopic detail. Ernest E. Just discerned that African Americans were too emotional which was not productive? Only through rigorous scientific methods could African Americans hope to determine their own future. For Ernest E. Just, "science could be a savior of black people, their road to an improved life" (Manning, 1983, p. 329).

Edwin R. Embree (1935), president of the Julius Rosenwald Fund said that: "Dr. E. E. Just of Howard University is not a great Negro biologist, he is a great biologist." When Ernest E. Just's work was cited by his peers, it was simply no different than for any other scientist. Moreover, publications by other African American scientists such as Moddie Taylor, Roger Arliner Young, Shiefflin Claytor, Henry C. McBay, Adolphus A. Milligan and Shirley Ann Jackson gave little or no clue as to the race of the author. White scientists who had never met Just, for example, would have had no way of telling from his work that he was African American – except perhaps his affiliation with Howard University, and even that was no clear indicator, because there were a number of white scholars at Howard (Logan, 1969; Winston, 1971). Because the work was judged on merit alone, science had a built-in basis for equal opportunity that inevitably appealed to African Americans aspiring to careers in the field. African American scientists could think of the scientific world as one where racism held no sway and where only the laws of nature governed (Manning, 1983).

Nonetheless, many African American scientists, Just included, noted a curious pattern over the course of their careers: that their work was cited more frequently in European than in American journals. This pattern of particularism was counter to the notion of objectivity. African American scientists were correct to assume that their relatively low rate of citation on one side of the Atlantic was related to their racial status. However, this is not to argue that European scientists were more accepting of African Americans. Rather they seemed to have had fewer ways than did white Americans of discerning race and, therefore, of acting on their prejudices. European scientists did not know the African American scientists personally, nor were they generally aware of predominantly black institutions (Manning, 1983, p. 332).

To escape the vestiges of race, some light complexioned African Americans became "white" by "passing." Although passing usually involves lighter complexioned African Americans, some of the darker ones pass by self-identifying as Filipinos, Spaniards, Italians or Mexicans (Conyers & Kennedy, 1963; Myrdal, 1944). Generally, passing occurs only for selected areas of life – such as the occupational or recreational; however, it can occur in all areas. Passing may be temporary or permanent, voluntary or involuntary; with or without knowledge on the part of the passer. Also, it may be individual or collective (Myrdal, 1944). One Cohort I interviewee described this experience with a colleague who was passing:

> I knew of a black chemist with a master's degree who was working in industry but he was passing as white. There were a lot of very fair blacks in_. He was passing as a white chemist at_Company in_(Northeast). I had a chance to talk to him about chemistry as a career. At the time, there were no opportunities for blacks in the sciences because industry didn't hire blacks. _only got his job because he was passing. He ran into a problem because of his passing.

He lived in a black neighborhood (because of residential segregation) with his black wife who was also from my hometown. When his white colleagues came to town and wanted to visit, he had a problem because he couldn't bring them to his home . . .

It is difficult to determine the extent of passing because many who have passed conceal it. In fact, some descendants of those who have passed permanently may be unaware of it themselves because their families purposely hid the knowledge from them. Passing is believed to be more common for men than for women. One explanation holds that passing usually involves economic advantages to African American males who must compete in a white man's world, but economic disadvantages for African American females who could get a white husband only from the lower classes, but possibly an African American husband from the upper classes (Myrdal, 1944).

By World War II, the United States' scientific enterprise was stronger than it had been a quarter of a century earlier. The utility of science in World War I had been impressed on many Americans through the popular press and the public information programs of scientific societies. Chemists, for example, had been publicized widely for their work on explosives, smoke screens, and war gases and the associated protective devices. More important in the long run, both government and industry had recognized the value of science in solving problems; both had begun to spend more liberally on research and development. Universities built more courses in the sciences into their curriculums. Between 1920 and 1940, for example, the number of industrial laboratories in the U.S. increased dramatically – from about 300 to 3,500. Also, their scientific staff rose from 9,000 to 70,000 (Skolnik & Reese, 1976).

The landmark achievement of the period, whether for good or for bad, was the discovery and harnessing of nuclear fission. In 1938, Otto Hahn and Fritz Strassmann at the Kaiser Wilhelm Institute were able to obtain a small amount of barium by bombarding uranium with neutrons. The energy produced in the reaction far exceeded that produced in any previous transmutation reaction. The Allies converted the discovery to the atomic bomb. Many of Europe's most eminent physicists already were refugees from Hitler's Europe. The Austrians Lise Meitner (one of Hahn's collaborators) and Otto Frisch were in Sweden; the Italian Enrico Fermi; the Hungarian Leo Szilard; and the German Albert Einstein were in the United States. In March 1939, when the Hahn-Strassmann results became known, Fermi tried but was unsuccessful in convincing the Navy Department of the importance of atomic fission. Later, Alexander Sachs and Leo Szilard drafted a letter describing the potential of the phenomenon signed by Einstein and delivered to the President by Sachs on October 11, 1939. In February 1940, $6000 was provided to begin research on a bomb (Skolnik & Reese, 1976).

WORLD WAR II

After 1940, science increasingly came to be more closely dependent on industry and government, particularly in military-related research. The project took on added significance when Japan attacked Pearl Harbor on December 7, 1941. In January 1942, a schedule was developed to have a bomb ready within three years. In June 1942, the War Department organized the Manhattan District to lead the project. Glenn T. Seaborg and his team devised a means of isolating plutonium from fission products and uranium. On August 20, 1942, the team isolated the first visible quantity of the element. Harold C. Urey of Columbia University was working on the gaseous diffusion process for enriching uranium; at the University of Virginia and Standard Oil Co. (N. J.) scientists were investigating the centrifuge method for the same purpose; E. O. Lawrence and his colleagues at Berkeley were studying electromagnetic methods for extracting uranium-235 and plutonium. Meanwhile, facilities were under construction at Oak Ridge (Tennessee), Hanford (Washington), and (Los Alamos) New Mexico. The sites represented the manufacturing sites for specific phases of the project. The Du Pont Company was charged with designing, building, and operating the Hanford works, while Union Carbide had the administrative responsibility for Oak Ridge. The bomb was designed and assembled at the Los Alamos facility which was headed by Robert Oppenheimer. Overall, the Manhattan District employed some 150,000 people (Skolnik & Reese, 1976).

With the United States' entry into World War II, the demand for scientists and engineers escalated. This was the first significant window of opportunity for African Americans to secure employment as scientists and engineers in industrial and governmental laboratories. The demand for professionally trained scientific and technical personnel became so acute that the federal government implemented courses to train persons for the rapidly growing chemical industry. According to Cohort I interviewees, it was during this period that many laboratories hired African American scientists and technicians on an experimental basis. The success of these pioneers led to the employment of African Americans in new venues. African American scientists made the most of this window of opportunity: several found work in large industrial laboratories and major research universities; and some worked at the Army and Navy research laboratories, and the National Bureau of Standards. In addition, an estimated 30 to 40 African American scientists worked on the Manhattan Project (*A Monthly Summary of Events and Trends in Race Relations,* 1945; Atkins, 1949).

During World War II, African Americans were able to enter new industries, rise to skilled jobs and join unions, although they still remained at a disadvantage relative to whites. Some cities and states passed Fair Employment Practice (FEP) laws to assure equitable treatment by employers. World War II drastically affected the status of African Americans. To some extent, the conscience of whites was stirred by the fact that the Nazi enemy proclaimed a racist ideology, which stood in sharp contrast to the democratic ideology. The inconsistency of the southern tradition with the American creed became more apparent (see Gavins & Hill, 2004; Litwak, 2004; Woodard, 1957). The tremendous need for human resources, the federal FEPC, and the policies of national labor unions created a solid economic advance for a number of African Americans (Karon, 1975).

Chemical education was essentially in standby status once the U.S. entered World War II, in December 1941. Although the scientific and technical achievements of the war left the U.S. with a strong sentiment in favor of expanded research and scientific education, it took several years and a boost from the space race to spur action. After the war, schools were crammed with returning veterans. In 1949, a revised set of minimum standards was sent to all U.S. institutions offering a degree in chemistry (Skolnik & Reese, 1976).

Essentially, the nation's scientists and engineers submitted data for the National Roster of Scientific and Specialized Personnel. Relatively few were called from the Roster for special duty, although the data were used regularly in considering deferments from the military draft and for other purposes. Scientists were not exempt from the draft and the indiscriminate drafting of chemists and chemical engineers troubled both the chemical industry and educational institutions. Throughout the war, the ACS battled with Selective Service over the critical nature of the work of chemists and chemical engineers in the war effort (Skolnik & Reese, 1976). Ironically, during the same period, Franklin and Moss (1994) report that African Americans were victims of systematic discrimination by the Selective Service, especially in some parts of the South.

During World War II, chemists at various universities and in the pharmaceutical industry developed a series of anti-malarial drugs that saved many American lives in the Pacific. Other contributions were new sulfa, antibiotic, anesthetic, analgesic, hypnotic, autonomic, and cardiac drugs. During the war, the Office of Scientific Research and Development had some 600 contracts in this area with approximately 150 institutions and involving about 5,500 people. Results of these contracts included methods for large-scale production of: atabrine, a malaria suppressive; pure albumin (from blood plasma), which was effective against shock; penicillin, which provided unprecedented control of bacterial infections; and DDT, which was used widely against disease vectors such as lice (typhus), mosquitoes (malaria, yellow fever), and houseflies (gastrointestinal diseases) (Skolnik & Reese, 1976).

After the World War II, a few white universities opened up opportunities for African Americans on their science faculties and in their graduate program. Nevertheless major problems confronting African Americans' pursuit of careers in science persisted. This was due to a host of reasons, (some of which persist today) including: (1) a lack of access to high-quality K-12 science and math preparation (Williams, 1981); (2) weak undergraduate curricula in black colleges (Ginzberg, 1956); (3) exclusion from certain opportunities at white colleges (Garvins & Hill, 2004); (4) the high cost of graduate training (Clement, 1939; Greene, 1946). Furthermore, African Americans were subjected to overt discrimination in scientific organizations. For example, as late as the mid-1950s the American Association for the Advancement of Science (AAAS) continued to hold its meetings in segregated cities such as Atlanta and New Orleans, where African Americans were denied accommodations at the conference hotels (Manning, 1999).

Like many highly gifted African Americans in the earlier portions of the twentieth century, Percy L. Julian (1899–1975) did not have the money for advanced study. When the scholarships and fellowships for postgraduate study were obtained for the graduates in chemistry at DePauw and Julian was not a recipient, his advisor, Blanchard reported to have said "I'm still not sure you will find doors open to you in chemistry, but if you have the guts to try it, I'll help you" (Blanchard cited in de Kruif, 1946). Julian earned his Master's degree in one year, coming out again in the top group of his class. Although Harvard usually appointed men with high rank as teaching assistants; the administrators explained that they feared Southern white students might not accept him as a teacher.

Julian stayed at Harvard four years on minor fellowships, and then went back south to teach at the West Virginia State College for Negroes. His laboratory had next to no apparatus. He was the one-man chemistry faculty, laboratory storekeeper and janitor as well (de Kruif, 1946). Julius Stone, Jr., a Harvard classmate and the son of a leading banker and industrialist in Columbus, Ohio, came to Julian's aid. With Stone's financial backing and a General Education Board fellowship, he went to Vienna (de Kruif, 1946) and received a Ph.D. at the University of Vienna in 1931. Julian considered himself to be only the third native-born black to earn a Ph.D. in chemistry (de Kruif, 1946).

Julian replaced St. Elmo Brady as Chair of Chemistry at Howard University. Although Howard was the most prestigious historically black college or university, it was nevertheless a frustrating place to work for a gifted research scientist, according to Manning (1993). (Other gifted African American scientists would later share a similar experience.) In *Black Apollo of Science*, Manning chronicles Ernest E. Just's struggles to conduct cutting-edge research in cell biology in inadequate laboratory facilities, under chronic funding shortages and heavy teaching loads. The confluence of these and personal factors, eventually precipitated Just's departure from Howard to pursue his research in Europe. In 1932, Julian would leave Howard University under a storm of controversy. Prior to departing Howard University, however, Julian designed a new chemistry building. Two years later, the building was dedicated by then President Franklin D. Roosevelt (Borman, 1993).

At several points in his career, Julian received critical support, encouragement and guidance from several mentors, mostly whites. The first and most important was William Blanchard of DePauw, who first inspired Julian's love of chemistry. Blanchard wanted Julian to be chair of DePauw's chemistry department. He would be the first black professor of chemistry in any white institution in America. However, Blanchard's enlightenment was not universally shared by some of his colleagues who deemed such an appointment as "inadvisable" (de Kruif, 1946).

White chemists E. P. Kohler of Harvard and Ernst Spaeth of the University of Vienna also nurtured Julian's career at critical times. Blanchard and DePauw President G. Bromley Oxnam recommended Julian's appointment to the faculty. However, the Board of Trustees rejected his appointment. Like many white universities of the time, DePauw was not ready for a black professor. (Some thirty years later, Julian was elected to the Board.) According to Borman (1993), the University of Minnesota declined to appoint Julian as well. Consequently, Julian applied for and was offered a position as a researcher at the Institute of Paper Chemistry (IPC) in Appleton, Wisconsin. This failed to materialize as well because IPC executives discovered an Appleton statute that forbade "housing of a Negro overnight" (Borman, 1993).

The magnitude of Julian's accomplishment should be placed in historical context. Julian's appointment took place more than a decade before Jackie Robinson broke the color line in baseball. In 1949, Julian developed and published a new corticosteroid synthesis that came to be used in commercial production of the anti-inflammatory drug – cortisone (Borman, 1993). In the late 1940s and early '50s, Julian and Glidden were key players in what chemical historians called the "Great Steroid Wars." Julian found a way to make the prohibitively expensive drug from soybeans; his work helped lead to dramatically lower prices – and relief for millions of arthritis sufferers. During his more than 17-year tenure at Glidden, Julian was responsible for numerous discoveries. Under Julian's direction, Soya phosphatides, soya oil, and lecithin granules (a soy-derived food supplement) became major products for Glidden. From soy protein, Julian's group developed a commercially important paper coating and a fire-retardant compound used in Aero-Foam, chemical foam used by U.S. troops to fight gasoline and oil fires during World War II (Borman, 1993).

In a year, Julian turned a sizable annual company loss into major profits. He played a leading role in designing and supervising the building of a protein plant at a cost of nearly $1,000,000. Glidden rewarded Julian for his outstanding research. He enjoyed a freedom that was atypical in academe. In his laboratory, Julian supervised a team of more than 50 white and black chemists (de Kruif, 1946).

In 1953, however, Julian decided to resign his position at Glidden to found Julian Laboratories. Julian's company specialized in steroid chemistry and the production of steroid drugs from Mexican yams. In 1961, Julian sold his profitable company to Smith, Kline & French Laboratories for more than $2.3 million. However, Julian remained as president of the company (Borman, 1993). Later, Julian repurchased one of his laboratories and established a nonprofit research organization known as the Julian Research Institute. In collaboration between the Institute and the graduate center of the University of Illinois, Julian directed doctoral dissertation research. He also served as a mentor to countless young African American chemists (Borman, 1993).

In 1973, Julian was elected to the National Academy of Sciences. On April 19, 1975, he died of cancer at the age of 76. Julian received numerous posthumous honors. Science buildings were named after him at DePauw; MacMurray College, Jacksonville, Illinois; Illinois State University, Normal, Illinois; and Coppin State College, Baltimore. At least four public schools have been named after him. An annual lecture series in his honor is held at DePauw, and a scholarship established by the family supports many DePauw students. A painting of him hangs in the clinical center of the National Institutes of Health in Bethesda, Maryland. In 1990 he was inducted into the National Inventors Hall of Fame (Borman, 1993).

Although his race made Percy Julian an anomaly in the chemical industry in 1936 (see Bechtel, 1989), his decision to leave academe for industry was not unusual for white chemists of his time. As has been shown, the chemical industry was in the midst of a great expansion. In a 1967 interview in the *New York Times*, Julian was candid about being black and a scientist in the U.S. He is quoted as having said: "We were taught a pretty little lie – excel and the whole world lies open before you. I obeyed the injunction and found it to be wishful thinking" (Borman, 1993, p. 11).

Many African American scientists regard Julian's appointment at Glidden as the watershed for the employment of African Americans outside of science departments at historically black colleges and universities. According to physicist Branson (1955), Julian was the most successful African American employed in the chemical industry, and the most prolific African American producer of scholarly scientific papers.

While it is difficult to determine the actual number of African Americans employed as chemists (all degree levels) in major industrial research laboratories in 1940, Ferguson claimed that there were at least 300. However, he speculated that most were probably employed as technicians or on the lower professional levels because they published little and were not widely known in black professional circles. Historically black colleges and universities played a pivotal role in the production of African American scientific talent, due largely to discriminatory practices in admissions to predominantly white colleges and universities, especially in the South (see Clement, 1939; Ginzberg, 1956; Pearson, 1985). In the 1940s, the National Institute of Science (NIS) was founded as a predominantly African American scientific society. A primary goal of the society was to encourage scientific research by African Americans at historically black colleges and universities. During the war, the few historically black colleges and universities with research capacities were recipients of nationally competitive research grants.

According to Branson (1952), Howard University's Department of Chemistry, which held contracts with the Office of Naval Research and the Atomic Energy Commission, was the premier research department among all historically black colleges and universities (see also Ferguson, 1949; Logan, 1969). One Cohort II interviewee asserted: *"Several of the Blacks at research universities came through Howard at one time or another. The best and the brightest have been through Howard but left."* Branson considered Harvard-educated R. Percy Barnes to be Howard's most productive member. Other productive members identified by Branson included: S. R. Cooper (Ph.D., Cornell); Kelso B. Morris (Ph.D., Cornell); Victor Tulane (Ph.D., Michigan); Lloyd N. Ferguson (Ph.D., University of California, Berkeley). He also noted talented scientists at Howard's Medical School: Vernon Wilkerson (M. D., Iowa; Ph.D., Minnesota), professor biochemistry; Charles R. Drew (M. D., McGill; D. M. S., Columbia) in blood plasma; H. D. West (Ph.D., Illinois) in chemistry. During the same period, Tuskegee's Carver Research Foundation was staffed by an outstanding group of young chemists headed by Russell W. Brown (Ph.D., Iowa State), Clarence T. Mason (Ph.D., McGill) and Edward Belton (Ph.D., Iowa). In industry, outstanding research was also being produced by chemists John L. Jones (Ph.D., Stanford) and James E. LuValle (Ph.D., Caltech) (see Brown, 1949). In 1946, chemists at Tuskegee's Carver Foundation (Clarence T. Mason) and Tennessee State College (Carl Hill) received research grants from the Research Corporation of New York. In the late 1940s, they were joined by chemists at Morehouse College (Henry McBay) and Fisk University (James Lawson).

This period also marked the expansion of scientific employment opportunities for African Americans outside of historically black colleges and universities (Atkins, 1949). These changes did not come without pressure from the federal government, however. In fact, much of the progress has been attributed to the efforts of the FEPC, which was mandated to draw on all of the United States' human resources during a national crisis. In short, a critical shortage of scientists and engineers expedited the recruitment of African American scientific talent (*A Monthly Summary of Events and Trends in Race Relations*, 1945, p. 6).

Atkins (1949) attributed the under participation of African Americans in chemistry to: (1) substandard educational facilities for African Americans in the South; and (2) nationwide restricted employment opportunities prior to World War II. He contends that employment in the South for African Americans with degrees in chemistry was limited to low-paying teaching positions in underfinanced segregated institutions. These conditions led aspiring African Americans to seek training and jobs outside of the South.

Statistics, particularly those on the status of early African American Ph.D. recipients in chemistry must be viewed with caution – for reasons other than the number of African Americans who passed as members of other racial/ethnic groups. For example, Greene (1946) asserts that at least 36 African Americans held doctorates in chemistry before 1944. However, an examination of his enumeration reveals that he identifies 37 African American doctorate recipients. Of these, two were identified as having specialties in chemistry and education. Thus, it is unclear whether these degrees were awarded in science or education. Elsewhere, Ferguson (1949) contends that by 1949, an estimated 55 African Americans held doctorates in chemistry. Because Ferguson does not discuss the source of his data, it is unclear how that figure was derived.

POST WAR POST WWII

In 1957, the Soviet Union's launching of Sputnik had an immediate impact on both U.S. domestic and foreign policy. The event prompted increased emphasis on scientific education, especially in the physical sciences and engineering, and influenced funding priorities in research that could lead to advances in the next generation of accelerators, missiles, and space satellites. These priority areas created expensive "big science" projects that required Congressional approval. Additionally, strong public support was required for enormous expenditures of money in scientific areas related directly to defense as well as other key areas, such as health, energy, and agriculture (Nye, 1996; deSolla Price, 1986).

As the Cold War was accelerating, the United States and its western allies were in a dog fight with the Soviet Union and its eastern bloc allies for supremacy on several fronts. On the scientific front, much of the preeminent research focus was on nuclear fission. It was only a matter of time before foreign scientists would master fission technology. Many U.S. scientists were concerned about the future if fission technology remained under the control of the military. These concerns prompted scientists to organize the Federation of Atomic Scientists in 1945. However, the next year the organization was renamed the Federation of American Scientists. In August 1946, the Atomic Energy Commission (AEC) was established to assume control of both the military and peaceful uses of atomic energy. In September 1949, the Soviet Union exploded a fission device. Within months, President Truman directed the AEC to proceed with the development of a fusion (hydrogen) bomb. The U.S. exploded its first fusion device in May 1951. By August 1953, the Soviets exploded a similar device (Skolnik & Reese, 1976).

In 1950, the National Science Foundation was established to channel federal support into basic research. The model for the National Science Foundation grew out of the success of the wartime Office of Scientific Research and Development (OSRD. Appropriations for the Foundation rose sharply from $225,000 in fiscal year 1951 to $14 million in fiscal year 1955 and to $153 million in fiscal year 1960. In the period 1953–1960, U.S. spending on R&D grew from $5.13 billion to $13.55 billion and the federal share of the total climbed from 54 to 65% (Skolnik & Reese, 1976).

In the two decades following World War II, many of the new chemistry and chemical engineering graduates found employment in the chemical industry. The results of a 1944 survey of executives focusing on postwar opportunities for young professionals beginning their business careers reveal that more than half of those surveyed indicated that the chemical industry was the most promising sector for employment. For many financial analysts, chemical research was viewed as a barometer of future opportunities for the industry. Various economic analyses identified the chemicals and allied products industry as an example of spectacular economic growth (Thackray et al., 1985). Sales in the chemical industry (especially synthetic organic chemicals) rose from about $13 billion in 1947 to $27 billion in 1960. This growth occurred despite recessions in 1953–1954 and 1957–58. From 1947–1960, the industry's annual output of organic chemical intermediates climbed 370% to 9.6 billion pounds; medicinal chemicals, 230% to 114 million pounds; plastics materials, 490% to 6.1 billion pounds; surface active agents 530% to 1.5 billion pounds; and pesticides and other organic agricultural chemicals, 520% to 648 million pounds (Skolnik & Reese, 1976, p. 45).

While the chemical industry enjoyed high praise from industry and government it began to attract its share of critics, especially after scientists began to report minute amounts of organochlorine pesticides in the environment, adverse effects of oral contraceptives, and the radiation hazard of television sets. Rachel Carson's *Silent Spring* stimulated a storm of protests over the impact of pesticides on the environment, thus, setting into motion a movement of activism that continues until this day. Although some of these problems were unanticipated, others were expected but accepted because of the belief that the benefits outweighed the costs. Corporate mishandling and consumer misuse of troublesome products and practices prompted other concerns. The U.S. Congress began to play a stronger regulatory role on environmental matters. In 1955, for example, Congress passed a series of regulations that put the Federal Government in charge of the nation's environmental effort. For example, it passed a water pollution control act. Around the same period, Congress also amended the Food, Drug, and Cosmetic Act of 1938 in order to stiffen controls on substances, such as pesticide residues, food additives, and prescription drugs. When scientific experts take strong but directly opposite positions on the same issue, the public is often confused. The public became increasingly skeptical of scientific research (Skolnik & Reese, 1976).

CIVIL RIGHTS MOVEMENT

During the late 1950s and early 1960s, growth in chemicals and allied products slowed from its pace after the war. According to Thackray and his colleagues (1985), this situation was precipitated by the industry's reputation for sustaining high earnings and profits. This high profile began to attract the attention of companies from other industries because of the perceived opportunity to increase profits by invading chemical markets. For example, oil companies such as Shell and Standard Oil of New Jersey, which had manufactured petrochemical products since the 1920s, began to expand their chemical operations to produce increasing amounts of petrochemicals from refinery by-products following World War II. Furthermore, former major customers of chemical manufacturers, such as tire and rubber companies began to produce their own synthetic rubber and other chemicals.

On Oct. 4, 1957 the Soviets stunned much of the world when it launched Sputnik I. Approximately one month later, Sputnik II, with the dog Laika aboard, was launched. Meanwhile, the U.S. space program was facing all sorts of challenges. On December 6, 1957, for example, Vanguard collapsed in flames on the launch pad. Shortly thereafter (January 31, 1958), the U.S. launched Explorer I. However, the Soviets held the advantage in propulsion research, which was a critical element in the missile race (Skolnik & Reese, 1976). In a strong reaction to the Soviets' success, on November 1957, President Dwight D. Eisenhower announced the appointment of James R. Killian as his special assistant for science and technology. Killian was responsible accelerating the missile program, stimulating basic research and scientific education. By mid-1973, President Nixon eliminated what had become the Office of Science and Technology. The director of the National Science Foundation assumed most of the office's functions (Skolnik & Reese, 1976).

Congress also reacted strongly and strategically to the Soviet's success. In 1958, it passed the National Defense Education Act which provided scholarships, loans and grants to improve science and mathematics education, and foreign languages; and other aids to education. In addition, Congress established the

National Aeronautics and Space Administration (NASA) which began operating on October 1, 1958 with a budget of $494 million. By the mid-1960s, the budget had grown to $5 billion. For Project Mercury (1958–1963), for example, the agency mobilized scores of prime contractors, subcontractors, and other workers – all total two million people. These efforts contributed to John H. Glenn, Jr.'s orbit of the earth in a Mercury spacecraft in February 1962. This even followed Yuri Gagarin's voyage on Vostok 1 about 10 months earlier. On July 20, 1969, the U.S. space program enjoyed even more success when Neil Armstrong and two colleagues landed on the lunar surface in Apollo II (Skolnik & Reese, 1976).

After Sputnik, the number of universities granting the Ph.D. degree in chemistry more than doubled. The growth was spurred mainly by federal support. Around 1968, however, there was a downturn in research and development (R&D) funding and the recession-aided weakening of the chemical job market. By 1975, academic openings in chemistry were relatively scarce (Skolnik & Reese, 1976).

Regardless of class, race, ethnicity or gender the space program and the federal emphasis on education in the sciences and engineering proved attractive to young Americans. The number of bachelor's degrees granted in chemistry climbed steadily, from 5,500 in 1954 to 12,000 by 1975. The number of Ph.D. degrees granted in chemistry remained level at about 1,000 during the 1950s, but then rose sharply, peaking at of 2,200 in 1969–1970. New Ph.D.'s in chemistry totaled about 10,000 in 1950–1960, but climbed to 15,000 in the next decade. By 1970, some 550,000 scientists and engineers were employed in research and development in the U.S. The growth in research output is reflected in the number of abstracts published annually by *Chemical Abstracts*. In 1957, it reached 100,000, passed 200,000 in 1966, and was about 300,000 in 1971 (Skolnik & Reese, 1976).

The ACS played an active role in public outreach. For example, in January 1961, the ACS News Service released the first program in its "Men and Molecules" series, a 15-minute science documentary produced weekly and distributed free to radio stations. The series featured noted scientists discussing their research in terms that the public could understand. Its main goal was to increase the public's understanding of the value of research. By the end of 1975, 785 programs had been completed and broadcast by 525 radio stations in all states (Skolnik & Reese, 1976).

By the mid-1960s, the ACS took particular interest in the divergent paths of academic and industrial chemistry. Students of chemistry were being trained to do highly specialized basic research. However, many of their goals included careers in research and peer recognition, which were problematic for industry because publication is limited by its proprietary nature. As the major employers of new Ph.D. chemists, companies found too many of them to be overspecialized, inflexible, and ill-prepared for the team research and economic context of industrial

R&D. But, companies could push their views only so far because most of the support of research in the schools came from federal funds (Skolnik & Reese, 1976).

The status of chemists in the eyes of executives was boosted by the successes of chemists in fields such as plastics, petrochemicals, and synthetic textiles. The industry's growing demand for trained chemists forged a new relationship with many academic chemistry departments. For example, universities supplied industry with chemists and with basic research to supplement work done in industrial laboratories. In turn, industry provided financial support to chemistry departments. Many of the increasing number of chemistry students in American universities were supported by pre- and post- doctoral fellowships from chemical corporations (Thackray et al., 1985).

In the late 1960s and early 1970s, a few chemical manufacturers began actively recruiting African Americans to their laboratories. Many African Americans, however, attributed this to affirmative action requirements rather than any industry-wide evolution in social consciousness (Gaines, 1996; Meier, 1982; Quarles, 1988). According to Meier, this view is supported by an October 25, 1976 article in *Chemical and Engineering News* reviewing changes in company hiring procedures and recruitment policies. The article concluded that the primary reason for the efforts to recruit African American chemists was the need for employers to comply with the federal laws and executive orders that prohibit job discrimination because of race, color, religion, sex, or national origin (see also Krislov, 1967). Meier (1982) further contends that the effect of affirmative action on the employment patterns of African Americans with degrees in chemistry was profound. He indicates that an estimated 70% of graduates from historically black colleges and universities were employed in industry. Despite this trend, the demographic characteristics of the corporate gatekeepers – White and male – remained relatively unchanged. That is, few African Americans advanced into major research or management positions in the chemical industry during that period.

1975–2004

Despite their under representation among professional chemists in the United States, African Americans have achieved a measure of success and recognition in the scientific community. For example, in 1973, Percy L. Julian was elected to the National Academy of Sciences; Walter Lincoln Hawkins was elected to the National Academy of Engineering in 1975; and in 1992, President George H. W. Bush awarded Hawkins the prestigious National Medal of Technologies for inventing plastic coatings for communication cable. Henry A. Hill was the first and only (as of September 2004) African American elected president of the American Chemical Society; he held this office from 1975 to 1977. Few Americans (especially scientists) are honored with their portrait on a United States postage stamp. However, at least one African American Ph.D. chemist has achieved this honor: Percy L. Julian in 1993 (see Borman, 1993).

Between 1978 and 1998 the production of African American Ph.D. recipients in chemistry has ebbed and flowed in double-digits. For example, in 1978 and 1979, annual outputs were registered at 26 and 28, respectively. This level of output was not equaled again until 1995, when 27 chemistry Ph.D.s were awarded to African Americans. In fact, the only other years the output equaled 20 or more during this period were in 1989 ($N = 20$) and 1994 ($N = 23$). All told, some 416 African Americans earned doctorates in chemistry during this 21 year period – that is a rate of about 20 per year (Commission on Professionals in Science and Technology, 2002). Data in Table 1.1 show that 46 chemistry doctorates were awarded to African American U.S. citizens in 1999, 36 in 2000, and 36 in 2001. Much of this growth is attributable to the increasing participation of African American women in chemistry. Since 1995 (except for 1997), they averaged double figure. In fact, they have accounted for more than two-fifths of the doctorates since 1997.

The history of chemistry has long been polarized between a focus on great chemists as innovators or originators of eminent chemical ideas, theories, and concepts and a more recent emphasis on the social composition of chemical societies and related professional forums, whose changing membership provides vital clues for understanding chemistry's shifting place in society, culture, and history (Abir-Am, 1993). Yet, the latter has neglected African Americans.

Differences in data collection practices make reliance on federal figures problematic. For example, some data on African American chemists are reported for "U.S. citizens and permanent visas" for certain years, while other data are reported for "U.S born citizens" for different years. Unfortunately, some data are reported for academic years, while others are presented for calendar years. Moreover, some data are aggregated as the "physical sciences," while other data are disaggregated by discipline. Some professional societies report data based only on their membership. To the extent possible, I shall report the most recent, complete data available on U.S. born citizens.

Throughout their history, African Americans have been underrepresented in chemistry in general and among doctorate chemists in particular (CPST, 2004). Nationally, they have typically comprised less than 3% of all chemistry degree recipients and less than 1% of those earning doctorates in chemistry in the United States. NSF (1997) figures for U.S. citizens and permanent visas degree recipients reveal that in 1995, African Americans were awarded 738 bachelors, 77 masters

Table 1.1. Chemistry Ph.D. Recipients by Sex and Race/Ethnicity (U.S. Citizens), Selected Years, 1978–2001.

Year	Total	Black Women	Black Men	American Indian Women	American Indian Men	Asian Women	Asian Men	Hispanic Women	Hispanic Men	White Women	White Men	Unknown Women	Unknown Men
1978	1,175	4	22	0	3	5	28	2	12	128	880	10	81
1979	1,240	4	24	0	1	8	24	5	8	140	928	13	85
1980	1,169	2	8	1	2	7	33	4	7	161	861	10	73
1981	1,235	2	11	0	1	4	22	4	16	163	939	6	67
1982	1,285	4	6	0	0	13	22	4	11	184	1,007	4	30
1983	1,357	2	9	0	3	12	27	13	7	206	1,046	2	30
1984	1,332	2	16	0	3	16	34	7	19	219	970	5	41
1985	1,345	4	15	0	2	20	37	4	10	229	990	4	30
1986	1,320	3	10	2	3	17	39	6	18	241	942	7	32
1987	1,381	2	9	2	4	13	36	13	27	261	982	5	27
1988	1,378	6	11	0	5	14	34	11	33	271	964	3	26
1989	1,298	7	13	0	5	8	34	15	25	310	857	2	22
1990	1,398	6	8	0	3	13	41	20	30	307	942	6	22
1991	1,350	4	15	2	7	15	46	8	31	305	896	2	19
1992	1,328	4	9	2	4	28	36	11	23	307	885	5	14
1993	1,272	8	11	1	1	36	38	14	29	291	828	2	13
1994	1,291	8	15	0	4	26	43	13	36	296	843	2	5
1995	1,238	16	11	2	3	39	51	14	24	333	733	5	7
1996	1,169	10	24	1	3	23	32	6	26	290	736	3	15
1997	1,233	8	23	0	6	30	51	10	26	292	748	11	28
1998	1,288	23	17	1	6	22	49	9	25	329	766	9	32
1999	1,256	19	27	2	3	35	53	20	21	281	773	5	17
2000	1,119	16	20	1	6	27	22	20	29	308	644	3	23
2001	1,126	18	18	2	9	35	37	15	24	284	652	11	21

Source: National Science Foundation Survey Data.

and 33 doctorate degrees in chemistry. Women accounted for 17 (or 52%) of the doctoral chemistry degrees. Data on bachelors and masters recipients were not reported by sex and race/ethnicity jointly (NSF, 1997). In 2001, African Americans accounted for 1,220 or 2% of all employed doctoral chemists (except biochemists) employed in the U.S. civilian labor force (NSF, 2003).

Models of Science

According to Merton (1973), advantages in science can accumulate in two ways: by addition or multiplication. These models are succinctly summarized by Zuckerman (1977, p. 60):

> In the additive model, people who begin their careers with certain ascribed advantages continue to benefit, to receive resources and rewards on grounds that are 'functionally irrelevant' – that is, irrespective of their occupational role performance. In the second model, people judged on functionally relevant criteria as the most likely to make effective use of the resources are the most likely to receive them. Recipients are advantaged in the sense of being more able to begin with, of getting more of what is needed to perform their roles, and of consequently achieving more. The resulting gap in attainment between the advantaged and the others is far greater than under the conditions of the additive model, in which the ability to use resources for further achievements is randomly distributed among recipients and non-recipients.

In the multiplicative model, those judged based on the quality of their performance are the most likely to make effective use of resources; thus, they are the most likely to receive them. As a result, their success is more likely to beget subsequent successes. The resulting gap in attainment between the advantaged and the others is much greater under the multiplicative model, for those already possessing the skills to effectively employ resources are the most likely to receive them. Resources are continually allocated to the same individuals based on the quality of their performance. Zuckerman (1977, p. 60) asserts that "over the course of their careers, discrepancies in attainment tend to grow ever larger between the initially advantaged and everyone else." Due to the allocation of resources to certain individuals, the resulting distribution of attainments tends to be sharply stratified. Those deemed most likely to effectively employ resources ultimately receive them and are at the top of the pecking order. Zuckerman (1977, p. 61) contends that "such a process produces elites of achievement and permits the elite to develop self-serving justifications for their continued receipt of resources."

The normative structure of science, with its abiding emphasis on extending certified knowledge, calls for the application of universal or meritocratic criteria in distributing resources for scientific investigation and rewards for contributing to science. The sooner individuals are identified as meritorious – in science, this means being judged as a "comer" or "rising star" – the sooner they gain privileged access to resources, the earlier they begin to develop, and the greater their head start over other young professionals judged less capable or not noticed at all. Great expectations must ultimately be buttressed by scientific productivity if scientists are to continue to receive scarce resources for research (Zuckerman, 1977).

According to Zuckerman (1977), a similar process of cumulative advantage is applicable to organizations. For example, the most distinguished universities tend to attract a stronger pool of applicants. Students acquire prestige from having attended these universities and, in turn, lend prestige to their alma maters later in their careers. The universities are more generously supported and thus have facilities that attract accomplished faculties.

Elites in science come disproportionately from the middle and upper socioeconomic classes. Nobel Laureates often described themselves as agnostics, without formal religious affiliation or commitment to a body of religious doctrine. Writing in the 1970s, Zuckerman (1977) reports that Jewish faculty are most heavily represented in the dramatically advancing fields of biology (bacteriology, molecular biology, virology and microbiology, biochemistry). She argued that these fields were singled out for recognition by Nobel Prize committees. Most Laureates are graduates of elite undergraduate and graduate schools. Further, more than half of those who conducted their prize-winning research in the U.S. had been a student, postdoctoral fellow or junior collaborator under an older Nobel laureate. Most prize-winning Laureates had accomplished their research by age forty-one. (The relevance of this discussion to African Americans is addressed more fully in Chapter 5.)

DISCRIMINATION IN SCIENCE

According to Bowen and Bok (1998), the issue of race is so pervasive in the U.S. that it affects in substantial ways an individual's experiences and attitudes. One of the most compelling results of their study was the finding that regardless of their attempts to control those variables that are certain to account for the many differences associated with race, racial gaps of all kind remained. Significantly, most studies of discrimination in science have focused on Jewish Americans and white women (Cole, 1987; Cole & Cole, 1973; Long, 2001; Zuckerman, 1977). Zuckerman (1977) asserts that Jewish academic scientists traditionally are more likely to be physicists than chemists because of the long-standing hostility to them in the chemistry field. Rossiter (1982) argues that American Jews were well aware that they were not welcome in industry in the 1920s and 1930s. Despite the dramatic increase in the proportion of American Jews in science following World War II, Lipset and Ladd (1971) report that American Jews were heavily concentrated in biochemistry and bacteriology, fields closely related to the highly prestigious field of medicine. According to the authors, American Jews believed that they were least subject to prejudice and discrimination in these fields.

Rossiter (1982) paints a stark picture of (white) women in science in the early 1900s. She argues that having advanced degrees in science did not necessarily lead to desirable employment for (white) women. Moreover, high quality research and major publications did not necessarily result in advancement or better working conditions for (white) women, as was the standard case for their male peers. Rossiter claims that it was not uncommon for (white) women of outstanding scientific accomplishment to hold positions that were not commensurate with their training and skill level. Furthermore, the many talented (white) women who received recognition for their scientific contributions did so only belatedly; often, this occurred years after their achievements or in their obituaries (see, for example, Watson, 1968). Generally and quite notably, science faculties at major research universities were more willing to educate (white) women than to employ them. Similarly, universities tended to promote only the most exceptional (white) women scientists.

According to Rossiter (1982), young white male scientists were seen as the salvation of the scientific enterprise in the 1920s and 1930s. She asserts that white women, African Americans, and Jewish scientists seeking industrial jobs were the victims of highly discriminatory employment practices. Rossiter contends that even when the advertisement did not include the phrase "male Christians only" it was common knowledge that only they need apply.

World War II opened employment opportunities in industry and expanded employment in government for (white) women scientists. Wartime personnel shortages in the chemical industry provided greater employment opportunities for (white) women scientists. Typically, (white) women's employment opportunities involved traditional areas of "women's work" (Rossiter, 1982). Historical and sociological research primarily on the careers of white men and women scientists show marked gender disparities in academic rank at the senior levels in terms of salary, promotion rates, positions of influence, and honorific awards (Rossiter, 1982; Zuckerman, 1987). Only recently have scholars begun significant efforts to search for evidence of African Americans' contributions to science (see Manning, 1983; Pearson, 1985). It is not uncommon for the National Academy of Sciences to induct an entire class without any African American representation. In 1995 only two of the 1,848 members of the academy were African Americans (*The Journal of Blacks in Higher Education*, 1995). The achievements of many African American scientists have been largely hidden, ignored, or diminished in importance. The lack of recognition of W. E. B. DuBois' contributions to sociological research methodology, for example, is a telling parallel in the social sciences.

In recent years, diversity has become a critical dynamic of the government, academe, and industry hiring process (Jacobs, 2002). Writing in the 1960s, Blalock (1967) claims that if an employer can point to a few African Americans in semi-responsible positions, he or she can usually clear himself/herself of the charge of discrimination. If such African Americans are highly visible to members of their own community, the employer may actually gain favor with that community, given the existing level of discrimination by his/her competitors. Blalock (1967) argues that further gains for minority individuals must come at the expense of increased outside pressure on the employer and increased vigilance in locating and demonstrating discriminatory behavior.

By way of illustration, Blalock points out that prior to 1947, baseball players of African American descent were completely excluded from the major leagues. As a result of this exclusion, the Negro Baseball League developed into a pool of first-rate African American athletes whose abilities were superior to those of many Whites of major league caliber. When Jackie Robinson joined the Brooklyn Dodgers, the racial barrier was broken and there was an almost immediate rush from major league management to tap this pool of highly skilled players. While not free of discrimination, Blalock contends that professional baseball, as an occupation, seems remarkably free of racial discrimination in terms of opportunity.

According to Blalock, one of the factors that contribute to baseball's perceived equal opportunity environment is that skill and performance are quantifiable and therefore easily evaluated. There exists a series of precise measures of performance that are standardized across teams and players – batting averages, slugging averages, home runs, runs batted in, fielding averages, earned-run averages, strikeouts, win/loss records, etc. Each player can easily be compared with another. There is absolutely no uncertainty about which hitters have batted in the most runs or which pitchers have the best records. In few occupations is individual performance evaluated so easily. In this case, high levels of performance work to the advantage of the team in terms of both prestige and income. Although rivalries among teammates may develop, the fact that teammates share in the rewards of outstanding performance tends to channel such competition into more or less good-natured rivalry (Blalock, 1967).

High productivity is highly correlated with high prestige. Moreover, high productivity on the part of some individuals does not result in fewer jobs for others. Players receive rewards and incentives based on the quality of their individual effort. A player cannot rely on the poor performance of others to increase his/her worth.

Persons in authority (coaches, managers, player/personnel executives, etc.) are usually retired rather than active players. As a result, there is little or no threat of the African American teammates becoming the white players' boss. An additional source of resistance to employing African American players is thereby removed (Blalock, 1967). Although there are more African American managers today than at the time of Blalock's writing, the statement remains relatively accurate today.

In baseball, the training necessary for high-level performance is accessible by all. A similar analogy could be drawn for basketball. Blalock noted that baseball training does not require a college education, as is generally the case with football, or expensive equipment (e.g. golf), or access to restricted facilities (e.g. swimming). Blalock contends that baseball is as much a lower-class as a middle-class sport. Although some parks and recreation departments, churches, or communities may possess better facilities, white athletes cannot obtain a monopoly on training facilities.

According to Blalock, another important factor that has worked to the advantage of African Americans in organized baseball is that performance depends only to a slight degree on interpersonal relations and manipulative skills. Blalock argues that the greater the importance of high individual performance to the productivity of the work group, the lower the degree of minority discrimination by employers. The greater the competition among employers for persons with high performance levels, the lower the degree of minority discrimination by employers. When an individual's performance level is accurately evaluated with ease, the degree of minority discrimination by employers is lowered.

Finally, Blalock concludes that academic and scientific professions should offer similar opportunities as baseball to minorities. He reasons that performance is readily evaluated in terms of research contributions or publications and does not depend primarily on interpersonal skills. There exists extensive competition for outstanding personnel and total productivity is not sharply limited by consumer demand. Unlike baseball, training for academic and scientific careers is prolonged, expensive, and requires some degree of interpersonal skills. There exists no pool of talented African American scientists with skills superior to those of their white counterparts, as was the case in professional baseball. Despite the prestige bestowed upon an institution or organization due to quality work produced by one of its scientists, many talented African American scientists are shunned. Traditionally, the world of science was the private domain of white males. Despite decades of interest in diversifying science and engineering (S&E), the overwhelming majority of S&E faculty are still white males (Parks, 2004).

Studies of the careers of white women doctoral scientists beginning in the 1970s have proliferated; however, the same cannot be said of African Americans. Attempts to assess the status of African Americans in science are often sketchy (see

Cole & Cole, 1973) and occasionally inaccurate (see Rossiter, 1982). Consider, for example, Rossiter's (1982) contention that during the 1920s and 1930s, the best African American chemists, Percy Julian and L. A. Hall, could not get jobs in industry (p. 384, 14f). This assertion is contradicted by the very source she cites i.e. Louis Haber's *Black Pioneers of Science and Invention* (1970). Haber writes: "Julian began his work with the Glidden Company in 1936" (p. 94). Regarding Hall, she states, ". . . in 1916, his chemistry background secured him a position as a chemist in the Chicago Department of Health Laboratories, where, one year later, he rose to the position of senior chemist. Two years later, he left to become chief chemist for the John Morrell Company in Ottumwa, Iowa, where he remained for two years" (p. 105). Nevertheless, Rossiter's point is that industrial employment opportunities for African American scientists were virtually non-existent during this period of American history.

Bechtel (1989) argues that the scientific community reflects the values of the larger American society in its social structures, beliefs, and attitudes. Therefore, like American society in general, American science (including much of the literature in social studies of science) reflects the dominance of whites, especially males. Bechtel argues that historically the African American scientist was viewed as an anomaly.

Although Zuckerman (1988) later concludes that science appears to exhibit some of the same structures of discrimination as other occupations, she cautions that available data at the time suggest that the scientific community is marked by an intense commitment to achievement over ascription. She contends that her thorough review of the relevant literature reveals a lack of compelling evidence of discrimination in the American scientific community. Today, few scholars of the social studies of science accept this view. White women have, without a doubt, made substantial progress in science careers over the last two decades. Nonetheless, in many areas, full gender equity still remains elusive (Long, 2001).

In 2000, *Chemical & Engineering News* editors examined statistics on the representation of women in the chemical industry; the situation is relatively good at lower levels but still it remains poor higher up (Jacobs & Storck, 2000). Later the same year, statistics on the "top 50" chemistry departments in research expenditures showed that only about 10% of the 1641 tenured/tenure track faculty were females (Long, 2000). In its most recent study of gender differences in the careers of doctoral scientists and engineers, the National Research Council reported that controlling for length of time in a profession, the rate of advancement for women falls below that for men. On average, women had fewer years' work experience than men who received a Ph.D. at the same time (Long, 2001). In general, the number of years working in the profession affects tenure and promotion in academia. Because the average female faculty member has had fewer years of professional experience than the average male, there are proportionately fewer female full professors. This is true for administrative and gatekeeping roles, such as journal editorships and department heads as well.

The relevance of Zuckerman's conclusions for African American chemists is questionable. Most studies of U.S.-born doctoral scientists do not include racially comparative samples (see Long, 2001; Sonnert & Holton, 1995). One of the few exceptions is Pearson's (1985) study of the career patterns of a national sample of 722 white and 565 African American Ph.D. scientists. The results of the study call into question the extent to which the U.S. scientific community adheres to the norm of universalism. While some African American Ph.D. scientists were employed in other than historically black colleges and universities, most believed that their careers were restricted in some way because of their race. Manning's (1983) excellent biography of Ernest E. Just raises serious questions regarding the extent to which American science is guided by the norm of universalism.

According to Thackray and his colleagues, despite some challenges, American chemistry offers a strategic site for research. They assert that because of chemistry's methods, concepts, theories, and techniques merge with those of physics and biology, it occupies as critical place among the natural sciences. Moreover, chemistry plays a prominent role in the interchanges between science and technology which are characteristic of modern science. As has been shown, chemical activity and chemical products are pervasive in American society.

THE SOCIAL ORIGINS OF AFRICAN AMERICAN CHEMISTS

This chapter focuses on the birth region, familial, religious, and marital status of interviewees. (See Appendix for data sources.) Most early studies of the social origins of American scientists (Goodrich et al., 1962; Hardy, 1974; Harmon & Soldz, 1963; Knapp & Goodrich, 1952; Roe, 1953; Zuckerman, 1977) have not included racially comparative samples. Previous studies of African American scientists have reported similar geographic distributions (Jay, 1971; Young & Young, 1974). This chapter focuses on the birth region, familial, religious, and marital status of interviewees. Most early studies of the social origins of American scientists (Goodrich et al., 1962; Hardy, 1974; Harmon & Soldz, 1963; Knapp & Goodrich, 1952; Roe, 1953; Zuckerman, 1977) have not included racially comparative samples.

REGION OF BIRTH

Pearson (1985) reported significant race differences in the geographic origins of scientists. He found African Americans to be nearly four times more likely than Whites to have grown up in the South. Previous studies of African American scientists have reported similar geographic distributions (Jay, 1971; Young & Young, 1974). Compared with census data of the study periods, Pearson reports that the North and West may have slightly overproduced black scientists compared to other regions; the North was overproducing white scientists.

Like other race/ethnic groups, the African American population is not randomly distributed across the nation. Historically the population has been concentrated in the South. Therefore, it is not surprising that 70% of the interviewees were born in the South, while 23% had their origins in the Midwest, followed by the Northeast with 9%; none were born in the West (Fig. 2.1). In general, survey data confirm these geographic distributions. It was noteworthy that there has been a decline

31

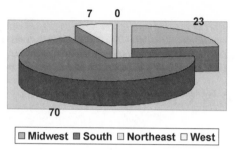

Fig. 2.1. Percent Distribution by Region of Birth [Interviewees].

in the percentage of African American respondents having their birth origins in the South after 1984. Nevertheless, the region continued to be the top producer of African American chemists. In sharp contrast, 70% of white respondents were born in the Northeast and Midwest (Fig. 2.2).

CURRENT RESIDENCE

In comparison to the interviewees' region of birth, a considerably smaller portion of the them resided in the South at the time of the interviews (Fig. 2.3). In fact, only slightly more than half of the interviewees reside in the South, followed by the Midwest (25%), Northeast (16%) and West (9%). While the general regional distribution pattern remains, it is clear that the East and particularly the West reflect greater percentage shares than was the case for birth regions. Opportunity structures

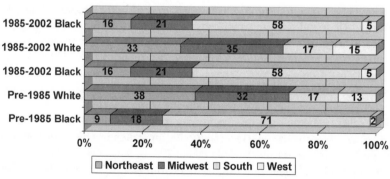

Fig. 2.2. Percent Distribution of Region of Birth by Race and Cohort [Survey Respondents].

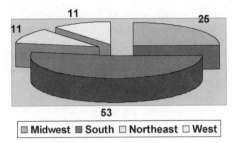

Fig. 2.3. Percent Distribution by Current Residence [Interviewees].

resulting from various civil rights legislation, court decisions, executive orders and personal preferences had much to do with many of the residential choices.

One Cohort II interviewee from the Midwest remarked: "I was never interested in applying for jobs in the Midwest. I wanted to be somewhere . . . warm and near the ocean." In contrast, a Cohort IV interviewee from the East commented: "I didn't want to go to the Midwest where I thought I was going to encounter racial prejudice." For most interviewees, however, opportunity seemed to be the deciding factor in determining their current residence.

FAMILY ORIGINS

A majority of interviewees (93%) grew up in two-parent households. Only three interviewees had their origins in single-parent households usually because of divorce. One interviewee was raised by someone other than a biological parent. The number of siblings of interviewees ranged from none to eight. Thirty percent of the interviewees had no brothers, and 14% had no sisters. Nearly two in five interviewees were first-borns, while roughly one in five was the youngest.

PARENTAL EDUCATION

Data in Table 2.1 show the parental attainment levels for interviewees. Approximately two-fifths of both mothers and fathers of the interviewees were not high school graduates. Three of the Cohort III interviewees reported that their parents were illiterate or functionally illiterate.

Some interviewees had to overcome barriers imposed by their parents. In one case, the father (a sharecropper) did not see the value of a formal education for his son. According to the interviewee, his father actively discouraged academic

Table 2.1. Percent Distribution by Parental Education [Interviewees].

Level of Education	Parent	
	Mother	Father
Doctorate/Professional degree	5.0	7.0
Masters	9.0	2.0
Some graduate work	2.0	2.0
College	5.0	11.0
Some college	7.0	9.0
High school	32.0	20.0
Less than high school	39.0	41.0
Don't know	2.0	7.0
Total	100.0	100.0

Note: Percentages may not sum to 100 because of rounding.

achievement. The interviewee explained that after middle school, his father encouraged him to quit school and work full-time on the farm. The Cohort III interviewee explained: "I left home after middle school and stayed with various relatives until I finished high school." Fortunately, teachers and other relatives recognized his brilliance. It was this support and the interviewee's motivation and determination that facilitated his completion of secondary school with honors.

Another Cohort III interviewee described his father as a successful and independent farmer. Having himself attained less than an elementary school education, the father refused to allow his son to attend classes beyond elementary school. The father insisted that his son work on the farm. The son worked long hours and attended school infrequently during the planting and harvesting seasons. However, the son secretly read his sister's texts (she was in the same grade as a result of his skipping grades) to keep up with his classes. The interviewee's mother and teachers pleaded with the father to permit the son to attend school on a regular basis. The father reluctantly agreed to allow the son to attend school most of the year. During the interview, it became clear that this was a painful and perhaps long repressed experience. Evidently, the father abused alcohol and frequently physically abused the son. Once the interviewee completed high school, he did not return to his hometown until his father died. In a third case, the interviewee indicated that her family's impoverished lifestyle motivated her to excel academically in order to escape poverty.

Generally, fathers were considerably more likely than mothers to hold a college degree, an academic doctorate or a professional degree. Interviewees were somewhat more likely to know their mother's (98%) than father's (93%) educational attainment level.

Table 2.2. Percent Distribution by Parental Education by Cohort and Race [Survey Respondents].

| | Cohort | | | |
| | Before 1985 | | 1985–2002 | |
	Black	White	Black	White
Mother's education				
Doctorate/Professional Degree	D	0.6	2.2	1.8
Master's/Some Professional	6.7	6.8	21.1	15.6
College	11.9	17.4	10.5	23.5
Some College	15.5	17.8	20.6	21.1
High School	31.1	44.4	29.4	32.9
Less Than High School	34.7	12.9	16.3	5.0
Total	100.0	100.0	100.0	100.0
Father's education				
Doctorate/Professional Degree	4.7	0.2	7.2	12.1
Master's/Some Professional	5.2	12.1	16.0	21.3
College	13.0	19.2	12.4	22.2
Some College	12.4	13.7	17.5	15.4
High School	19.7	30.8	27.8	21.9
Less Than High School	45.1	18.0	19.1	7.1
Total	100.0	100.0	100.0	100.0

Note: Percentages may not sum to 100 because of rounding and/or suppression of counts. D = Suppressed for reasons of confidentiality.
Source: Survey of Earned Doctorates.

Survey data reveal that slightly more than a third of mothers of African American chemists earning their doctorates before 1985 did not complete high school (Table 2.2). An even greater proportion of fathers (more than two-fifths) of survey respondents were not high school graduates. Mothers were more likely than fathers to hold a high school diploma, have some college credits and a masters/some professional degree. Fathers were considerably more likely to have a doctorate degree or equivalent. However, a similar percent of both mothers and fathers held bachelor's or Master's degrees. The parents of white respondents attained higher levels of education than the parents of black respondents. The notable exception being among fathers where 5% of black fathers compared with less than 1% of white fathers held a doctorate or postdoctoral degree. In terms of the bachelor's degree and higher, the differential between mothers was more narrow than that between fathers.

For the 1985–2002 cohort, some 80% or more of both mothers and fathers of black respondents finished high school. This was considerable more than the 60% in the previous cohort. The parents of black parents in the second were more likely than those in the first cohort to hold a graduate degree. Fathers of black survey respondents continued to hold an edge over the mothers with regard to doctorate or postdoctoral degree. Generally, the parents of white peers in both cohorts were somewhat better educated than those of African Americans. However, there are noticeable variations. For example, among mothers, blacks were more likely to hold a Master's degree and equally likely to hold a doctorate or postdoctoral degree. whites were twice as likely than blacks to hold a college degree and equally likely to have at least some college credits. Among fathers, whites held an advantage at every degree level. Furthermore, few parents of white respondents did not finish high school.

In recent decades, the education gap between African Americans and whites has been closing among adults aged twenty-five and older. This is due, in part, to improvements in school retention rates. For example, the black dropout rate among persons sixteen to twenty-four years old declined from 17% in 1980 to 11% in 2002, compared to dropout rates for Whites of 11 in 1980 and 7 in 2001. However, the 2002 Black dropout rate was the lowest ever recorded. The 2002 Census Bureau revealed comparable numbers of high school graduates with no college (36% for African Americans and 34% for whites). Differences remained, however, in the category of high school graduate or more education (79% black and 89% white). In 2002, 17% of all African Americans, had a Bachelor's degree or more, while the comparable percentage for whites was 29% (Parrillo, 2005).

Data in Table 2.3 show the parental occupations of the interviewees across cohorts. Ten interviewees reported that their mothers were housewives. The occupations of the mothers who worked outside of the home spanned the economic spectrum from sharecropper to physician, although most were not employed in professional or white-collar occupations. The occupations of the fathers mirrored those of the interviewees' mothers.

Previous studies report that historically African American fathers compared to white fathers receive a much smaller return on their educational investment, particularly in terms of occupational prestige. Moreover, highly-educated African Americans fared less well relative to comparably educated whites, than did less educated African Americans to their white peers (see Freeman, 1976). Data in Table 2.4 show little change in black percentage of white median family income in the past thirty years. While acknowledging that salary and occupational discrimination along racial lines traditionally have been greatest at the top, both economist Richard Freeman (1976) and sociologist William J. Wilson (1978) suggest that such forms of overt discrimination have virtually faded. This has been

Table 2.3. Distribution by Parental Occupation During Senior Year of High School by Cohort [Interviewees].

Cohort I Before 1955		Cohort II 1955–1964		Cohort III 1965–1974		Cohort IV 1975–1984		Cohort V 1985–1995	
Mother	Father	Mother	Father	Mother	Father	Mother	Father	Mother	Father
Teacher	Teacher/ Farmer	Seamstress	Motorboard Operator	Teacher	Sharecropper	Dental Tech.	Teacher	Teacher	College Professor
Seamstress	Farmer	Laundress	Small Business	Physician	P. O. Clerk	Security Officer	Truck Driver	Small Business	Farmer
Piece Work	Brakeman	Domestic	Farmer	Secretary	Presser	Housewife	Army Sgt.	College Prof.	Small Business
Housewife	Mortician	Housewife	Minister	Seamstress	Physician	Nurse	Factory Worker	Housewife	Principal
	Factory Worker		Laborer	Domestic	Stock Room Manager		Contractor	Child Care	Laborer
	State Clerk			Farmer	Farmer		Real Estate Broker	Government	Carpenter
	Federal Employee			Laborer	Principal			Clerk	Forklift Operator
				Housewife	College Administrator				
				Book Store Manager	Painter				
				Receptionist	Laborer				
				Cafeteria Worker	Janitor				
				Sharecropper	Mail Carrier				
					Steelworker				

Table 2.4. Distribution of Median Income of U.S. Families by Race.

Year	White (Dollars)	Black (Dollars)	Percentage of White Income (Black)	Income Gap (Dollars) (Black)
1950	3,455	1,869	54.3	1,576
1960	5,835	3,233	55.4	2,602
1970	10,236	6,516	63.7	3,720
1980	21,904	12,674	57.9	8,061
1990	36,915	21,423	58.0	15,492
2000	53,256	34,192	64.2	19,064

Source: Adapted from U.S. Bureau of Statistics.

attributed to a number of factors, including anti-discrimination laws and market competition for the best talent.

Pearson's (1985) study confirmed that the highly educated fathers of his African American scientists did not find employment commensurate with their academic training and abilities. This is particularly true for some of the fathers of scientists who earned their doctorates before 1965. This point is best illustrated in the case of a chemist who explained that although his father held a professional degree from one of the nation's most prestigious research universities, he spent his entire professional career as a federal employee. According to the interviewee, his father was frustrated that he could not find suitable employment in private business because of his race. In recent years, some progress has been made in closing the income, education, and occupational gaps between African Americans and whites. However, Orr (2003) cautions those substantial racial differences in wealth continue to effect opportunities and life chances. Among native-born African Americans nearly 80% consists of working- or middle-class people, who tend to earn about one-fourth less than non-Hispanic whites with comparable educational backgrounds. Orr sees this situation as a possible indicator of the persistence of racial discrimination. The remaining 20% consists of African Americans who live in poverty at a rate triple the percentage for white Americans. The black/white poverty ratio has remained constant for nearly 50 years (Parrillo, 2005).

In 1978, William Julius Wilson published an influential and important book, *The Declining Significance of Race,* on the status of African Americans in the U.S. Cose (1993) is probably correct in his assessment that many individuals read the title and assumed that Wilson was arguing that race no longer mattered in America. A close reading of the text would suggest otherwise. Cose asserts that Wilson was more subtle and less exact in his argument. Wilson concluded that the life chances of individual African Americans were determined more by economic class position than by the daily encounters of whites. As evidence,

Wilson showed the increased movement of African Americans in white-collar jobs and attendant life styles similar to their white peers; however, he speaks to the issue of career mobility and final positions commensurate with their education and career experience. Wilson's primary concern focused on the plight of the black underclass-whose life chances could not be attributed solely to race. Furthermore, economic trends that changed the structure of work limited the socioeconomic positions of the very poor regardless of race or ethnicity (Cose, 1993).

MARITAL STATUS

Survey data reveal that regardless of racial groups earning their Ph.D.s before 1985, males considerably more likely than females to be married. In fact, African American male respondents were the most likely to be married, while African American females were least likely to report being married. African American females were nearly twice as likely as any other demographic group to be widowed, separated or divorced. The results for chemists earning doctorates between 1985 and 2002 show a decidedly different picture. For example, African Americans are considerably more likely than their white peers to have not married through 1990 or never married after 1990. African Americans were somewhat more likely than their white peers to report that they were in a marriage or marriage-like relationship (albeit small percent). White males were most likely of all demographic groups to be married, while African American females continued the most likely to be not married through 1990 or never married after 1990 (Table 2.5).

Data in Table 2.6 reveal that slightly more than half of the interviewees were married. In fact, about half of the interviewees were married while pursuing the doctorate. The age at first marriage ranged from 18 to 48 years, and the median age was 26 years. Interviewees expressed a wide array of opinions about their marital life. The following are representative comments. One woman felt that if she were to complete her doctorate, she had little choice in making the decision to "defer marriage until after my Ph.D." One male interviewee explained that: "Being married has affected my work because my family is my top priority . . . Getting married did not adversely affect my work. But work adversely affected my marriage!"

Another female interviewee said: "It is often difficult to divide time between home and work life." A female interviewee commented: "Being female and trying to balance family and career demands played a role in my tenure difficulties. I enjoy research but when you have family, you can't always stay in the lab 24 hours a day. This did affect my research productivity." One interviewee from industry remarked that: "Marriage brought out the best in me. My wife is highly motivated

Table 2.5. Percent Distribution of Martial Status by Race, Sex and Cohort [Survey Respondents].

Marital Status	Cohort							
	Before 1985				1985–2002			
	Black		White		Black		White	
	Female	Male	Female	Male	Female	Male	Female	Male
Married	43.0	72.0	54.0	66.0	33.0	45.0	49.0	52.0
Marriage-like relationship	[a]	[a]	[a]	[a]	3.0	2.0	2.0	1.0
Widowed/Separated/Divorced	18.0	7.0	10.0	9.0	4.0	3.0	3.0	2.0
Not married (thru 1990)/Never married (after 1990)	39.0	21.0	37.0	26.0	61.0	50.0	46.0	45.0
Total	100.0	100.0	100.0	100.0	100.0	100.0	100.0	100.0

Note: Percentages may not sum to 100% due to rounding.
Source: Survey of Earned Doctorates.
[a]Less than 1%.

Table 2.6. Percent Distribution of Marital Status by Sex [Interviewees].

Marital Status	Sex		Total
	Female	Male	
Married	14.0	60.0	52.0
Never married	43.0	3.0	9.0
Divorced	29.0	19.0	21.0
Remarried	14.0	11.0	11.0
Widowed	0.0	8.0	7.0
Total	100.0	100.0	100.0

Note: Percentages may not sum to 100% due to rounding.
Source: Survey of Earned Doctorates.

and she has always pushed and encouraged me." One male interviewee exclaimed, "Being married helped me to become more proficient!" Another male agrees:

> Being married has a stabilizing influence in that I am more focused on what I have to do in my career as opposed to wasting time. My wife knows that as an untenured assistant professor, I need to keep long hours in the lab initially. I try to be considerate of her in the actual number of hours I spend in the lab. Because my wife and I are employed in professional occupations, I know that I will have to scale back once we have children. By then, I plan to have tenure.

> An interviewee from industry commented: "In certain corporate cultures, I believe management views a married black male more positively than a single black male."

Nearly one in ten interviewees had never married. As was the case with the survey respondents, there were striking gender differences with females more likely to have never married. These findings are consistent with those reported by Pearson and Earle (1984) in their study of African American and white doctoral scientists. They found that African American women were far more likely than any race-gender group to have never married.

Demographic data reveal that at any given time in the United States since the World War II, there have been a greater number of women than men who are eligible for marriage and looking for a partner. Sociologists have defined this imbalance in the ratio of marriage-aged men to marriage-aged women as a "marriage squeeze," where one sex has a more limited pool of eligibles. The marriage squeeze limits the range of choices of mates for women, although its impact is experienced differently across race and age and even geographic location. Studies suggest that statistically, African-American women appear more vulnerable to the marriage squeeze (Tucker & Mitchell-Kernan, 1995). The lower life expectancy for African-American men (lower than that for white males and all females), coupled with an ever-increasing number of young African-American men who are victims of homicides and the disproportionate numbers who are incarcerated contribute greatly to this trend (Majors & Gordon, 1994; Staples, 1999).

By the time African-American women reach 18 years of age they begin to outnumber African-American males. White women do not begin to outnumber white men until age 32 (Spanier & Glick, 1980). According to Staples (1999), this phenomenon will continue to deny large numbers of African-American women a mate of comparable status. Crowder and Tolnay (2000) point to an additional factor that exacerbates that marriage squeeze for African American women, especially, well-educated, professional. These researchers point to recent interracial marriage trends among African American males. Their findings show that African American men married to non-black women (usually white) are more likely than those married to African American women "to have higher incomes, education, occupational prestige, and rates of employment" (p. 804).

DIVORCE

In the general population, African Americans tend to have higher divorce rates than whites. Some analysts attribute the higher rate of divorce among African-Americans to the legacy of slavery (Frazier, 1939). Subsequent scholarship, however, has found that the increase in black marital instability is a more recent development, accelerating since 1960 and corresponding to a decline in the economic situation of large numbers of African-Americans, especially males (Cherlin, 1981; Gutman, 1976; Tucker & Mitchell-Kernan, 1995). There is some support for the argument that higher divorce rates among African-Americans reflect greater economic hardships. Goodwin (2003) asserts that the fragile economic situations of African Americans place considerable stress on their marriages. She reveals that African American marriages are more likely than whites (47% vs. 32%) to end in divorce within 10 years. Overall, African Americans are less likely than whites to evaluate their marriages as positive. Significant black/white differences in marital stability may also be explained by differences in levels of education and income (Jaynes & Williams, 1989).

Among ever-married chemists, African American women had the highest divorce rates and lowest rates of remarriage following divorce. Divorce rates tend to be higher among women with five or more years of college education but the pattern does not occur among comparably educated males. Although the reasons for these divergent patterns are not as yet well understood, Eshleman (2003) speculates that the higher level of divorce for women may reflect lessened dependence on men for economic support, viable alternatives to marriage and conflicts involved in balancing work and family responsibilities. This may be exaggerated in the case of African American women because they contribute disproportionately to finances of their households. Furthermore, women holding professional jobs are less likely to be financially dependent on a spouse and thus can afford to leave an unsatisfactory relationship. One woman explained: "Prior to the divorce, we were having some problems, which I think were related to my moving ahead much faster than my husband. He would not admit that that was a problem." Compared to their white peers, African American marriages are viewed as more equalitarian. Nevertheless, gender equality remains an issue in African American marriages (Goodwin, 2003).

Survey data are available only in the aggregated form of widowed, separated and divorced. These data reveal that significant race-gender differences emerge for the pre-1985 cohort. African American female chemists comprised the largest portion of those in the category widowed/separated/divorced. For the 1985–2002 cohort, race-gender variations were negligible. Regardless of race, females dominated this category. Based on previous studies, the number of widows cannot account for this finding. One-fifth of the interviewees had experienced a divorce and was unmarried at the time of the study. Slightly more than a tenth of the interviewees were remarried. Approximately 7% of the chemists were widowed. Some interviewees indicated that the period prior to, during and after divorce took a heavy emotional and physical toll on them.

One male interviewee recalled "My first marriage had a lot of turmoil and it affected my career in a sense that I was not receptive to being mobile." Another male interviewee reflected: "After the divorce, I realized that it took a greater toll than I thought." One male interviewee had this to say about his short-lived marriage: "Marriage affected my research because we had different ideas about how to live and about work ethics. This became a major issue with us. So, I decided to get a divorce."

A twice-divorced male interviewee explained:

> My second marriage lasted less than a year because it distracted greatly from my work. She wanted to distract me from my work. She actually brought some personal issues into my workplace. The whole thing started because she refused to believe that I couldn't take her on all my business trips. She just couldn't understand why I couldn't take her on all of them. She thought that if I was not taking her that I must have been taking someone else . . . the fact that I had marital problems affected management's perception of me. At the time, I was on the management track. As a result of the divorce and resulting stress, I ended up back on the technical track, which was not my preference.

One female interviewee, who viewed divorce positively, said that: "Getting a divorce actually enhanced my work." One male interviewee extolled the virtues of remarriage: "I have been married twice. My first marriage ended in divorce

Table 2.7.   Distribution by Occupation of Current Spouse [Interviewees].

Wife (*N* = 26)	Husband (*N* = 2)
K-12 Teacher	Community College Instructor
Housewife	University Professor
Social Worker	
Biologist	
Freight Coordinator	
Computer Technician	
Business Manager (Academe)	
Graduate Student	
Community College Instructor	
Government Regulatory Specialist	
Vice President (Non-profit Organization)	
Secretary	
Data Processor	
Nurse	
Attorney (Private Practice)	
Speech Pathologist	
Small Business Owner	

after years. Following a two-year hiatus, I came to know a woman (who is 14 years his junior) in our laboratory and we have been married ever since. We have two children. Every morning while I am home, we do a two-mile walk where we chat about various things."

The two currently married (including one remarried) females were married to men employed in higher education. The largest occupational category for the wives of interviewees was the teaching profession, primarily at the K-12 level. However, the next highest category was housewife. A couple of the male interviewees were married to white-collar professionals (see Table 2.7).

The number of children of ever-married interviewees ranged from zero to five. The typical family consisted of two children. Typically, the interviewees' median age when the first child was born was 31 years, although the range was from 20 to 52 years. Overall, few interviewees reported that a child was born during a critical point in his or her career. Of those who did, the following comments are illustrative. One interviewee said: "Having children motivated me to get things accomplished so that I could be a good provider for my family." Another interviewee explained: "I was not prepared for having so many children and so close together. Plus, these kids were unplanned. I felt like I was being run down a gauntlet. I had to deal with whatever came along. I did what was necessary to get my work done but it was very stressful." One male interviewee remarked: "Having children made me more aware of various career options." However, a female interviewee emphasized

"Children affected my work because I had less time to devote to research." One interviewee comments:

> Without a child, I would probably be more work-driven and enjoy smelling the roses less. My daughter adds a different dimension to my life. She brings joy into my life. I think that it is very important to provide a balance between work and other things in life).

Another interviewee elaborated:

> When I was transferred from a small city in the Northeast to a large city in the Midwest, my children had a difficult time adjusting. Shortly after moving into the neighborhood, I discovered that black folks were not very well accepted. For my children's well being, I went to management and asked to be transferred back to my former site. I am convinced that this had some negative impact on my career mobility.

This chemist's decision to protect his children from racism may not be so atypical from other black professionals. Cose (1993) provides considerable anecdotal evidence that some of the most affluent African Americans – graduates of prep schools and Ivy League colleges and universities – make concerted efforts to shelter their children from unpleasant racial experiences. He claims that in order to protect and enhance the self-image and self confidence of their children, many affluent black parents send their children to prestigious historically black colleges and universities, such as Howard University and Spelman College. Many of Cose's interviewees spoke of the difficulty of raising middle-class black children. Parents want to provide the highest quality of education and exposure to the larger world, while sheltering them racism. This conundrum was also very much on the minds of some of the chemist interviewees in this study. The dilemma of being black and middle-class in the racialized U.S. has been the subject of commentary over the expanse of history. E. Franklin Frazier's (1939), *Black Bourgeoisie* sparked controversy and condemnation among some African Americans, especially the middle class. The psychological aspects of being black middle class parents may be even more challenging today than in the more racially segregated nation of the past. Cose (1993, p. 148) contends that "even if one assumes that black children need to be taught to cope with the burden of race, how relevant is the experience of parents who were raised in a time when certain racial barriers were much higher than they are today, and in an era when racial attitudes now widely deemed unacceptable were freely exhibited without censure or embarrassment?"

RELIGIOUS AFFILIATION

Scholarly interest in the role of religion in the lives of scientists is longstanding (Glock & Stark, 1965; Greely, 1965; Lehman, 1974; Leuba, 1934; Merton, 1973;

Roe, 1953; Wuthnow, 1985; Zuckerman, 1977). Overall, African Americans are less likely than whites to evaluate their marriages as positive. Significant black/white differences in marital stability may also be explained by differences in levels of education and income (Jaynes & Williams, 1989). However, Murry et al. (2001, p. 916) emphasize that "one source of stress that is unique to the African American experience is racial discrimination." They assert that exposure to chronic racial discrimination actually amplifies other stressors on the African American families.

Most published studies of the role of religion in the lives of scientists are limited to whites. The major exceptions are studies by Pearson (1985) and Pearson and Ellis (1988) which included samples of African American and white doctoral natural and social scientists. These studies confirmed the findings of previous studies of white scientists regarding the prevalence of Protestants. According to Pearson (1985), African Americans were considerably *more likely* than their white peers to be Protestant, *equally likely* to be Catholic and *less likely* to be Jewish.

Compared to the general public, Pearson and Ellis (1988) report that both African American and white scientists are *less likely* than their non-scientists peers to be Protestant or Catholic. Only among whites were Jews and those citing "other" affiliation overrepresented among scientists. Regardless of race, scientists were far *more likely* than the general population to be unaffiliated with a religion. Among natural scientists, however, Pearson and Ellis reveal striking race variations with whites *more likely* to be nonaffiliates (slightly more than one-fourth vs. slightly less than one-fifth), Jewish (10% vs. less than 1%) and *less likely* to be Protestant (slightly less than half vs. slightly less than three-fourths). Additionally, African Americans were found to be *more likely* than their white peers to be Baptists. This is not surprising given that most African Americans had their origins in working class or low socioeconomic status families in the South, a region where the Baptists predominate (Steinberg, 1974).

In the present study, Fig. 2.4 reveals that nearly two-fifths of interviewees reported no religious preference. This is somewhat surprising given the results of previous findings on the religious affiliation of African American Ph.D. natural scientists (see Ellis & Pearson, 1988). Of those reporting a religious preference, the pattern was similar to those reported in previous studies: mostly Protestant, a few Catholics or "other" religions (e.g. Asian or African religions). Not surprisingly, those expressing no religious preference were the least likely to attend religious services. A greater proportion of the Protestants than others reported attending services frequently. In a measure of ritualistic religiosity – participation in prayer and church attendance (Glock, 1962), Pearson and Ellis (1988) report that among natural scientists African American were significantly more likely than their white

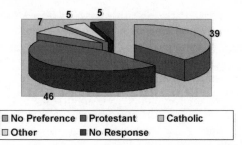

Fig. 2.4. Percent Distribution by Religious Affiliation [Interviewees].

peers to attend church. Although scientists reporting Jewish affiliation were *least likely* to attend church, the authors found no statistically significant race differences among the various denominations.

One interviewee had this to say about religion: "My childhood preference was Baptist. This preference was socially driven because most people whom I knew attended the Baptist church. However, I no longer consider that a preference." Another interviewee asserts: "I have been a member of almost every conceivable traditional religion. I have now decoupled from traditional religion." One interviewee identified himself as a "non-practicing Roman Catholic," while another commented, "I am a Protestant and that is about as much of a distinction as I make." Some interviewees were ambivalent about traditional religions. Another interviewee reported this transformation:

I guess I am a Baptist now. I joined the Episcopal Church when I got married, but I've sort of gravitated back to my roots. I grew up in the Baptist church...I attend church services quite infrequently, now. I attend maybe once or twice a year...I have a real problem with traditional religion... The fact that I don't go to church doesn't mean that I don't believe in Christianity. As a matter of fact, I have very strong beliefs. It's just that I am the kind of person who believes that if something is right, then that should govern your daily life...I try to live my religion...I am having a bit of trouble because I grew up in the church and somehow that sticks with me that I ought to be going to church all the time...I just got out of the habit of going because I saw so many things that I thought were contradictory to what the people said they believed in... Growing up, church was the only thing that you could do on Sunday. Even then, I questioned, in my own simplified way, why there were all these roles for people who were Christians. I think that I have always seen the inherent contradictions in traditional religion. When I brought my terminally ill mother to live with me, not one person from my church came to see her... They didn't call to see how she was doing or anything like that. To me, that is not what church is supposed to be about... When I was experiencing marital problems, I called my minister and he came by once... Another minister who was to come to talk with us never came. Nobody was concerned that we were having marital problems... So, I started attending another church...but the minister ended up in jail... If there are rules, no matter what denomination you belong to, then you ought to follow them...I am a stickler for rules . . . there are people who go to church on Sunday; then, on Monday they're stabbing people in the back.

One interviewee reported belonging to a West African religion and attending services every Saturday. The interviewee claimed that his "religious beliefs have centered him." In short, the interviewee asserted that religion brought him an inner peace. One interviewee stated simply: "My faith is a source of strength." One interviewee relocated to be near the "home church" in order to be more engaged in its activities. At the time of the interview, this interviewee mentioned that "God" was more central than the professional career. The interviewee referenced getting the current job because of prayer. An interviewee had this to say:

> . . . I knew some people who conducted studies on the religion of African Americans in North and South Carolina . . . The results indicated that regardless of what a black person said he was, the basic philosophy was that of a Baptist . . . That goes all the way back to slavery . . . Because of the way it [religion] was taught during slavery, it enabled the black man to survive, because he could look forward to going to heaven to get his worldly goods. Therefore, he didn't have to worry about materialistic things on earth . . . Religion has done more than anything to hold the black man back! . . . He's going to get his reward in Heaven! . . . To me, religion is a bunch of hypocrisy! . . . They (whites) sold slaves in the church after services! . . . Now, I thought Christianity was based on the brotherhood of mankind! . . . Like Martin Luther King, Jr. said "The most segregated time in America is 11:00 am Sunday morning.

One notable characteristic of religious practice in the United States is the almost completely separate worship practices of African Americans and whites (Schaefer, 2000). According to Lincoln and Mamiya (1990), a black sacred cosmos emerged historically that cut across denominational lines. They posit that regardless of denomination a qualitatively different cultural form of Christian expressions is found in most black churches. Moreover, the authors contend that there has always been a small sector of "unchurched" black people – young African American males or maverick types determined to resist the powerful social control of black churches in the small rural towns and in urban areas. One interviewee cautiously stated:

> I am a black nationalist . . . I don't talk about this publicly because it will make things even more difficult for me . . . This is going to sound radical but I really believe that we (African Americans) are in a struggle for survival.

For many interviewees, religion provides a source of strength, a solace in times of need. For others, although they may have had a religious upbringing, various experiences have altered the role of religion in their adult lives. In fact, many had simply disengaged from traditional religious affiliation.

EDUCATIONAL EXPERIENCES: FROM GRADE SCHOOL TO GRADUATE SCHOOL

In 1954, the U.S. Supreme Court in *Brown v. Board* unanimously decreed segregated public schools unconstitutional. Some fifty years later, a significant proportion of black children attend separate and inferior schools (Freedman, 2004; Orfield & Yun, 1999; Pinkney, 2000). The racial and class composition of schools is associated with both economic and educational resources insofar as residential property taxes generate revenues to fund public schools. Therefore, returning to the concept of neighborhood schools creates a new form of segregation in terms of spending on education and achievement in many urban areas throughout the United States (Condron & Roscigno, 2003).

In the state of Illinois, for example, nearly two in five black students compared to less than 1% of white students attend one of the 335 schools on the state's "academic watch" list. Moreover, a student attending a majority black school is nearly six times more likely than one attending a non-majority black school to receive instruction from teachers who are not fully state-certified in Illinois. Approximately seven in 10 black students attend a majority black school, while nine in 10 white students attend a majority white school (*Black Issues in Higher Education*, 2000).

Society suffers economically when the schools and the young abandon each other. Lack of education is both a cause and an effect of poverty. Among all families living in poverty, one-fifth of all heads of household are not high school graduates. This proportion increases dramatically for African American children. Furthermore, children of the poor are less likely than those of the nonpoor to graduate from high school or to enter college. Many of these children are doubly victimized because they receive little or no academic encouragement at school and/or have parents who cannot assist with homework at home. Also, some

49

teachers will have low expectations for their achievement. The confluence of these unfortunate circumstances often intensifies the children's low achievement, which results in them leaving school. Those who manage to remain in school are likely to receive a substandard education. Both the rural and urban poor are overrepresented in these schools which are not conducive to teaching and learning (Parrillo, 2005). Consequently, a considerable share of these children will end up in what Wilson (1978) describes as the underclass – with low paying jobs or no jobs at all. Too often, this leads to intergenerational poverty.

Residential segregation is a major contributor to school segregation. Eminent historian John Hope Franklin also points to segregation in housing as a barrier to school desegregation (Suggs, 2004). When African Americans move to the suburbs, whites move even farther away, thereby causing the inner suburbs to turn increasingly black. Increasingly, more and more middle-class African Americans are joining their white peers in seeking the relative security and quality of private schools. As a result, urban public schools become the province of lower-class racial minority children. Often, these schools are deteriorating and in need of major repairs. Critics argue that a deteriorating school environment makes children less likely to learn. A minority child is also three times more likely than a white child to be enrolled in vocational education or in classes for the mildly mentally retarded (Parrillo, 2005).

Busing was introduced to bring racial balance to segregated school districts. However, the practice resulted in most minority students being bused to predominantly white neighborhoods. Over time, minority parents objected to the long bus trips for their children. In particular, minority parents were outraged because their children were met by angry and sometimes violent adults. Additionally, white flight from affected areas tended to undermine attempts at racial balance. In its ruling in *Milliken v. Bradley* (1974), the U.S. Supreme Court held that desegregation efforts could not be imposed across school district lines to apply to an entire metropolitan area. The decision is believed to have further encouraged white flight. In 1986, the U.S. Supreme Court agreed that Norfolk, Virginia could end busing in order to reduce white flight. A few years later (1991), in *Board of Education of Oklahoma City v. Dowell*, the U.S. Supreme Court reversed its previous decision on busing as a remedy by releasing all segregated school systems from court-ordered busing-based methods of desegregation (Parrillo, 2005).

To date, studies of the effects of busing have produced inconclusive results. Some studies report improved achievement of minority students but under certain conditions. For example, if their education began early in a desegregated school with a multicultural curriculum. However, other studies report negative effects on minority student achievement – especially when the minority students are placed in desegregated schools where they differ from white students in terms of socioeconomic status and academic preparation (Parrillo, 2005). For many black and white parents, busing as a strategy to bring about racial balance in the schools and high-quality instruction for all students has not been satisfactory.

Public school reform has been evolving more and more toward parental choice, which has taken two primary forms: (1) charter schools; and (2) magnet schools. Generally, charter schools have some flexibility from district and state regulations. However, the schools are required to meet student performance standards. Proponents believe that schools have an advantage over traditional schools because the instructional methods and managerial styles are more innovative. Magnet schools tend to be more specialized. For example, curriculum content tends to focus on a particular area, such as maths and science, fine and performing arts or design. Proponents see this approach as more effective than involuntary busing because students volunteer to attend (Parrillo, 2005).

In 2000, the percentage of high school graduates with no college was comparable for African Americans and whites (36% and 34%, respectively). However, among those with high school diplomas or more education, race differences are considerably larger (79%, black and 89%, white). Moreover, about 64% of recent white high school graduates compared with 56% of African Americans enrolled in college (Parrillo, 2005).

Generally, interviewees report fond memories of their elementary and secondary school years. In particular, most singled out their math and science courses. Usually, their interest in mathematics emerged prior to that in science. This, of course, is due in large measure to earlier exposure to mathematics. By the end of middle school or early high school, most interviewees were interested in pursuing some type of career in science. Once exposed to a chemistry course or a chemical experiment, interviewees were more definite in their disciplinary choice. A small minority reported that prior to high school they wanted to pursue a career in chemistry (see Fig. 3.1). The vast majority decided to pursue a career in chemistry in high school (usually around the junior year), while approximately one-fourth did so after high school – usually in college. As early as 1953, Roe reported that although a majority of (white) scientists in her study decided to pursue a career in science during their junior or senior year in high school, a few made the decision much earlier. In their study of African American natural science doctorate holders, Young and Young (1974) found that more than half decided to pursue a scientific career by the sophomore or junior year in high school. That interviewees report decisions to pursue a career in science at various points along the educational continuum suggests multiple pathways to a scientific career.

As reported in previous studies of African American scientists, the vast majority performed exceptionally well in their high school academic courses. Data in

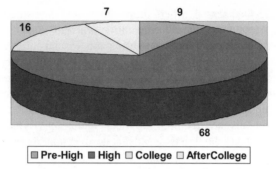

Fig. 3.1. Percent Distribution by Age at Initial Choice of Chemistry as a Career [Interviewees].

Table 3.1 reveal that an overwhelming number of the interviewees graduated in the top quartile of their senior classes.

Roughly one in ten interviewees graduated from a private high school, while the remainder earned a diploma from a public school. Whether private or public, the vast majority of interviewees graduated from high schools where they were in the racial majority. Although this was more typical of the South, the pattern was not substantially different in the North and East. These data reflect the pervasive nature of both residential and school segregation in the U.S. (Taeuber & Taeuber, 1965). Pearson (1985) also found significant differences in the racial composition of the schools attended by the scientists in his study. He reported that nearly all (99%) of white scientists attended high schools where they were in the racial majority. Contrastly, approximately three-fourths of black scientists attended high schools where they were the racial majority. However, Pearson found that these patterns varied according to region. For example, African Americans who matriculated high school in the South were considerably more likely than those from the North,

Table 3.1. Percent Distribution by High School Graduating Class by Quartile [Interviewees].

Quartile	Percent
First	93.0
Second	7.0
Third	0.0
Fourth	0.0
Total	100.0

Note: Percentages may not sum to 100 because of rounding.

West, and East to have attended high school where they comprised 50% or less of the student population. Often, the racially segregated schools (both now and in the past) had teachers who were not certified in a mathematics or science field teach those subjects (see also, Smith, 1994). One interviewee recalled: "The only real math I had was Algebra. We had something beyond that, but somebody who was not a mathematician taught it."

CATALYSTS FOR CHOOSING CHEMISTRY

Regardless of race, a preponderance of scientists cite "personal interest" or the desire to know more about nature as the primary reason to pursue science as a career. A greater proportion of white scientists than African American scientists cited this as their primary reason. African American scientists are more likely than their white peers to report that the influence of others contributed greatly to their decision to pursue a career in science (Pearson, 1985). Similar to previous studies, the majority of interviewees in this study cite the influence of others as the leading catalyst for selecting a career in chemistry. One interviewee reported this:

> I had a very interesting junior high school science teacher. I was the best student in my science class. I was his prize student. Once I came in contact with chemistry – symbols, formulas, equations, and all the different things you could do – I just fell in love with chemistry!

Another interviewee recalled:

> I think along with the particular curiosity about how things worked, it had to do with this intriguing name chemistry, ads in *Popular Science* and *Popular Mechanics*,[1] and buying a chemistry set from one of those ads and seeing pictures that were generally elaborate chemical setups. I found that intriguing. So, I thought that I wanted to do that.

Several male interviewees reported that advertisements in these magazines attracted them to science – especially chemistry.

One interviewee explained his decision to pursue chemistry this way:

> I was always good in math. In high school, I took chemistry and physics courses and did well. So, I knew I wanted to be a science major. I probably became chemistry major because my sister was in chemistry and I had high admiration for her. If I had different exposures, I may have pursued engineering.

Another interviewee recalled two key experiences that influenced his choice of a science career:

> First, a science fair project that involved the distillation of gasoline to separate the hydrocarbons into their component parts. Second, my high school science teacher had me making stock solutions and things like that. At that point, I knew that I had some talent toward science, and specifically in chemistry.

One interviewee provided this response:

> When I took my first course in chemistry, I was a junior in high school. I put it that way because
> we were required to take biology, but it never moved me. The next science course was either
> chemistry or physics, and I chose chemistry. Taking chemistry, which was a senior course,
> permitted me to take more mathematics, which was also an interest of mine.

Another interviewee explained: "I selected chemistry because I thought it was more challenging and had more things to discover than biology. Biology was too routine for me." One chemist said that he decided to pursue a career in chemistry because of the influence of a chemistry teacher, whose highest degree was a master's in French.

One interviewee explained:

> My science teacher in junior high school, where I initially gained some interest in science,
> was a black male. Part of the value of going to an all black junior high school is that you can
> emphasize some things to a greater extent than what is done in integrated settings. Oftentimes,
> he [science teacher] would assign extra topics as research or reading projects. Looking back
> on it now, I can see the disparity in the class and he probably recognized that at the time too.
> He would always assign those extra things to me and a couple of other people who excelled in
> school to report back to the other people in the class. I guess that was his way of generating
> interest from some of the other members of the class . . .

Another interviewee said:

> I remember in high school that I really didn't want to be a MD. I just thought about the repetition
> and that you would be doing the same thing over and over. I went to the library and read about this
> thing called "Research" and it sounded like something new and challenging to do. That's when
> I started thinking that I really wanted to do something different and intellectually challenging.

Several interviewees became interested in a scientific career after reading the biography of George Washington Carver. Some were influenced after reading articles about Percy Julian related to breaking the color barrier in industry during the 1930s. One respondent said: "A friend of the family worked for Percy Julian but I really didn't know what he did. However, I did know the children of another black industrial chemist by the name of Hall."

One interviewee pointed to the influence of the war effort on the decision to pursue a career in science:

> I can't point to anything other than the publicity and the news surrounding the atomic bomb and
> atomic energy. The things that I heard a lot about piqued my curiosity. First, I became interested
> in physics, then in chemistry. What most piqued my curiosity were the discussions about how
> atomic energy was going to revolutionize our society and the world.

A Cohort III interviewee recalled being impressed with the DuPont advertisement: "Better Things for Better Living Through Chemistry." The interviewee reflected:

"I remember thinking, I would like to create some special compound that would improve the quality of life."

One interviewee commented:

> I was riding my bike through the local university when I came across a professor [African American male] and we talked for about four hours. He sketched out an idea on a piece of paper for making a homemade chromatograph. I don't think he really thought I would do anything with it. I used the university library to research it. Then, I realized that I could make it out of scrap material. I built a chromatograph. A student teacher, who was intrigued by it, helped me to write up a report. My teachers helped me enter a statewide contest . . . which I won! Ultimately, I received a scholarship to attend (a prestigious public university). At that point, I realized I could make money doing science. That got me into science in a big way.

An interviewee who decided to pursue a science career while in college recalls:

> I realized that I was very interested in science. Around my sophomore year . . . I started taking some chemistry courses and liberal arts courses. I worked so hard in those liberal arts courses but I could never get Bs in them. I went to a prestigious liberal arts college where there was no grade inflation and it was unusual to get an A. No matter how hard I tried, I had so much trouble getting good grades in liberal arts courses. Finally, it dawned on me that I was not very good in liberal arts courses. At the same time, I was taking chemistry and biology courses as well, and I was doing very well in them. That's how I gradually got into science. The thing that really made me decide that I was more interested in graduate school than medical school, was when I took a genetics course. DNA research was hot. It was exciting. I decided that I wanted to pursue a career as a research scientist.

A majority of interviewees reported that they had been encouraged by various persons to pursue their studies beyond high school. Data in Fig. 3.2 show that parents exerted the most important or significant influence on the interviewee's decision to attend college. The next most influential person was likely to be a teacher. In an earlier study of American doctoral scientists, Pearson (1985) found that after parents, African Americans were more likely than whites to cite a "teacher" as the person who most influenced them to attend college. In contrast,

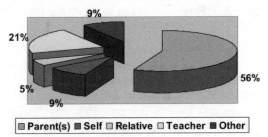

Fig. 3.2. Percent Distribution by Person Who Most Influenced Decision to Attend College [Interviewees].

whites generally cited themselves as the most important influence on their decision to attend college.

In 1997, President Clinton devoted one-quarter of his State of the Union address to education and issued a "Call to Action for American Education." Among the several ambitious goals he set for the nation was to have a well-prepared teacher in every classroom (Clinton, 1997). President Clinton's successor, George W. Bush, also recognized the need to improve the quality of teaching and learning for all children. President Bush's "No Child Left Behind" initiative had a strong focus on mathematics and science (No Child Left Behind Act of 2000).

The quality of classroom teaching is the most important in-school factor for improving student achievement (Sanders & Rivers, 1996). Teachers guide students toward higher levels of knowledge, understanding and personal development. Learning is a personal process that occurs largely through regular, direct interactions between students and their teachers. Good teachers engage students in the process of understanding the vast accumulated knowledge using it constructively, and communicating it effectively. These are serious responsibilities which can only be fulfilled by dedicated professionals who have received specialized training. One interviewee recalls:

> I went to a public high school where the chemistry/physics teacher was just brilliant. He gave special attention to anyone whom he thought had that extra get-up-and-go. There were two of us in his class to whom he gave special projects such as extra math, chemistry, and physics problems. He taught us stuff that he couldn't cover with the rest of the class. One day, he took me aside and said, "You need to go to college." Then the principal took me aside and said, "What can I do to help you attend college?" The principal got me a basketball scholarship. There were a lot of people in the school system who encouraged me to go to college. My mother told all of us (siblings) that to have a better life we needed a college degree.

One interviewee who grew up in a small Midwestern city recalled:

> At a high school reunion, I saw my favorite high school teacher (a white male). When I told him that he motivated me to go to college, he broke down and started crying. He said that I was the only one of his students who expressed an interest in science who got a Ph.D. in science. He was so proud. That made me feel good because my sister and I were two of only three African Americans in the graduating class at that reunion.

One woman said that she was influenced to attend college by the teachers at her high school, but also by the fact that: "I was running from the fields or domestic work because those were the only other (occupational) choices."

The interviews revealed that high school counselors, especially in schools where African American students were in the minority, often played insignificant or deleterious roles. For some interviewees, attending college was threatened by the lack of financial aid. Accessibility to a college or university is often determined by one's ability to pay. In studies of academic persistence, financial aid emerges as one of the most prominent factors having a direct impact on the process (*The New York Times*, 2004). While financial concerns affect the general population of students, they are particularly acute for African American students. However, recent studies (see, for example, Glenn, 2004; *Journal of Blacks in Higher Education*, 1999) reveal that African Americans have higher graduation rates at the most selective colleges and universities. In fact, some of the historically black colleges and universities have some of the nation's highest attrition rates. Moreover, African American students continue to have attrition rates higher than white students. This is related to selectivity of the type of institution attended by African American students as well as other factors, such as inadequate financial aid (see Arenson, 2004). For example, nearly 80% of the U.S.-born black population consists of working- or middle-class people, who tend to earn about one-fourth less than non-Hispanic whites with comparable educational backgrounds (*The Journal of Blacks in Higher Education*, 1996/1997). This differential is one indicator of persistence of racial discrimination in the marketplace. Often, the racially segregated schools (both now and in the past) had teachers who were not certified in a mathematic or science field to teach those subjects (see also, Smith, 1994). One interviewee recalled: "The only real math I had was Algebra. We had something beyond that, but somebody who was not a mathematician taught it."

The remaining proportion of black people lives in some level of poverty. This proportion of poverty-stricken blacks is triple the percentage for whites. This ratio has remained fairly constant for nearly fifty years (Parrillo, 2005). This suggests that many African American families will continue to depend on the availability of financial aid for their children to attend college. One interviewee commented:

> I had assumed that, like my siblings, I wasn't going to go to college. Even with the college scholarship that I received, there was no guarantee that my family could afford the room and board. Consequently, my mother only agreed to one year of college at a time.

Another remarked: "I had scholarships to go to_, _, _, and somewhere else. I found out I could go to_as a state student cheaper than with the scholarship going to_, that's why I went to_."

Undergraduate Education

In 1952, Knapp and Goodrich published one of the earliest studies of the baccalaureate origins of U.S. Ph.D. scientists. Institutional productivity was measured with an index based on the rate per thousand at which graduates of the institution between 1924 and 1934 continued to the doctoral level. The sample was drawn from individuals listed in the 1944 edition of *American Men of Science*. The authors found that small liberal arts colleges comprised a majority of the 50 most productive institutions in their sample. In 1968, Goodrich et al. again confirmed that most American doctoral scientists earned their undergraduate degrees at small liberal arts colleges. Also, they found that institutions located in the Midwest were the top producers of undergraduates who subsequently earned a doctorate in science.

Noting the absence of women in the Knapp and Goodrich study, Tidball and Kistiakowski (1976) studied gender variations in the baccalaureate origins of scientists. The authors report that women's colleges out produced coeducational institutions. Proponents of women's colleges argue that when women at these schools are enrolled in physics or chemistry classes, they are not discouraged by being in the minority and there is no peer pressure from male friends not to be smart (Sapiro, 1986). According to Stoecker and Pascarella (1991, p. 403), "the environment of a women's college may socialize women in ways that enhance self-confidence, drive for success, and prominence within occupational strata."

These studies have focused on whites or, at least, they do not disaggregate findings by race and gender. Consequently, they fail to inform the reader of the relevance of the findings for African Americans. One of the earliest studies of the educational backgrounds of African American doctoral scientists was conducted by James M. Jay (1971) who identified and rank-ordered those undergraduate institutions that were most productive in contributing to the pool of African-American Ph.D. natural scientists. He found that historically black colleges and universities dominated the list. This finding was confirmed by Young and Young (1974) in their study of African American doctoral natural scientists. In 1985, Pearson reported significant race differences in the types of institutions in which American Ph.D. scientists have their baccalaureate origins. He found that both groups were more likely to earn bachelor's degrees from institutions where they were the racial majority. Pearson and Pearson's study (1985) found that both natural and social scientists earning baccalaureate degrees from historically black colleges and universities decreased from three-fourths before 1955 to approximately two-thirds in the period from 1955 to 1974. Pearson and Leggon (1993) found a dramatic increase in the rate of this decline among their sample of African-American Ph.D. natural and social scientists: about two-firths of the 1975–1984 cohort had their baccalaureate origins in historically black colleges and universities, while less than one-fourth had such origins in the 1985–1989 cohort. Findings from Leggon's (1993) study of African Americans earning doctorates in the sciences between 1975 and 1992 indicate that more than half of the biologists and slightly less than half of the physical scientists had baccalaureate origins in an historically black college. In sharp contrast, only three in 10 social scientists earned baccalaureate degrees from historically black college/university. Similar to the findings reported by Tidball and Kistiakowski (1976), Leggon and Pearson (1997) report that women's colleges played an important role in the production of African-American women who subsequently earned doctorates in the sciences. These studies did not specifically focus on chemists.

One of the few studies focusing on the undergraduate origins of Ph.D. chemists was published more than a decade ago by Hall (1984). The top 10 baccalaureate institutions in Hall's study were: Swarthmore, DePauw University, Harvey Mudd, Oberlin, Kings (Pennsylvania), Union (New York), Trinity, Reed and Wabash (tie), and Worcester Polytechnic Institute. In a 1999 study of the undergraduate origins of American Ph.D. chemists, Pearson, Ness and Hoban found striking differences by racial and ethnic groups. The University of California-Berkeley led all baccalaureate institutions in the production of both whites and Asian-Americans, while Howard University was the top producer of African-Americans. When the baccalaureate institutions were categorized by Carnegie classifications, research institutions were the dominant baccalaureate institutions of whites, Asian Americans and Mexican Americans. In sharp contrast, African-Americans and Puerto Ricans were more likely to have their baccalaureate origins in institutions. Additionally, African-Americans and Puerto Ricans are unique insofar as BAII institutions (usually predominantly black or Puerto Rican) play a significant role in the production of individuals later earning the doctorate in chemistry. Top institutional produces tend to be located in those regions where a given racial and ethnic group was most heavily concentrated. Only five of the 48 institutions on the list for African Americans appear on that for whites. For whites, the leading producer for males was the University of California, Berkeley, while Rutgers University held that position for females. For white women, it is noteworthy that a women's college, Mt. Holyoke, tied with the University of Michigan-Ann Arbor as the second leading producer.

Among African Americans, Morgan State University, a historically black MAI institution, led all institutions in the numbers of its female baccalaureate recipients earning Ph.D.s in chemistry; Howard University led in the production of males. Some support is provided for Tidball's (1986) and Astin's (1963) argument that elements of the academic environment differentially affect women and men. Among African Americans, nearly a fourth of the undergraduate institutions on the men's list are classified as research-level universities, compared to about one third of those on the women's list. Slightly over a fifth of the men's institutions are classified as bachelor's level, compared to over two-fifths of those institutions on the women's list. These results should be interpreted cautiously because of the small numbers of institutions producing the females (e.g. three research and four baccalaureate institutions). Interestingly, predominantly black Spelman College was the only women's college to appear on the combined gender list for any racial and ethnic group (see also Leggon & Pearson, 1996). This finding lends some support to Pascarella's (1984) and Tidball's (1986) conclusions about the importance of women – both faculty and peers – in shaping the decisions and directions taken by women students (Pearson et al., 1999).

Historically Black Colleges and Universities

Given the significance of historically black colleges and universities in the production of African American scientific talent, these institutions deserve special attention. Prior to the Civil War, most African Americans lacked access to higher education. This was due in large measure to public policy and certain statutory provisions that prohibited the higher education of African Americans, especially in the South. Between 1826 and 1910 only 693 African Americans were graduated from predominantly white colleges in the United States. Even City College of New York, which had almost no admission requirements and an institutional mission to serve the dispossessed, had educated only two black graduates by 1910. By 1954, African Americans made up only 1% of freshmen at predominantly white institutions. This percentage did not increase above 2% until the late 1960s. It is true that a few colleges, usually religiously based, such as Oberlin, Berea, Bowdoin, Amherst, and Middlebury admitted a few African Americans as early as the 1820s, but this occurred only on a token and highly selective basis (Slater, 1994). Founded in Cheyney, Pennsylvania in 1837, the Institute for Colored Youth was the first higher education institution for African Americans. It was followed by founding of two other black institutions – Lincoln University, in Pennsylvania (1854), and Wilberforce University, in Ohio (1856). Even by the standards of the time, these institutions were "universities" in name only because much of their mission in their early years was to provide primary and secondary schooling for African American students (U.S. Department of Education, 1991).

In 1890, the Second Morrill Act required states to establish a land-grant institution for black students whenever a land-grant institution was established and restricted for white students. Eventually, 16 black land-grant colleges were established. Most course offerings were in agricultural, mechanical, and industrial subjects, but few offered college-level courses and degrees. In 1896, the U.S. Supreme Court's ruling in *Plessy v. Ferguson* established the "separate but equal" doctrine in public education. Theoretically, racially segregated institutions were to be equivalent to one another. Black colleges focused more on teacher training to provide a pool of instructors for the racially segregated primary and secondary schools (U.S. Department of Education, 1991).

In 1954, the U.S. Supreme Court decision in *Brown v. Board of Education* overturned the *Plessy* decision. Nevertheless, most African American students continued to attend racially segregated historically black colleges and universities with inferior facilities and budgets compared with traditionally white colleges and universities (U.S. Department of Education, 1991). Soon after the Brown decision, Congress passed Title VI of the Civil Rights Act of 1964 to provide a mechanism for ensuring equal opportunity in federally assisted programs and activities. Title III of the Higher Education Act of 1965, as amended, authorizes funds for enhancing historically black colleges and universities. The statute authorizes the "Strengthening historically black colleges and universities Program" and the "Strengthening Historically Black Graduate Institutions Program." In April 1989, President George Bush issued Executive Order 12677 to strengthen the capacity of historically black college/university to provide quality education and to increase their participation in federally sponsored programs (U.S. Department of Education, 1991).

Fifty-six of the 107 historically black colleges and universities are under private control. More than two-thirds of the nearly 230,000 students in historically black institutions are enrolled in the public institutions. Eighty-seven of the institutions are four-year colleges or universities, while 20 are two-year institutions. Although historically black colleges and universities enroll about 20% of all black undergraduates, they award 40% of baccalaureate degrees earned by black college students (U.S. Department of Education, 1991).

Overall, 59% of the interviewees matriculated in historically black colleges and universities, while 41% began their undergraduate studies in predominantly white colleges and universities. However, there were cohort and gender differences. For example, most of the interviewees from the South matriculated in historically black colleges. Overall, males (62%) were more likely than females (43%) to matriculate in an historically black college. Data in Table 3.2 show that almost three-fourths of the interviewees entered college intending to major in chemistry, almost one-fourth intended to be pre-med majors.

Interviewees provided several explanations for choosing chemistry as a major. One interviewee explained: "When I entered college, students told me not to major in chemistry because it was hard. I think we [interviewee and friends] did it (majored in chemistry) because it sounded like a challenge." One remarked: "It seemed like it was a powerful discipline to me. You could make, discover and invent new things."

One female interviewee who initially prepared for a teaching career, explained:

I don't deal well with youngsters . . . I was not accustomed to being around younger kids. That is probably a fault in my make up. During my student teaching, I knew that I was not cut out to be an elementary school teacher. Fortunately, I realized that I needed to concentrate on college level teaching.

Table 3.2. Percent Distribution by Intended College Major and Cohort [Interviewees].

Major	Cohort					
	Before 1954	1955–1964	1965–1974	1975–1984	1985–1995	Total
Chemistry	60.0	78.0	72.0	60.0	57.0	68.0
Pre-Med	40.0	11.0	28.0	0.0	29.0	23.0
Biology	0.0	0.0	0.0	0.0	14.0	2.0
Physics	0.0	11.0	0.0	20.0	0.0	5.0
Chemical Engineering	0.0	0.0	0.0	20.0	0.0	2.0
Total	100.0	100.0	100.0	100.0	100.0	100.0

Another interviewee had this to say:

> Initially, I thought about going into biology, but I didn't think there was anything I could do but teach with a biology degree. While I was in high school, I had a lot of chemistry demonstrations. So, I saw that chemistry had a wide range of applications.

One interviewee, who decided on a chemistry career during the senior year of college, recalled:

> When I decided not to pursue a medical career, I started doing research on my own by reading more about black scientists. I saw science as a possible career. After talking with some of my professors and others, I decided that chemistry would be something that I was interested in pursuing as a career.

Along these same lines, one interviewee had this to say:

> I went to college with the expectation of going to medical school . . . I changed my mind when we dissected a cat. I was a chemistry and math major. So I analyzed what the future would hold between those two majors. Then, I decided to take my chances with chemistry.

One interviewee explained: "In my community, if you were studying science or chemistry when you went to college, you were going to be a doctor." Another interviewee explained: "It was an evolutionary process. Basically, I was a pre-medical student in college . . . It was only after graduating from the military that I started looking around for careers and one happened to evolve into a career of research at_. It was not a crisp decision. I was 27 years old." A related comment came from an interviewee who said: "When I entered graduate school, I thought that I would apply for medical school after a few years . . . However, the medical school desire was out of my system once I got to graduate school and found out what research was all about. Then, I realized I wanted to do chemistry."

Another interviewee explained:

In high school, I didn't know what a scientist did. When I got to college, I didn't really go into chemistry because I thought "I want to be a scientist" or because I'd seen all these scientists. I just sort of fell into it . . . probably by default.

While in college, approximately 19 interviewees reported having attended a scientific society meeting. A greater number of those attending historically black colleges and universities ($N = 14$) than historically white colleges and universities ($N = 5$) indicated attendance at a scientific meeting. A majority of the meetings attended by students from historically black colleges and universities were predominantly black scientific organizations, such as Beta Kappa Chi, National Institute of Science (NIS) and National Organization of Black Chemists and Chemical Engineers (NOBCChE). However, a majority also attended American Chemical Society (ACS) meetings. In sharp contrast, all of the graduates of historically white colleges and universities attended ACS meetings.

Although six in ten interviewees had their baccalaureate origins in an historically black college, there were marked differences along gender lines. For example, data in Fig. 3.3 show that males are more likely than females to earn their bachelor's degrees at historically black colleges and universities.

Table 3.3 shows striking race differences in the baccalaureate origins of survey respondents. The data confirm the results of previous studies regarding the concentration of whites in same race colleges and universities. The data also reveal a virtual reversal in the racial composition of the undergraduate institutions of African American chemists from the pre-1985 cohort to the 1985–2002 cohort.

Table 3.4 shows the top baccalaureate institutions of chemists by race and gender. These data confirm earlier findings by Pearson, Ness and Hoban (1999) that different institutions appear to produce very different racial and gender groups for

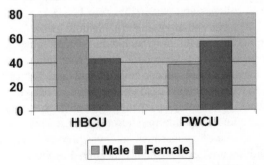

Fig. 3.3. Percent Distribution of Baccalaureate Origin by Racial Composition of College or University by Sex [Interviewees].

Table 3.3. Percent Distribution by Baccalaureate Origins by Racial Composition of College or University, Cohort and Race [Survey Respondents].

Bachelor's Institution	Cohort			
	Before 1985		1985–2002	
	Black	White	Black	White
Historically Black College or University	61.0	0.0	34.0	0.0
Historically White College or University	39.0	100.0	66.0	100.0
Total	100.0	100.0	100.0	100.0

Note: Percentage may not sum to 100 because of rounding.
Source: Survey of Earned Doctorates.

the U.S. chemistry doctoral talent pool. Among African Americans, for example, the predominantly white institutions in the top 20 are not the same for males as for females. While there is some overlap in historically black colleges and universities, an equal number of institutions do not appear on each list. Spelman College is the only women's college appearing on African Americans' list of the top 20 institutions. In other words, Spelman College is the only women's college listed by African Americans. Noticeably absent is the presence of research universities, especially those ranked in the top 50. In contrast, the list for white survey respondents is dominated by research universities, especially for males. For white women, three liberal arts colleges (including two women's colleges) appear on the list of top producing institutions. The University of Michigan, M.I.T., and the University of North Carolina, Chapel Hill appear of the list for both whites and African Americans.

Overall, graduates of historically black colleges and universities expressed greater satisfaction with their undergraduate education than graduates of historically white colleges and universities (see Fig. 3.4). Similar findings have been reported by Gurin and Epps (1975), Fleming (1984), Allen and Wallace (2001), and Bennett and Xie (2003). These authors found evidence of more positive experiences on measures of psychosocial development among African American students attending historically black colleges and universities than historically white colleges and universities. Gurin and Epps, for example, report high levels of positive self-images, strong racial identity, and high aspirations. Fleming's research revealed more favorable psychosocial adjustments. Allen and Wallace conclude that regardless of campus racial composition, students who have positive relationships with faculty, express high educational aspirations, and have strong pre-college preparation tend to be more successful in academic performance in college.

Table 3.4. B.A.-Granting Institutions of Chemistry Doctorates by Race and Sex, U.S. Citizens and Institutions Only [Survey Respondents].

Black Men		Black Women	
Institution	Number	Institution	Number
Morehouse College	20	Howard University	18
Morgan State University	12	Spelman College	12
Howard University	11	Jackson State University	8
Alcorn State University	10	Southern University and A&M College	6
Jackson State University	10	Fisk University	4
Fisk University	9	Furman University	4
North Carolina Central University	9	Tougaloo College	4
CUNY City College	8	University of North Carolina at Chapel Hill	4
Lincoln University	7	Clark Atlanta University	3
Massachusetts Institute of Technology	7	Georgia State University	3
Southern University and A&M College	7	Louisiana State University & AG&MECH & Hebert Laws Ctr	3
North Carolina Agricultural and Technical State University	6	North Carolina Agricultural and Technical State University	3
Tuskegee University	6	Prairie View A&M University	3
University in Michigan – Ann Arbor	6	University of the District of Columbia	3
Xavier University of Louisiana	6	Xavier University of Louisiana	3
Alabama A&M University	5	Alcorn State University	2
Texas Southern University	5	Chicago State University	2
Alabama State University	4	Hampton University	2
CUNY Brooklyn College	4	Kent State University – Main Campus	2
Dillard University	4	Moran State University	2
Top 20 Institutions	156	Top 20 Institutions	113
Total Institutions Reported (230)	467	Total Institutions Reported (131)	213
White Men		White Women	
Institution	Number	Institution	Number
University of California – Berkeley	302	University of Michigan – Ann Arbor	67
University of Illinois at Urbana – Champaign	295	Rutgers University – New Brunswick	64
University of Michigan – Ann Arbor	242	Pennsylvania State University – Main Campus	58
Pennsylvania State University – Main Campus	238	Carleton College	56

Table 3.4.   (*Continued*)

White Men		White Women	
Institution	Number	Institution	Number
University of Wisconsin – Madison	233	College of William and Mary	55
Massachusetts Institute of Technology	229	University of California – Berkeley	54
Rutgers University – New Brunswick	212	University of Illinois at Urbana – Champaign	54
Purdue University – Main Campus	211	Massachusetts Institute of Technology	51
Rensselaer Polytechnic Institute	196	Mount Holyoke College	49
University of North Carolina at Chapel Hill	196	Purdue University – Main Campus	48
University of California – Los Angeles	176	SUNY at Buffalo	48
University of Minnesota – Twin Cities	169	Cornell University – Endowed Colleges	47
Brigham Young University	163	University of North Carolina at Chapel Hill	47
SUNY at Buffalo	163	University of Wisconsin – Madison	44
Cornell University – Endowed Colleges	158	Bryn Mawr College	43
University of California – San Diego	155	University of Delaware	43
Michigan State University	154	Northwestern University	42
The University of Texas at Austin	150	University of Florida	42
University of Florida	148	University of California – San Diego	39
		University of Kansas – Main Campus	39
Top 20 Institutions	4,092	Top 20 Institutions	1,100
Total Institutions Reported (1,077)	26,787	Total Institutions Reported (919)	7,012

Source: Survey of Earned Doctorates.

These authors conclude that African American students at historically black colleges and universities tend to have positive social and psychological environments comparable to those experienced by white students at historically white colleges and universities. They argue that students generally thrive in environments where they are valued, socially connected, protected and accepted. In short, Allen and Wallace assert that historically black colleges and universities

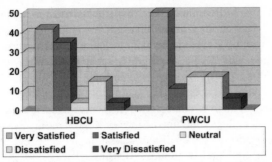

Fig. 3.4.   Percent Distribution by Level of Satisfaction with Undergraduate Education by Racial Composition of College or University [Interviewees].

provide this more favorable environment for African American students. Their African American respondents attending predominantly white colleges and universities were more likely to report incidents of racial discrimination, feelings of alienation, and isolation.

A Cohort V graduate of a predominantly white high school in the Midwest recalled that his counselor kept steering him away from the top colleges, even though he was an honors student in chemistry.

> In college, I tried to sign up for an additional advanced math class and the secretary told me that it was closed. When I turned around to leave she said "there is an honors section but you wouldn't want that." She assumed that I was not an honors student. But, I was. So, I was able to get in. Things like that accumulate. I know that I am going to encounter racism and I deal with it as best I can. But, I am very concerned when an attitude turns into behavior that can directly impact my future. While in college, I discovered that one physics classmate was in the class because of placement. I didn't know anything about advanced placement tests or AP courses. My counselor never mentioned this to me. Now, I know that knowledge empowers people.

In a more recent study, Bennett and Xie (2003) conclude that African American students at historically black colleges and universities tend to be more integrated into the campus life than their peers attending historically white colleges and universities. They assert that historically black colleges and universities are very effective in accomplishing their historical mission of educating African Americans. Furthermore, Bennett and Xie argue that historically black colleges and universities have a history of accepting and nurturing African American students who might not have been admitted to other 4-year colleges and universities. They point out the criticality of historically black colleges and universities in not only accepting these students but also promoting their graduation, which exceeds those of their African American peers in historically white colleges and universities. Moreover, students attending historically black colleges and universities were found to have closer relationships with the faculty and more involvement in campus organizations and activities. The authors argue that the environment at historically black colleges and universities tends to be more welcoming and nurturing. Additionally, Bennett and Xie believe that another important attribute is that African American history and culture are more integrated into the curricula at historically black colleges and universities compared to historically white colleges and universities.

Despite these positive characteristics, some interviewees who attended historically black colleges and universities especially during the first two cohorts pointed to deficiencies in the quality of education that they received in the poorly financed and ill equipped institutions (DuBois, 1977; Poe, 2002; Schexnider, 2003). Given the significance of historically black colleges and universities in the production of African American scientific talent, these institutions deserve special attention (Drewry & Doermann, 2003; Hill, 1996). For example, reflecting on the curricular offerings of his undergraduate school, one Cohort I interviewee said:

> It [college education] was marginal. We had good teachers. Both_and_were very good teachers. I was pretty satisfied with my undergraduate courses with them . . . However, my graduate school classmates were from these top schools – MIT, Harvard, and Oxford – and they had an extensive chemistry education (more undergraduate courses) whereas I just had a minimum.

Another Cohort II interviewee commented: "I appreciate all that my teachers did for me but I had a great deal of catching up to do. I had to work extremely hard. I had quiet a barrier to get over . . . The deficiency was the rigor of my courses and the extent of them. " It should be pointed out that none of this interviewee's college science professors held graduate degrees. A Cohort III interviewee agrees: "In retrospect, it was not as strong as I thought it was going to be and as it should have been . . . None of my chemistry professors had more than a master's." The interviewee adds: "Although my preparation wasn't the strongest . . . _ (historically black college), it gave me the confidence that sustained me through challenging academic times in grad school because I didn't want to let the school, my teachers and my family down." A Cohort III interviewee gave this description:

> I went to a small liberal arts college (an historically black college) where I had four years of chemistry. In graduate school, I was competing with folks who were graduates of technical universities. Most of them had a chemistry degree, plus some graduate work. On average, these students had six years of chemistry. So, I had an extreme deficit.

A Cohort V provides a similar experience: "Many of my white classmates were the sons and daughters of professors and doctors. They had a little bit more of a privileged background. As a result, they had attended more prestigious colleges."

A Cohort II graduate at a historically black college relates this experience:

During my sophomore year, one of my professors encouraged me to consider a career in chemistry. He encouraged me to pursue graduate studies. During my senior year, I applied for admission to_(a prestigious research university). Somewhere in my files, I have a letter from the Dean explaining why I shouldn't come there. I persisted and eventually I became the first graduate from an historically black college to be admitted. They had never heard of my undergraduate school. Every time I read it (the letter), I get two different feelings. At first, it made me angry because it seemed to be saying that the (graduate) school was too challenging. They had placement exams that determined the courses you took. The exams were given in three general areas of chemistry. They sent it to me over the summer. Each exam was about eight pages and took three hours to complete. The organic one really had me kind of worried. Meanwhile, I had also applied to_(another prestigious research university) and I had been accepted. A second thought I had was that the letter was saying that I was from the_coast and maybe I should consider a school closer to my home. Nevertheless, I thought it was a condescending letter.

The interviewee continues:

Because I received a_fellowship, I attended a weeklong orientation with recipients from across the country. At the meeting, I ran into a white fellow from_(an Ivy League school) who excelled in organic chemistry. I gave him that exam to work and he couldn't work it. So I said, _(graduate school), here I come." Up until that time I hadn't really decided whether I was going to enroll there. Once I enrolled, I found out that he (the Dean) was trying to be helpful . . . I admit that I was intimidated upon my arrival at the school. But I thought that this school was the place for me. Later, I found out that it was a very prestigious institution. It had all the things I needed. I was very fortunate. I got the individual attention that I really needed to make up for my undergraduate deficiencies.

Another Cohort II interviewee reflected:

Today, I would say that I was very satisfied with my undergraduate education. Like many students, I was not very satisfied while attending_(a private historically black college/university). After I entered the doctoral program at_(a top-ten university at the time), I discovered that my college professors were well respected. There were one or two times when I needed some specific help on something. When I went to see my professors, they would put you at ease by asking, "Well, who works there (interviewee's undergraduate college)?" I would say, "Well, I guess_was the best organic chemist." They would automatically recognize the name. They had seen him at a professional meeting. As I talk with people in my generation about who was an influence on their careers, we find the same names coming up. They did something, which we don't do as much today. They were concerned about their students in that they wanted to make sure they went to graduate school.

A Cohort II interviewee who served as a senior administrator at an historically black college/university, which had a joint program with a neighboring historically white university, made the following observation about African American students taking courses at the latter:

They have been excellent students, but when it gets down to graduation time, they [the white professors] have no interest in them. A young man in the joint program was nearing the end of his junior year, perhaps the beginning of his senior year with a 4.0 average in courses at both campuses. Apparently, some white professor happened to look at his transcript and saw that he had all A's. You can't graduate with a "C" in your major field. Don't you know they [the white professors] began to drop some C's on that young man. I knew a young lady in the same program who was determined to get the joint degree. But she had a white professor who sat down and told her she ought to transfer to_(the historically white university) because she would get out easier. There are any numbers of African American students who have had this experience. These are the kinds of things that young African American students have to deal with. They need somebody who will help them fight that, because they can't do it alone. We have got to get more African Americans in the program. We will never graduate them if we don't get them in. I think that we have got to work with them to make this happen.

Another perspective comes from a Cohort IV graduate of a predominantly white research university, who noted:

All of my undergraduate professors were supportive. [No African Americans were on the chemistry faculty.] I was invited to work in a laboratory. _is a very big school, yet the chemistry faculty knew me. They guided me when they felt I needed it. They always let me do the talking or whenever I needed something they were very, very helpful. That avenue was opened to me through the undergraduate research experience. It also helped me to find out what courses I needed to take. By working with graduate students and postdocs and listening to them talk about their graduate school experiences, I got to know what courses they took. By my senior year, I was taking graduate courses with first year graduate students.

One interviewee who attended undergraduate school at a predominantly white university had this to say about the quality of instruction:

It didn't provide the level of academic challenge that I was looking for. But, I didn't realize that when I started. But after I had been there for awhile, I recognized that I had kind of outgrown the institution and department.

Another interviewee who attended undergraduate school at a predominantly white university had this to say about the quality of instruction:

It didn't provide the level of academic challenge that I was looking for. But, I didn't realize that when I started. But after I had been there for awhile, I recognized that I had kind of outgrown the institution and department.

A Cohort II graduate of a historically white university explained:

I found that I had a knack for_chemistry. I had undertaken some very challenging and difficult assignments as an undergraduate research assistant and I was good at it. I discovered that I really wanted to invent, discover and make things. I suppose that my love for chemistry may have been part of my fascination with my mother's cooking. I observed her mixing ingredients and making some dishes. In high school, I was always involved in experimentation of one kind or another.

In general, interviewees continued the pattern of achievement evidenced in high school. In fact, some 70% graduated from college with honors. As can be seen in Table 3.5, regardless of race or cohort, most survey respondents earned a

Table 3.5. Percent Distribution of College Major by Race [Survey Respondents].

Major	Cohort			
	Before 1985		1985–2002	
	Black	White	Black	White
Other Fields	5.0	4.0	10.0	7.0
Biological Sciences	10.0	15.0	16.0	21.0
Health Sciences	D	1.0	2.0	1.0
Engineering	D	1.0	1.0	1.0
Chemistry	84.0	78.0	71.0	69.0
Physics	D	1.0	D	1.0
Total	100.0	100.0	100.0	100.0

Note: Percentages may not sum to 100 because of rounding and/or suppression of counts. D = Suppressed for reasons of confidentiality.

Source: Survey of Earned Doctorates.

bachelor's degree in chemistry. The biological sciences was second most popular major.

GRADUATE SCHOOL

For most interviewees, the decision to attend graduate school was made while in college. When asked who or what most influenced their decision to attend graduate school, the top response was "self," followed closely by "mentor" (see Fig. 3.5). As was true for the decision to attend college, teachers once again played a pivotal

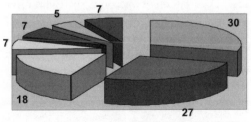

| ▨ Self | ▨ Mentor | ☐ Career Mobility | ☐ Parent(s) | ▧ UG Research | ☐ Lack of Med School Funds | ▨ Other |

Fig. 3.5. Percent Distribution by Person Who Most Influenced Decision to Attend Graduate School [Interviewees].

role in influencing interviewees' decision to pursue higher levels of education (see Pearson & Warner, 1998).

The follow comments highlights some of these influences. One interviewee recalled: "All of my principal teachers were impressive to me. _cemented my notion of going to graduate school. He excited all of us about being scientists. He had a tremendous ability to encourage his students." Another interviewee explained his decision to pursue graduate studies in chemistry this way:

> After I decided that I wasn't going to medical school, I looked around to find out just what I really wanted to do. I started reading literature. That's when I became interested in chemistry. I started talking to various people and they told me where the best schools for chemistry were in the country. Since I had a fellowship that paid for preschool visits, I was able to visit three schools.

Although interviewees reported a variety of academic and professional reasons for selecting their particular graduate school, occasionally a departmental staff member tipped the scale. Consider this comment by a Cohort III interviewee: "I choose_because the secretary wrote such a warm letter of acceptance and indicating his willingness to assist if I had any difficulties. I felt that the department was much friendlier than the others."

With respect to research specialties, the largest proportion of interviewees concentrated in organic chemistry, followed by physical chemistry (Table 3.6). Few concentrated in analytical chemistry. There were some cohort differences. For example, organic chemistry dominated the specialties in Cohorts I (before 1955), III (1965–1974), and IV (1975–1984); while both organic chemistry and physical chemistry led Cohort II (1955–1964); and physical chemistry was the leading specialty of those earning doctorates in Cohort V (1985–1995). The cohort distribution of specialties is consistent with annual ACS survey data. In 2002, U.S. institutions awarded approximately 1,822 doctoral degrees in chemistry. Of

Table 3.6.   Percent Distribution of Specialties by Cohort [Interviewees].

Specialty	Cohort					
	Before 1955	1955–1964	1965–1974	1975–1984	1985–1995	Total
Organic	80.0	33.0	50.0	60.0	14.0	45.0
BioChemistry	0.0	11.0	17.0	0.0	14.0	11.0
Physical	20.0	33.0	17.0	20.0	43.0	25.0
Analytical	0.0	22.0	0.0	0.0	0.0	7.0
Inorganic	0.0	0.0	17.0	20.0	14.0	9.0
Other	0.0	0.0	0.0	0.0	0.0	2.0
Total	100.0	100.0	100.0	100.0	100.0	100.0

Table 3.7.   Percent Distribution of Specialties by Cohort and Race [Survey Respondents].

Specialty	Cohort			
	Before 1985		1985–2002	
	Black	White	Black	White
Analytical	10.0	13.0	18.0	18.0
Other Chemistry	18.0	19.0	31.0	25.0
Inorganic	16.0	15.0	13.0	15.0
Organic	33.0	33.0	27.0	26.0
Physical	24.0	21.0	11.0	16.0
Total	100.0	100.0	100.0	100.0

Note: Percentages may not sum to 100 because of rounding.
Source: Survey of Earned Doctorates.

these, 27% were awarded in organic chemistry, followed by physical and analytical chemistry at 16% each. U.S. citizens earned 59% of all chemistry doctoral degrees awarded in 2002 (National Science Foundation, 2003).

Data in Table 3.7 confirm the distributional pattern by specialty for the cohort of survey respondents earning doctorates prior to 1985. For example, organic and physical chemistry were the first and second most popular specialties for both African American and white respondents. A somewhat different pattern prevailed for the 1985–2002 cohort with "other" and organic chemistry being the first and second most preferred specialties for African Americans. These specialties were also the most preferred by whites (see Table 3.7).

FINANCIAL SUPPORT FOR GRADUATE EDUCATION

Table 3.8 shows the primary source of graduate support by race for survey respondents in the 1985–2002 cohort. There are significant race differences in the type of support used to fund graduate education. In terms of institutional support, white respondents (60%) were considerably more likely than African American respondents (40%) to hold some form of assistantship. Specifically, white respondents held proportionately more research assistantships, compared to less than a fifth of African American respondents. Further, nearly two-fifths of white respondents were supported by a teaching assistantship, compared to slightly less than one-fourth of African American respondents. Relatedly, more than two-fifths of African American respondents but less than one-fifth of white respondents were supported by fellowships. The relative financial position of white respondents

Table 3.8. Percent Distribution of Primary Source of Graduate Support by Race, 1985–2002 [Survey Respondents].

Primary Source of Support	Race	
	Black	White
Own Resources	12.0	20.0
Teaching Assistantship	23.0	38.0
Research Assistantship	17.0	24.0
Fellowship	43.0	16.0
Other Support	6.0	3.0
Total	100.0	100.0

Note: Percentages may not sum to 100 because of rounding.
Source: Survey of Earned Doctorates.

manifests itself in the fact that 20% of them compared to 12% of African American respondents supported their graduate study with personal resources. To sum up the situation, one Cohort I interviewee made this comment about financing graduate studies:

> The place where I worked for room and board didn't give me enough to eat. I got leftovers and it was never enough. For breakfast, I got a piece of toast and a cup of coffee and would have to last me all day. I was pretty thin! And I was hungry all of the time. That was the worst part of graduate school. I'd stay up until 2 am and then get up 6 am each day. That first semester was real tough.

Previous studies have reported similar findings regarding doctoral students in general (Blackwell, 1981) and science in particular (Pearson, 1985). Blackwell found major differences in the manner in which African American and white students finance their graduate education. He reported that white students were more likely than African American students to have their graduate studies supported by teaching and research assistantships. Pearson reported that 30% of the white scientists in his study held some form of assistantship, compared to 19% of African American scientists. African Americans, however, were more likely than their white peers to hold a fellowship (23% vs. 14%).

The importance of assistantships on careers has been noted by a number of scholars. Blackwell (1981) is representative of these scholars when he asserts that recipients accrue significant training and experience which may prove immensely valuable in developing those teaching and research skills which are vital in enhancing career success. However, it is not merely the existence of financial aid that has an impact on persistence; the actual type of assistance and timing, can greatly affect the effectiveness of the aid. For example, fellowships or assistantships have been correlated with full-time attendance, student retention and the rate of progress students make towards their degree.

Doctoral Granting Institution

Because of the small numbers and consequent efforts to protect anonymity, the Ph.D.-granting institutions of interviewees are not identified. Nevertheless, data in Table 3.9 show the prestige rankings of the interviewees' Ph.D.-granting institutions. It is recognized that national rankings are not without critics (see Wilson, 1995), especially the Gourman Reports (see Stephenson, 1997). Some critics accuse those producing national rankings of engaging in no more than a popularity contest. While divergent producers of rankings such as *U.S. News & World Report* and the National Research Council publish their rating criteria and methodology, Gourman has been criticized for failing to disclose his methodology. Among the factors weighed in Gourman's Reports are: facilities, administrative policies, support of faculty members, cooperative among professors, relationships between professors and administrators methods of professorial/administrator communications, openness of the administration, use of consultants and committees to solve problems, attitudes about scholarly research and overall cooperation of the administration (Selingo, 1997). Compared

Table 3.9. Distribution of Prestige of Ph.D.-Granting Department by Cohort [Interviewees].

Cohort I, Before 1955 $(N = 6)$[a]	Cohort II, 1955–1964 $(N = 9)$[b]	Cohort III, 1965–1974 $(N = 17)$[c]	Cohort IV, 1975–1984 $(N = 5)$[d]	Cohort V, 1985–1995 $(N = 7)$[e]
(4) Distinguished/ Eminent	(1) Distinguished	(5) Top Ten	(2) Top Ten	(2) Top Ten
(1) Strong	(4) Strong	(2) Second Ten	(1) Second Ten	(1) Second Ten
(1) Foreign Institution not included in U.S. Ratings but would rank first in its country	(4) Good	(10) Other	(2) Other	(4) Other

[a] Ratings by Embree (1935), Cartter (1966).
[b] Ratings by Cartter (1966).
[c] Ratings by Gourman (1980).
[d] Ratings by Gourman (1993).
[e] Ratings by the National Research Council (1995).

to interviewees earning their doctorates after 1965, those receiving their Ph.D.s prior to 1965 tended to do so in ranked institutions. There appears to be no question about the high quality of Ph.D.-granting departments of those earning doctorates in Cohorts I and II. However, over time an increasing number of interviewees earned their doctorates in unranked institutions. This may be related to the growth of doctoral programs, especially in the South. Traditionally, the prestige rankings of departments have been dominated by non-Southern, predominantly white universities (see, for example, *The Journal of Blacks in Higher Education*, 1995). As more universities began to offer doctoral programs in chemistry, many were not highly rated. As has been mentioned, historically African Americans were not granted admission to southern universities. As a result, the practice in many Southern states was to cover much of the cost for their black citizens to pursue graduate education elsewhere (Kluger, 1975). African American students were gradually admitted to traditionally white graduate and professional schools if their program of study was unavailable at historically black colleges and universities. According to Jacobs (1999), academic departments located in universities with "State," "A&M," or regional designations ("North," "Southern") in their names, departments with larger proportions of female graduate students, and departments in urban, public, largely commuter schools receive significantly lower prestige rankings net of any effects of productivity (See Burris, 2004).

Data in Table 3.10 show the top doctorate granting institutions of chemistry doctorates by race and gender across both cohorts. Howard University emerged as the top producer of African American chemistry doctorates, while the University of California, Berkeley was the leading producer for whites. Among African Americans, Howard University was the top doctorate producers of males, while Louisiana State University, Baton Rouge held this position for females. Contrastly, the University of California, Berkeley was the top producers of both white males and females. Additionally, the table reveals that while nearly all white chemists, regardless of sex, earn their doctorates in top 50 research universities, a strikingly different pattern holds for African Americans. Regardless of sex, few African Americans earned doctorates in top 50 chemistry departments. African American men, however, were more likely than African American females to earn a doctorate from a top 50 chemistry department. Moreover, only one historically black university – Howard University – appears on the African American males list, while two – Howard University and Clark-Atlanta University – appear on the list of African American females. At the time of this writing, Howard University is the only historically black university designated as a research university in the Carnegie classifications. Given the earlier findings on the striking race differences in baccalaureate origins of survey respondents, the overall doctoral origins are not surprising.

Table 3.10. Top Doctorate-Granting Institutions of Chemistry Doctorates by Race and Sex, U.S. Citizens and Institutions Only [Survey Respondents].

Black Men	Number	Black Women	Number
Howard University	47	Louisiana Sate Univ. & AG & MECH & Hebert Laws Ctr	16
Louisiana Sate Univ. & AG & MECH & Hebert Laws Ctr	12	Howard University	14
University of Illinois at Urbana – Champaign	11	University of North Carolina at Chapel Hill	12
University of California – Berkeley	10	Emory University	10
CUNY Graduate School and University Center	8	Clark Atlanta University	5
University of Maryland – College Park	8	Georgia Institute of Technology – Main Campus	5
Wayne State University	8	University of California – Davis	5
North Carolina State University at Raleigh	7	Ohio State University – Main Campus	4
University of North Carolina at Chapel Hill	7	Purdue University – Main Campus	4
Georgia Institute of Technology – Main Campus	6	University of Florida	4
Georgia State University	6	University of South Carolina at Columbia	4
Massachusetts Institute of Technology	6	Virginia Polytechnic Institute and State University	4
Michigan State University	6	American University	3
Ohio State University – Main Campus	6	Auburn University – Main Campus	3
Purdue University – Main Campus	6	Loyola University Chicago	3
Temple University	6	Massachusetts Institute of Technology	3
Texas A & M University	6	Texas A & M Univeristy	3
University of Cincinnati – Main Campus	6	University of California – San Francisco	3
University of Florida	6	University of Chicago	3
University of Kansas – Main Campus	6	Univeristy of Georgia	3
Univeristy of Pennsylvania	6	University of Kansas – Main Campus	3
Top 20 Institutions	202	Top 20 Institutions	126
Total Institutions Reported (139)	467	Total Institutions Reported (88)	213
University of California – Berkeley	1,027	University of California – Berkeley	220
University of Wisconsin – madison	804	University of North Carolina at Chapel Hill	182
University of Illinois at Urbana – Champaign	782	University of Wisconsin – Madison	173
Purdue University – Main Campus	699	University of Illinois at Urbana – Champaign	168

Table 3.10. (*Continued*)

Black Men	Number	Black Women	Number
Pennsylvania State University – Main Campus	499	Purdue University – Main Campus	155
University of North Carolina at Chapel Hill	469	Pennsylvania State University – Main Campus	137
Ohio State University – Main Campus	460	Northwestern University	136
Cornell University – Endowed Colleges	441	University of Minnesota – Twin Cities	130
Massachusetts Institute of Technology	435	Massachusetts Institute of Technology	120
California Institute of Technology	432	The University of Texas at Austin	110
University of Florida	424	University of Colorado at Boulder	110
Stanford University	423	University of California – Los Angeles	104
Indiana University – Bloomington	411	Cornell University – Endowed Colleges	101
University of Minnesota – Twin Cities	404	California Institute of Technology	100
Iowa State University	403	University of Michigan – Ann Arbor	100
Texas A & M University	401	University of California – Davis	98
The University of Texas at Austin	394	University of Pennsylvania	98
Harvard University	389	Yale University	97
Northwestern University	369	Stanford University	96
University of Michigan – Ann Arbor	359	Texas A & M University	96
		University of Washington – Seattle Campus	96
Top 20 Institutions	10,025	Top 20 Institutions	2,627
Total Institutions Reported (213)	26,787	Total Institutions Reported (212)	7,012

Source: Survey of Earned Doctorates.

In terms of geographic origins of the Ph.D.-granting institution, most interviewees earned their degrees in the Midwest, followed by the Northeast, South, and West (Fig. 3.6). No interviewees earned a doctorate from a Southern institution prior to 1965. A number of interviewees earning their bachelor's degrees in the

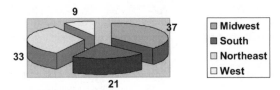

Fig. 3.6. Percent Distribution by Geographic Origin of Ph.D. Degree [Interviewees].

South before 1965 stated that they were forbidden to pursue doctoral studies in Southern historically white colleges and universities because of racial segregation. Interviewees from the so-called "Deep South" reported that their native states provided funds for them to attend graduate school outside of the state. This confirms the earlier discussion of the historical participation of African Americans in U.S. higher education.

Few interviewees reported that African Americans were on the faculties of their Ph.D.-granting department. In fact, no interviewees in Cohorts I, II or IV reported African Americans on the faculties of their department. One of the 17 interviewees in Cohort III reported the presence of one African American faculty member. Three interviewees in the last Cohort (V) indicated the presence of African Americans on the faculty (i.e. one in each department). Figures for the two interviewees who earned their Ph.D.'s at an historically black college are not included because both faculty and students were predominantly African American at the time the interviewees earned their degrees. These finding are not surprising given the fact that historically few predominantly white colleges or universities hired African American scholars (*The Journal of Blacks in Higher Education*, Summer 1995). The history of U.S. higher education is replete with examples of eminent African American scientists who were denied employment opportunities in American research universities. After the Civil War, for a period of almost one hundred years, distinguished Negro academics such as Carter G. Woodson, Alain Locke, W. E. B. Du Bois, Ernest E. Just, E. Franklin Frazier, John Hope Franklin, Sterling A. Brown, Charles R. Drew, and Rayford Logan were not acceptable as scholars at most of America's great institutions of higher learning. There was no black faculty member of Harvard College until the appointment of Ralph Bunche in 1950, 314 years after the founding of the university (Cross, 1998; Slater, 1998/1999; *The Journal of Blacks in Higher Education*, 2000; Wideman, 1978). These data further demonstrate the extent to which African Americans were and continue to be underrepresented on the faculties of graduate chemistry departments at historically white colleges and universities.

Of the 1,638 Ph.D. chemists employed by the "Top 50" chemistry departments in 2001, Nelson et al. (2001) report that only 18 or a mere 1.1% were African Americans. The fact that only one African American Ph.D. chemist was appointed as an assistant professor in a tenure-track position at one of the nation's top 50 chemistry departments in 2000 provides further evidence that African Americans continue to be virtually absent from these faculties (Bhattacharjee, 2003). In a report released by Dartmouth College (2003), a key finding was that faculty diversity tends to lag well behind student diversity.

Langford (2003) views the underrepresentation of African Americans on the faculties of science departments at top-rated research universities as a major challenge for equity in higher education. Benjamin (1991, p. 124) agrees that, in general, African Americans are "less likely to be employed in the most prestigious colleges and universities." She estimates that most African Americans (two-thirds to three-fourths) are concentrated on the faculties of historically black colleges and universities. Pinkney (2000) asserts that at least half of all African Americans on the faculties of major research universities have their baccalaureate origins in historically black colleges and universities.

Conversely to the findings of virtual invisibility of African American faculty at major research universities, interviewees were more likely to report the presence of African American classmates at some point during their doctoral studies. Cohort I graduates reported six African American classmates. The comments of a cohort member are illuminating:

> I got a letter from the admissions committee, admitting me to the master's program at (a prestigious university). However, I was confused when I arrived because a teacher told me not to register for organic chemistry. I thought maybe this meant I should go to another department. Later, I found out what really happened. university allowed only one black per year in chemistry and only 38 in the whole university. There was considerable prejudice at the time. For example, they only allowed 12–14% Jews in chemistry . . . Because, there were no blacks in chemistry, and I was the quota for the year. As long as I was there, no other black was enrolled in the program. Even when I came back for my doctorate, a black had just finished. There was only one black at a time. When one black left another would come.

Experiences with discrimination in admissions were commonplace among the interviewees, especially those earning doctorates before the early 1970s. Historically, discrimination in the admissions process was a common occurrence. Although Percy Julian earned Phi Beta Kappa honors and graduated valedictorian of his class at DePauw, he found the scholarship doors closed to him because of his color, and his graduate education was thereby delayed (Jenkins, 1984, p. 478).

Those earning doctorates in Cohort II reported having 12 classmates. Cohort III graduates reported 37; and seven were reported by Cohort IV graduates. Those earning Ph.D.s in the last cohort reported only five African-American classmates. The relatively high number of classmates in Cohort III is somewhat misleading because the doctoral studies of several interviewees overlapped in the same departments. As Table 3.11 shows, a substantial majority of interviewees completed their doctorates in less than five years of full-time enrollment. Few interviewees completed their Ph.D.s in less than three years or more than six years. The latter figure reflects the small minority who transferred to a second program due to academic difficulties in the first department.

During the course of their doctoral studies, most interviewees attended at least one meeting of a scientific society. In fact, 32 of the 40 interviewees who responded to this item reported that they had attended a professional meeting, usually ACS

Table 3.11. Percent Distribution of Enrolled Time to Completion of Ph.D. Degree [Interviewees].

Months	Percent
Less than 36 months	5.0
36–47 months	32.0
48–59 months	32.0
60–71 months	25.0
72 or more months	7.0
Total	100.0

Note: Percentages may not sum to 100 because of rounding.

(regional or national) or NOBCChE. However, one Cohort V interviewee said: "I wish I had more exposure to national, high quality meetings. I wish I had been forced to present at meetings other than NOBCChE."

Data in Table 3.12 show that 90% of interviewees were very satisfied or satisfied with the quality of their doctoral education. For many, the level of satisfaction was tied to their relationship with a mentor or key faculty member. Ellis (2000) reports a similar finding. For example, she concludes that doctoral students who reported good relationships with advisers usually rated the environment of their departments as good. In contrast, those who reported poor relationships with their advisers reported negative feelings about their departments. Advisors and mentors were viewed as key links to departmental resources, both human and financial. Ellis points out that when such links did not exist, students were more likely to be unsuccessful in making academic and social transitions into their departments. She concludes that white men were more likely than African American men and women and white women to report a close working relationship with a

Table 3.12. Percent Distribution by Level of Satisfaction with Doctoral Education [Interviewees].

Level	Ph.D.
Very satisfied	64.0
Satisfied	25.0
Neutral	7.0
Dissatisfied	5.0
Very dissatisfied	0.0
Total	100.0

Note: Percentages may not sum to 100 because of rounding.

mentor or adviser. Additionally, she found that African-American women were less likely than white women, African-American or White men to have mentors or advisers whom they reported working closely with during their doctoral study. Bowen and Bok (1998) confirm that African Americans pursuing their studies in predominantly white universities are less likely than whites to have faculty mentors.

One Cohort V interviewee gave this description: "My advisor showed me how he wrote grants and prepared for class. In fact, several faculty members gave me their lecture notes when I decided to take an academic job. They really helped me in that way." This excerpt was provided by a Cohort V interviewee: "Perhaps the most difficult adjustment has been the isolation, especially in terms of my research. Also, having attended a predominately white institution where I received very little encouragement, I still have to fight through a lot of self-doubts. It is a problem for me. Now, I can see how it affects my performance."

One Cohort II interviewee said:

> I am very satisfied with my doctoral education because: The faculty allowed me to grow and pursue knowledge in a very open way. The professors were marvelous and actively engaged in cross-disciplinary research. Although I was specializing in_, I was exposed to some of the leading researchers in_(another chemistry specialty and another scientific discipline). The department was small enough so that I knew everyone.

Another Cohort II interviewee recalled:

> We had a marvelous set of professors who engaged in cross-disciplinary training. Although I was a_chemist, I got a chance to be engaged with some leading scholars in inorganic chemistry and the biological areas. The groups there were small enough that you knew almost everyone in the department. I found this experience very helpful.

A Cohort I interviewee had this to say about the quality of doctoral education:

> I rate_(a prestigious university) as excellent, no nonsense, no crap, excellent ideas. We were always bouncing ideas back and forth. You didn't try anything without really considering several alternatives. You looked at your results critically. You did analytical work. We had an excellent analytical laboratory where we did everything. We were all pretty good glass blowers. Much of what I was doing in the lab was all new.

Another interviewee had this to say:

> The resources, interactions, requirements, and professional contact were all state of the art. _enjoyed an international reputation in_chemistry. I would sit out in the hallway and discuss with him problems that had occurred in the classroom. Accessibility to the faculty and other resources was nothing short of phenomenal. I know what helped me survive grad school at_(a prestigious department) was the fact that I graduated from a black school that trained be to be a total individual. So, when I came through a system which was non-supportive of whom I was as a person, not only intellectually but all other parts of me were rejected. Internally, I knew that had the capability and I could succeed.

A Cohort III interviewee provided this account:

> My advisor (and mentor) gave me the encouragement and support to continue when I was at a low point in grad school. In grad school, I think that it is important to find someone who respects where you are coming from and what you have done. I had numerous conversations with my advisor late at night in the lab. So many times we would be the only ones in the building late at night. One night, he said 'I know your background (ill prepared coming from an historically black college) . . . and I see where you are now. I just encourage you to stay the course, continue to work hard and I will help you.' That made a big difference to me.

Another Cohort III interviewee related this experience:

> Where I attended college (an historically black college), I was used to writing what I thought, what I read . . . feeding it back to the professor. I was not used to doing analytical writing and evaluating readings. It took me a year to really understand how to read and critique journal articles. My undergraduate education prepared me to teach but not to go to graduate school.

One interviewee stated: "I would work in the mornings, get my work done and go home. Because of that, I was penalized for not participating socially. I will say that the people who played the social game, got more fellowships, more notoriety, etc."

A few interviewees were neutral or dissatisfied with their graduate education. One Cohort V interviewee explained:

> My advisor and I didn't get along. He was very antagonistic. I don't think that he believed that someone with my low socioeconomic and educational background could make it through (a prestigious university). In the middle of my experiments, my data were stolen and I was told that some faculty members were not satisfied with the progress of my experiments. However, I was making significant progress and strides in my research because I was working my butt off. Out of frustration, I went to the Dean. The first thing he asked about was my academic standing. After determining that my work was in order and on time, he held a big meeting and told my advisor to stop giving me a hard time. Ironically, this poison turned into medicine because I had to become independent, work hard and be exact. Because of the conflict with my advisor, I learned to defend my work and not depend solely on others for support and to be self-motivated.

One interviewee expressed dismay at the quality of his graduate instruction:

> Although I went to an elite Ph.D. program (at the time), my courses were garbage. One of our best scientists used to walk in the classroom and lecture and then walk out of the room lecturing. There were no text books for the courses. Coming from a high-quality liberal arts college, I was not used to that . . . Plus, the professors just exploited us because publications and grants were the priorities.

Over time, some of the tension between student and advisor mellowed as they aged. One Cohort III interviewee explains: "My research advisor and I didn't get along for years. He was very antagonistic. Since both of us have gotten old, he has gotten a lot more pleasant."

Social discrimination in American colleges and universities is one of the most important means by which group attitudes are conditioned in this country (McWilliams, 1948). One Cohort V interviewee gave this explanation of the politics of her department:

> I was penalized for not participating socially. I'll give you an example. One time, a faculty member asked me why I didn't go to the departmental parties. I said that I was here to do work not party. Some faculty members told me that it was going to take me longer to complete my degree because I didn't socialize with them. Social interaction seemed to play a direct role on how well you progressed in that educational system. The people who played the game, so to speak, got more fellowships, more notoriety, so forth and so on.

One Cohort III interviewee remarked: "The course-work was horrible, but the research experience and my advisor were good. My satisfaction with my doctoral education was very mixed." A Cohort V interviewee recalled:

> During my first year at_, I overheard my mathematical methods professor talking about the "Negro" girl in his class. The two African Americans who were here when I visited, transferred to_following my first year. They moved with their faculty advisor. I think it had been twenty years before there had been a black person enrolled in the doctoral program. So, these folks didn't know what to do with me, especially one very racist professor. There were a couple of others who were just lazy. The racist was an older person. I refused to take any more courses from him. I was generally satisfied with the other courses.

The number of years between B.S. and Ph.D. degrees ranged from four to 17; while the median was seven years. In general, age at Ph.D. for interviewees ranged from 25 to 39 years, while the median age was 29 years. One Cohort II interviewee explained the time-to-degree this way: "At the time I was coming along, it was common to get a master's degree; then, work for awhile before returning for the Ph.D. Most blacks could not afford to go straight from college to a doctoral program and financial aid was not widely available." Survey data provided by NORC reveal that the median age at receipt of the doctorate for the pre-1985 cohort was 31 years for African American males and 30 years for African American females. For whites, 28 years was the comparable figure for both sexes. The median years for the 1985–2002 cohort was 31 for African American males, 29 years for African American females and white males compared to 28 years for white females. The median registered time to doctoral degree for survey respondents was similar for both racial groups. In the pre-1985 cohort, the median registered time for African Americans was six years compared to five years for whites. By the 1985–2002 cohort, the time was six years for both racial groups.

The largest number of interviewee doctoral recipients (two-fifths) came from Cohort III. This period (1965–1974) marks the beginning of the implementation of many affirmative action programs (Higginbotham, 1998; Wilson, 1996).

Postdoctoral Study

Postdoctoral study became more prominent among the interviewees beginning with Cohort III (1965–1974). For example, only one of six graduates in Cohort I pursued postdoctoral study, compared with two out of eight in Cohort II (1955–1964), eight of eighteen in Cohort III, two of five in Cohort IV (1975–1984) and six of seven in the last Cohort (1985–1995). Most interviewees pursuing postdoctoral study were pursuing careers outside of historically black colleges and universities. Interviewees earning doctorates prior to the mid-1970s indicated that the postdoctoral study was uncommon for their respective cohorts. One Cohort I interviewee said: "When I finished graduate school, it was not common to pursue a postdoctoral fellowship." One Cohort III interviewee provided this description:

> When I finished my Ph.D., I applied for two postdoctoral positions. One famous chemist said come on but bring your own money, and another reputable chemist offered funding. I didn't have any money and my wife refused to go to the place with money. So, I took a job in academe. I really didn't know how important postdoctoral positions were until I arrived at work to discover that nearly everyone had done a postdoc.

By the 1980s, however, it was common for scientists to pursue postdoctoral study to further specialize and produce more published research in order to be more competitive on the job market, especially in academe. One interviewee said commented: "When I was coming along, you only did a postdoctoral if you were going into academe."

Data in Table 3.13 reveal the postdoctorate plans of survey respondents. In the pre-1985 cohort, white respondents were twice as likely as their black

Table 3.13. Percent Distribution of Postdoctorate Plans by Race and Cohort [Survey Respondents].

Postdoc Plans	Cohort			
	Before 1985		1985–2002	
	Black	White	Black	White
On a postdoctoral fellowship	10.0	20.0	21.0	23.0
On a postdoc research associateship (FY 1969 to present)	7.0	23.0	16.0	24.0
On a traineeship, other study, internship, residency	2.0	2.0	2.0	2.0
Other employment	80.0	54.0	61.0	50.0
Military service/other plans	1.0	1.0	0.0	1.0
Total	100.0	100.0	100.0	100.0

Note: Percentages may not sum to 100 because of rounding.
Source: Survey of Earned Doctorates.

Table 3.14. Percent Distribution of Cumulative Indebtedness by Sex and Race [Survey Respondents].

Cumulative Debt	Race			
	White		Black	
	Male	Female	Male	Female
No debt	23.0	28.0	38.0	40.0
$5,000 or less	15.0	17.0	18.0	17.0
$5,001 – $10,000	19.0	16.0	18.0	16.0
$10,001 – $15,000	9.0	12.0	10.0	10.0
$15,001 – $20,000	7.0	7.0	5.0	5.0
$20,001 – $25,000	4.0	7.0	4.0	4.0
$25,001 – $30,000	7.0	4.0	2.0	2.0
More than $30,000	16.0	10.0	6.0	5.0
Total	100.0	100.0	100.0	100.0

Note: Data unavailable for the pre-1985 cohort. Percentages may not sum to 100 because of rounding.
Source: Survey of Earned Doctorates.

peers to plan additional training on a fellowship, and three times more likely than African American respondents to hold a research associateship. However, African American respondents were far more likely than white respondents to plan to pursue other employment (four-fifths vs. slightly more than one-half). By the 1985–2002 cohort, African American and white respondents were essentially equally likely to hold a fellowship for postdoctoral studies. Although a greater percentage of white respondents than black respondents held a research associateship (24% vs. 16%), the black rate was more than twice that for blacks in the pre-1985 cohort. Further, African American respondents were more likely than white respondents to have plans for other employment.

At receipt of the doctorate, white survey respondents (about two-fifths) were considerably more likely than African American respondents (one fourth) to report no indebtedness (see Table 3.14). Women of both races were somewhat more likely than males to have accumulated no debt. The gender differential was slightly greater among African American respondents (5 percentage points) than among white respondents (2 percentage points). African American respondents were more than twice as likely as their white peers to list debts of more than $30,000. Among race-gender groups, African American males reported the highest level of indebtedness. This may be related to greater financial demands resulting from family responsibilities.

NOTE

1. Several male interviewees reported that ads in these magazines attracted them to science, especially chemistry.

CAREER PATTERNS AND EXPERIENCES

In their study of members (of all degree levels) of the American Chemical Society (ACS), Strauss and Rainwater (1962) identified three primary employment settings of chemists: industry, academe, and government. Additionally, they found that a small proportion of their population worked in non-profit institutions. Non-profit institutions were combined with government to create the category "government and other." These researchers were concerned with the permeability of the boundaries of the sectors, and whether each sector draws equally from the others. Their findings reveal that the predominant pattern was a career in a single sector. However, they reported that 30% of chemists holding two or more jobs over their careers, moved from one sector to another. Few chemists reported movement across all three sectors. Industrial chemists were most likely to remain in one sector throughout their career, followed by academic chemist; however, chemists in government were the most mobile. Because Strauss and Rainwater did not disaggregate their findings by race and ethnicity or gender, it is unclear how relevant their findings are for African American chemists.

FIRST POSITION

After completing their doctoral and/or postdoctoral studies, most interviewees began their careers in academe, with industry a close second, and government and other a distant third. Previous studies consistently report a high correlation between the prestige of the departments in which academics received their degrees and the prestige of the departments where they obtained jobs, especially their initial jobs (Baldi, 1995; Berelson, 1960; Caplow & McGee 1958; Cole & Cole, 1973; Crane, 1965; Hargens & Hagstrom, 1982; Long et al., 1979; Reskin, 1979; Zuckerman, 1970). This effect holds independently of differences in pre-employment productivity (Baldi, 1995; Long, 1978; McGinnis & Long, 1988).

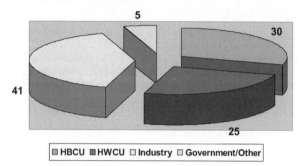

Fig. 4.1. Percent Distribution by Employment Sector of First Position [Interviewees].
Note: Percentages may not sum to 100 because of rounding.

However, this was not the experience for most interviewees who earned doctorates from some of nation's most elite doctoral departments. As was shown in Chapters 1 and 3, few gifted African American scholars were employed in elite departments. For the most part, these institutions were largely closed to African American scholars. In general, the interviewees entering academe were somewhat more likely to begin their careers in historically black colleges and universities (see Fig. 4.1). However, there were noticeable cohort differences (Table 4.1). For example, while the initial job placement of Cohort I interviewees (received Ph.D. before 1955) is similar to the general pattern for all interviewees, it is noteworthy that no appointments were in predominantly white colleges and universities. Only one interviewee's first job was in the "other" setting. With the exception that no one entered the government/other sector, the entry pattern in Cohort II is the same as Cohort I.

Table 4.1. Distribution by Sector of First Position by Cohort [Interviewees].

Cohort	Industry	HBCU	HWCU	Government and Other[a]	Total
I (Before 1955)	2	3	0	1	6
II (1955–1964	3	5	0	0	8
III (1965–1974)	8	4	5[b]	1	18
IV (1975–1984)	2	0	3	0	5
V (1985–1994)	3	1	3	0	7
Total	18	13	11	2	44

[a] Includes self-employed and non-profit organizations.
[b] Includes one non-tenure track appointment.

Table 4.2. Percent Distribution by Sector of First Position by Race and Cohort [Survey Respondents].

Sector	Cohort			
	Before 1985		1985–2002	
	White	Black	White	Black
Industry	70.0	53.0	72.0	66.0
Academe	15.0	29.0	15.0	14.0
Historically Black College/University	[0.0]	[20.0]	[0.0]	[4.0]
Historically Black College/University	[15.0]	[9.0]	[15.0]	[11.0]
Government/Other	16.0	19.0	14.0	20.0
Total	100.0	100.0	100.0	100.0

Note: Includes only those employed. Percentages may not sum to 100 because of rounding.
Source: Survey of Earned Doctorates.

Beginning in Cohort III, most interviewees' first positions were nearly as likely to be in industry as in academe. The trend began much earlier for white chemists. Significant more interviewees in this than previous cohorts held first jobs in predominantly white colleges and universities than historically black colleges and universities and industry. These general patterns continued over the remaining cohorts.

Data in Table 4.2 show results by race and cohort. As can be seen, before 1985, a majority of both African American and white respondents began their careers in industry. For African American respondents, academe was the second employment destination, especially historically black colleges and universities. The second destination for white respondents was equally likely to be academe – predominantly white colleges and universities – and government/other. By the second cohort, the black/white pattern in first position had converged even more; industry was, by far, the primary destination for both races. However, the black/white gap in the first cohort was reduced by more than one half. Government/other was the second most popular destination for African Americans, while white respondents continued their equal preferences for government/other and academe – predominantly white colleges and universities. The percentage of African American respondents pursuing an academic career was reduced by nearly one half (29% vs. 15%) from the first cohort. In fact, only 4% of African American respondents in the second cohort took their first jobs in historically black colleges and universities. Interestingly, no white respondents in either cohort began their careers in historically black colleges and universities. Similar findings were reported by Pearson (1985).

Although African Americans comprise roughly 14% of the U.S. population, they account for only 6% of all teachers at the college and university level (Cross, 1998; Slater, 1998/1999). According to a report published in *The Journal of African Americans in Higher Education* (Spring, 2000), liberal arts colleges been more successful in recruiting African American faculty than the nation's large research universities. Previous studies consistently report a high correlation between the prestige of the departments in which academics received their degrees and the prestige of the departments where they obtained jobs, especially their initial jobs (Berelson, 1960; Cole & Cole, 1973; Crane, 1965; Long et al., 1979; Reskin, 1979; Zuckerman, 1970). This effect holds independently of differences in pre-employment productivity (Long, 1978; McGinnis & Long, 1988).

A Cohort I interviewee made this observation regarding employment opportunities after completing his undergraduate education:

> At (a major research university), I was third in a class of 37 graduating physics majors. I thought I was going to have several job interviews. I was particularly struck by the way one company did its interview. They would request that a person from the list of graduating seniors come in for an interview. I was on the list. When I walked into the room, this fellow (recruiter) said to me, "Can I help you?" I said, "I am here for an interview." He said, "You're here for an interview? I don't think so. What is your name?" I told him. He said: "Oh, well, that's okay. We have your name on file . . ." That was the end of the interview. I had a couple of other interviews and they said the same things . . . Maybe . . . a couple of weeks after that, I was telling my parents that I had a job lined up because they have my name on file. Then my parents told me what that really meant. I have to admit that this was my first introduction to prejudice. And it was blatant!

The interviewee continues:

> After graduation, I didn't have a job. So, I started hitting the bricks. I found a job with a company in (a Midwestern city). I will never forget the white guy who hired me. He was very nice. I think about him all the time. It was during the war years. He hired me and we would talk from time to time, I told him about my experience with the recruiter. He didn't say much about it, but he told me that I was going to face that more and more because it is not really a free and equal society out there. After talking with him and my parents, that is when I got really angry about being discriminated against. I enjoyed my stay at_ . . . I remember a white guy in the physics department who was my advisor. He kept telling me to take some education courses. I told him that I didn't want to teach school. He just kept saying, "Why don't you want to take some education courses?" He knew that I wanted to go into research but he also knew that it was going to be rough for a black out there. But he never told me that. Years later, he was apologetic after I confronted him. I believe that he had an obligation to give the facts then and he didn't. He told me that he felt that I should pursue a scientific career because somewhere along the line something (racial discrimination in industrial research and development) was going to change. And he thought that I was the person to get it. I mentioned that I was disappointed that I hadn't been able to get a job. He said that he had told me to go into education because he knew that blacks probably couldn't get a job as an industrial scientist. He felt that I really didn't understand how prejudiced it was in the real world. I have to admit that I really didn't.

From grade school to high school, I was the only black in my classes except one. But, I always felt accepted by the white kids and white teachers.

One Cohort I interviewee related this experience about a campus recruiter:

He asked me, "Are you Indian or Hawaiian?" I said, "No, I am a Negro." His reply was, "Gee, that's too bad because it is illegal for us to hire Negroes in our laboratories." Each recruiter told me the same thing. Some fifteen to eighteen years later, one of these recruiter's company bought the company where I worked. This was before the Civil Rights days in the sixties. Because I was black, they had to change their whole meeting schedule. They couldn't hold the meeting in the hotels around their major research facilities because state (South and non-South) laws prohibited African Americans from staying at the hotels.

Another Cohort I interviewee argued that a prestigious research department was more willing to educate than hire African Americans. The interviewee relates the following case about an African American peer:

Although_was the only student to pass his prelims, he was not offered a job at_(a prestigious department). But a white classmate who failed his prelims was later hired in the chemistry department. If anybody should have gotten a job there, it should have been_. It was the reality of the time. The university was open and fair with respect to black graduate students studying there, but they were not expected to get a job in the chemistry department. This was one of the better chemistry departments for blacks to attend graduate school.

A Cohort II interviewee had this to say:

In 1951, I accepted an industrial job at_. My (white) supervisor had only a high school education. We had problems so seriously that when my chief supervisor left him in charge, he kept bugging me until I told him to get out of my lab. He reported me to supervision. That's when everything went haywire. I knew they needed me worse than they needed him. If this had happened between two whites it would have been a mole hill. They made a mountain out of the thing but I knew I was right. When my supervisor came back, he was so upset because they had spent hours and hours on what to do about my problem. That is what they thought of a black at that time.

The interviewee continues:

I left the company to complete my Ph.D. When I returned four years later (shortly after the Brown decision), things were entirely different. They laid out the red carpet. Apparently, some government regulation told them that they'd better hire a minority. I found out through devious methods that I fit the profile they wanted because I was fair skinned. The only problem was that I wasn't married. They were really upset about that . . . After three months on the job, I was placed on a project with a group located in another building. They had an organic chemist who had spent over a year working on the problem without success. They thought, let's put this hot shot chemist on this thing. The moment I arrived on the scene, an older white technician looked at me and sat on his rear for a week. He wasn't going to work for me. I still solved one of the major problems. As a result, I got four salary increases in fourteen months. But, this created conflict between me and a white coworker who only had a master's degree.

A Cohort II graduate of a prestigious department explained the choice of a career at an historically black college:

> I had a good offer from industry, but I decided to decline it. There were so few African Americans with Ph.D.s in chemistry that I decided to dedicate my career to increasing the talent pool. I decided to take the job at because it needed me more. The chemists there were conducting very little cutting-edge research, primarily because of a lack of resources. During my early years, I spent summers working in industrial labs. This was very beneficial because I was able to see first hand that industry was finally opening up to hiring African American scientists. Industry was also anxious to recruit African American scientists but discovered that the pool was very small. So, my colleagues and I began to develop a strategic plan to expand the pool, especially for master's level students to work in industry. We convinced some companies that we were the best department to produce high quality graduate students to meet their needs. We were extremely successful in attracting grants from foundations and industry. As a result, we more than doubled the number of graduate students we were producing each year.

Another Cohort II interviewee adds:

> I decided to work at (an historically black college) because this was to be my contribution to the Civil Rights Movement. I decided that since I hadn't marched, I would work at a black college. I reasoned that if I were a student at a black college, I would want to study with someone who had the training that I had from a prestigious department ... That's why I came ... It would have been difficult to get jobs at other places when I first graduated, because industry hadn't opened up to minorities, and certainly not to minority women. Predominately white institutions had not opened up to women as much as they have now, and certainly not black women, but I'm sure I would've gotten hired, because I've received job offers almost every year I've been here ... I came here because I really wanted to make a contribution.

One Cohort III interviewee also wanted to make a difference in the lives of young black aspiring scientists: "I took a position at (an historically black college) because it was fledgling and I thought that I could make a contribution in the development of the program."

Prior to the Civil Rights movement, African Americans were largely confined to historically black colleges and universities. As a result of the Civil Rights movement, the enrollment of African American students at predominantly white campuses increased. When African American students arrived on white campuses, they found a dearth of role models who looked like them. Many felt alienated and perceived hostility because of racial differences. According to the psychologist Fleming (1984), African American students who perceive racial discrimination from white faculty and peers avoid interaction with them outside of the classroom. She reports that African American students are less likely to seek help from professors or participate in extra-curricular activities with their white peers. As a result of the perceived discrimination, African American students began to protest and call for the hiring of more African American faculty. Benjamin (1991) indicates that historically black colleges and universities were a major source of talent from which African American faculty and administrators were drawn, creating a brain drain in those schools.

Benjamin (1991) asserts that at predominantly white colleges and universities there are few African Americans in senior decision-making positions to act as mentors for African Americans. She contends that African Americans in senior positions are often isolated from one another because of their heavy involvement in academic activities. According to Benjamin, African American academics have an additional role of performing as a "buffer" in the university with African American students and with the African American community. She believes that this produces a dilemma, creating both role strain and role conflict. Furthermore, walking this academic tightrope creates a serious tension. Benjamin argues that a disproportionate number of African American administrators in higher education are likely to hold titles as what she calls "a special-assistant-to-someone phenomenon." She claims that most African American administrators in predominantly white universities have little power and authority. She believes that the quality of the environment at predominantly white universities negatively affects the retention of African American academicians. The confluence of the role strain, role conflict, and social isolation takes a horrific psychological and physical toll on African American scholars working in predominantly white settings.

According to Benjamin, a disproportionate number of African American administrators and faculty hired at predominantly white colleges during the late 1960s and early 1970s found their careers limited by racial barriers. Benjamin concludes that even when African Americans are engaged in research, promotion and retention may still be difficult to obtain. One of her interviewees attributed his tenure denial to racism, elitism, and changing standards. Benjamin believes that it is no coincidence that the promotion and tenure standards change when a diverse population enters academe or any new marketplace.

The comments of one Cohort III interviewee at a predominantly white university are instructive:

> I had totally limited knowledge about how the university worked. I probably wouldn't have known how a company operated either. I wasn't given any information in graduate school about how those things operate, and I knew no one who looked like me who had come from those environments. Unlike my white grad school classmates at_(a prestigious university), I had no family history of higher education or professional employment. A lot of my classmates had fathers or relatives who worked in research universities and large corporations. I just didn't know anything. It was not until fifteen or twenty years later, that I found out that I was hired through the administration, and not the chemistry department. In hindsight, I didn't remember having an interview with the department. I got an appointment because I finished from a prestigious department and because of my letters of recommendation. I just showed up at the department one day, and I was told, here are your classes. I knew nothing about what I was supposed to

do. It turns out that a lot of stuff was happening that I didn't know about. The_(a white male senior administrator) had a vested interest in recruiting black faculty. The idea was that I was hired to help bolster him and his agenda. This never came out. In hindsight, the only hint was at a social gathering where he said something to the effect that it wasn't a social gathering, it was a meeting that had a social aspect to it. I overheard him say that I thought the chairman of the chemistry department was my boss, but he was really my boss. At the time, I didn't know what that meant. He (the senior administrator) was supposed to provide start-up funds for me to purchase equipment to do my research but it didn't happen. After four years, I didn't have equipment to do the research that I was trained to do. When I finally got it, I didn't have any research funds. Now, I am strapped with teaching and mundane administrative duties. I have no time or students to develop a research program. After I was here for a few years, I was unable to attract students. One white graduate student confided in me that some of the graduate students wanted to work with me, but that they had been told by the chairman that they shouldn't. In more than 20 years, I have had only two graduate students!

One Cohort II interviewee reinforces the latter comments by arguing that many very capable African Americans on the science faculties of major research universities experienced problems recruiting top graduate students. The interviewee asserts: "They (African American scientists at predominantly white research universities) experienced similar problems. All these people are excellent researchers. What they found was frustration. Because they are black they could not attract the best students."

Commenting on the difficulty of attracting top graduate students, a Cohort III interviewee had this to say:

I need graduate students. I have had grant money but no graduate students ... it is an uncomfortable situation. Presently, I have one grad student and two post docs ... I've not fared well in the competition for graduate students. I tried to recruit some black students from black colleges but their GRE scores were not competitive enough to get accepted into our program. I have been unsuccessful in persuading my colleagues to take a chance on some black students whose GRE scores are slightly below our cutoff. I have had only two Ph.D. students in over 20 years.

In the last Cohort (V), one interviewee employed at a predominantly white university explained how being married to another professional influenced his search for the first job in this way:

We looked for a large metropolitan area. My wife had strong feelings about seeking employment in certain areas, especially the south. We actually targeted the southeast. We were looking at either_or_as our first choice and because it would increase the probability of employment if my wife decided to practice_in the future. Also cultural factors were attractive in these cities.

Benjamin found that African American Ph.D.s have the lowest faculty promotion and tenure rate of any group. She concluded that "even when African Americans are invited for interviews, they are frequently treated insensitively, which discourages them from accepting a position" (Benjamin, 1991, pp. 124–125). A Cohort V interviewee relates this experience:

> My wife and I discussed geographic preference during the job search. Unfortunately, most of the available jobs in my specialty were in the Northeast. We didn't want to live in that region because of the distance from our families, cost of living, and population density. My impression of the initial contact with_(a large public historically white university) was that they invited me solely because of the fact that I was black and they were attempting to satisfy EEOC requirements for the interview process . . . because nothing was ever timely during that interview process. They called me when I initially submitted the application . . . the process tended to just drag out . . . eight months . . . Their tardiness and lack of interest or enthusiasm dissuaded me from accepting the job. So, we took an offer in the Midwest.

One Cohort V Ph.D. recipient had this to say about an interview at a small private historically white university:

> The guy was very open with me . . . they were interested in getting a black faculty member . . . The head of the department told me that . . . The Provost told me that when I met with him . . . They spared no expense . . . It was my longest interview . . . I never considered them seriously because I always had an interest in doing research and the faculty there was not doing much research.

Another Cohort V interviewee elected to pursue an academic career after an industrial postdoctoral assignment. The interviewee commented: "I have much more space to be creative and develop my own ideas in academia."

At the time of the interviews, 41% of all chemists had held only one job. As expected, cohort variations reflect professional age. That is, 71% of interviewees in the last cohort compared to 33 and 25% respectively, in the first and second cohorts were in their first position.

For example, interviewees beginning their careers in industry and historically white colleges and universities were equally (44% vs. 45%) likely to have remained in their first position. In contrast, only 31% of those with first jobs in historically black colleges and universities remained in their first positions. The one Cohort I interviewee who began in the government and other sector remained in that job. The following comments are representative of the explanations for remaining in the first job. One Cohort III interviewee had this to say: "I decided to stay at_(an historically white university) because they have treated me well. They want me here . . . Everything has pointed to that . . . I have no qualms about advancement and support." A Cohort V interviewee at an historically black college related this experience:

> Opportunities have actually come to me because I am at a black school. For example, I was in_(a foreign country) giving a paper, when one of my "Ph.D. advisor's boys" from_(a prestigious chemistry department), came up to me. I said, "Hi, how are you doing?" He asked, "What are you doing here?" I said, "Same thing that you are doing here. I am presenting a paper." He said,

"I didn't think they did research at." The negative side is that I am isolated sometimes, but the positive side is that the faculty supports me.

Feelings of isolation were common among interviewees at both historically black colleges and universities and historically white colleges and universities. In instances where the chemists were the only persons of color in the department or perhaps the first ones ever appointed to a faculty position in chemistry, many became discouraged and sometimes very depressed. Benjamin (1991) posits that the social isolation faced by many upwardly mobile African Americans often leads to stress, which can manifest itself in physiological disorders, such as hypertension, behavioral disorders, and even suicide. One Cohort V interviewee offered the following comments:

The script says I went to this school. I did everything I was "supposed" to have done... When the promotions and choice assignments don't come, you realize that the "color-blind psychological camaraderie" is really not there... You're still black... And there's almost a sense of loss, because in some ways, you're still a slave... You're no different than the guy who is the janitor. It's just that you have a Ph.D. and you are making a little bit more money... This has psychological effects... You become paranoid... You become obsessive and don't know where to turn. I was fortunate to have (an African American senior colleague) to talk to because there was something going on that I was not aware of... I think there are a lot of black professionals in this situation who need to go to psychoanalysis. Unfortunately, this is largely taboo in the black culture.

Despite a commitment to teach and conduct research, the overwhelming impact of isolation sometimes affects confidence. Many interviewees did not have opportunities to interact with other chemists of color until they went to professional meetings. Sometimes, even professional meetings failed to provide an opportunity for meaningful discussions and networking among African American chemists. An interviewee from an historically black college comments:

One of the things I used to see a lot when I went to professional meetings was some black chemists treating other black chemists as if they couldn't do anything for them... Another black person was the last person that they wanted to have contact with... I used to get sort of disgusted that some blacks would have nothing to do with other blacks.

One Cohort III interviewee gave this account of leaving the first job:

Because my graduate study was supported by a fellowship, one condition was that I pursue an academic career. When I got to (an historically black college), I realized immediately that I didn't want to be there. The politics and the environment were not good for me. So, I applied for an industrial job and received an offer. But my wife wasn't ready to move. Because my wife had supported me during my doctoral studies, she felt that it was time for me to be supportive of her while she gained some valuable career experience for a year or two. She held an administrative position on campus. My wife said that she wasn't ready to run from something. She wanted to run to something. So, we stayed another year. Then I took the job in industry.

A Cohort III interviewee explained a different situation:

> I left industry for academic employment because I lost faith in my primary project which turned out not to be economically feasible... Then, I found myself not really enjoying the lab that much... I knew that any other industrial position would require working on whatever the company dictated. I just felt that I didn't want that restriction anymore. I wanted to have the freedom to work on what I wanted... and a university environment provided that.

Twelve interviewees were employed at historically black colleges and universities. Of these, four began careers in industry, six in historically black colleges and universities, and one each in government and other, and an historically white university. In sharp contrast, four of the six interviewees who were employed at historically white colleges and universities began their careers in such institutions, while only one each reported first jobs in industry and at an historically black college. A majority of those employed in government and other sectors launched their careers in industry, while two listed first jobs in academe (one each at an historically white university and an historically black college). It is noteworthy that chemists tend to leave one historically white university for another. One Cohort IV interviewee gave this account:

> Actually, the department didn't have a vacancy. Because the university was under a federal consent decree, it had what is called a_program. Under this program, if a person from an underrepresented group inquires about a position, the school will interview that person. Fortunately, I was offered a tenure-track position. I accepted the offer because I was in a non-tenure-track position at a small historically white university. When I informed the department of my decision to leave, only then did they offer to convert my position to tenure track.

The interviewee added:

> The positive aspect of being in this department is that I can teach as well as do research. This was not the case at my first job where I could not do research. While there, I really missed being in the lab. I like being able to do both. I like being able to interact with students, not only undergraduates but graduate students too. Now, I have an opportunity to write proposals and papers. The major negative is that with the recent administrative change, the research is more or less not being done for fun like it used to be. Now, there is more pressure to bring in grant money.

Another Cohort IV interviewee at a predominantly white university commented: "The Provost here at the time, really was doing hard core recruiting of faculty of color, especially African Americans." Historically black colleges and universities tend to recruit African American chemists from other historically black colleges universities as well as industry especially retirees. Industrial chemists also moved to government and other jobs. Interestingly, chemists pursuing their first jobs in academe tended to do so in institutions with student racial compositions similar to that of their baccalaureate-granting institutions. For example, 10 of the 11 interviewees whose first jobs were in historically white colleges and universities, held bachelor's degrees from such institutions. Similarly, 11 of the 13 interviewees who began their careers at historically black colleges and universities were graduates of these colleges and universities. Regarding industry, historically black colleges and universities accounted for 14 of the 19 interviewees who began their careers in industry and the one whose first job was in the government and other sector. (For a more detailed discussion of the contributions of historically black colleges and universities to industry, especially in the late 1960s and 1970s, see Meier, 1982).

LAST OR CURRENT POSITION

Regarding the last or current job, a majority of the interviewees were employed primarily in academe (especially historically black colleges and universities), followed by industry. Few interviewees worked in the government and other sector. Nearly two-thirds of the academic interviewees were employed in public institutions. Of those employed at historically white colleges and universities, approximately 64% were in research universities. A comparable percentage of those at historically black colleges and universities were employed at comprehensive institutions. This is not surprising because few historically black colleges and universities are classified as doctoral or research institutions by the Carnegie Foundation for the Advancement of Teaching. Interviewees at historically black colleges and universities were more likely than their peers in historically white colleges and universities to report above average student course evaluations (77% vs. 58%). An equal percentage (8%) of faculty at both schools reported below average evaluations.

Data derived from the Survey of Doctorate Recipients reveal that white respondents more likely than their black peers (three fifths vs. two fifths) to be currently employed in industry (Table 4.3). There were no race differences in employment in government/other and historically white colleges and universities. Approximately one fifth of black respondents were employed in historically black colleges and universities, compared to less than 1% of white respondents. The most striking race variations emerge when current academic employment is disaggregated by Carnegie Classification. These data confirm the underparticipation of African Americans at doctoral/research universities, especially those designated as extensive. Overall, about two-fifths of the white respondents are employed at these institutions compared to slightly less than 10% of black respondents. Black respondents were considerably more likely than their white peers (half vs. three-fourths) to be employed in other than doctoral/research universities, However, black respondents were slightly more

Table 4.3. Percent Distribution of Current Job by Employment Sector and Race [Survey Respondents].

Sector	Race	
	White	Black
Industry	62.0	41.0
Historically Black College/University	[a]	21.0
Historically White College/University	27.0	27.0
Government/Other	11.0	11.0
Total	100.0	100.0

Note: Percentages may not sum to 100 because of rounding.
Source: Survey of Doctorate Recipients.
[a] Less than 1%.

likely than white respondents (11% vs. 16%) to be employed in doctoral/research intensive institutions.

Furthermore, the survey data show that an about equal percentage of black and white respondents are employed in the Northeast (Table 4.4). Black respondents are nearly twice as likely their white peers to be employed in the South. In contrast, white respondents were more likely than their black peers to be employed in the Midwest and West. These patterns are not surprising given the strong concentration of black respondents employed in historically black colleges and universities (most of which are located in the South.

In terms of career positions, data in Table 4.5 provide some insight into the career paths of interviewees who have held two or more jobs. Of the two chemists

Table 4.4. Percent Distribution by Region of Current Employment by Race [Survey Respondents].

Region	Race	
	White	Black
Northeast	29.0	28.0
Midwest	24.0	10.0
South	26.0	48.0
West	21.0	14.0
Total	100.0	100.0

Note: Percentages may not sum to 100 because of rounding.
Source: Survey of Doctorate Recipients.

Table 4.5.   Distribution by Sector of Last Position by Sector of First Position of Interviewees with Two or More Positions.

First Position	Current/Last Position				
	Industry	HBCU	PWCU	Government	Other
Industry	1	4	1	3	1
Historically Black College/University	1	6	1	1	0
Historically White College/University	0	1	4	1	0
Government	0	1	0	0	0
Total	2	12	6	5	1

whose last job was in industry, one's first job was in industry, while the other's was in an historically black college.

A sampling of comments regarding job experiences is instructive. One Cohort I interviewee explained the impact of desegregation on historically black colleges and universities in this manner (see also Malcom et al., 1996):

> One of the things that has happened with desegregation is the fact that the predominately white schools are going out and, let me use the word, "buying" the black students! They don't want the lower achieving ones, and those are the ones that the black schools have to accept. As a result, the black schools are doing more remedial work than they have in the past! The white schools are getting the higher achieving black students. Often they bring them in and then they become a number. They end up feeling isolated and they don't always perform at their highest level of capability. Frankly, I don't think many have achieved academically because of the prejudice and pressures they feel in that sort of isolated and unsupportive setting.

When explaining the dearth of African American Ph.D. chemists employed in high-level decision-making positions at major governmental agencies, one Cohort II interviewee had this to say:

> To be very honest, it is a function of racism. Having attained a senior-level position, I have been privy to some information regarding the comments that people have made about me. Like, "he is not technical enough!" The irony is that for a long time the decision makers at were primarily grads of the same department where I earned my Ph.D.

The same interviewee explained a personal reluctance to accept a managerial appointment:

> It is not the most satisfying job. To turn it down would signal that African Americans could not do the job. I view it as a trail blazing situation. My motivation is to prove that a black can manage a predominately white staff. All of the managers who report to me are White and male. I announced that one of my objectives was to change that make-up by promoting equally qualified women and minorities. I discovered that they were not even at the next tier. I have promoted about half a dozen people to the next tier so in about a year or so they will be ready to move to managerial positions.

One Cohort IV interviewee at a predominantly white research university had this to say regarding attempts to collaborate with white colleagues:

> I am talking about people saying, "Why don't you work with this person?" or someone calling me up and saying, "Have you ever thought about working on this particular project?" I have to seek them out and then I have to struggle to keep in contact with them, even when I think that I am doing work that is unique and topical. I think that we are suffering enormously from racial prejudice in this country. I think that is going to limit what African Americans achieve as a people for the foreseeable future.

SECTORAL EXPERIENCES

Interviewees were asked to describe how they chose their jobs and career experiences in various employment sectors. One Cohort III industrial interviewee accepted a job "primarily because of_'s (a well known company) reputation in chemical research and the size of its research effort in_chemistry." The interviewee continued:

> The likelihood of, I won't call it unlimited support, but much more of what I would call secondary support for the kind of work I wanted to do was attractive . . . If you wanted to get into an area that required unusual instrumentation or more expensive instrumentation, then chances are you wouldn't have much difficulty gaining access to it . . . You would also be working with people who had great reputations in their respective fields.

For many interviewees financial considerations were important factors in determining employment sector. One Cohort V interviewee chose a career in industry because it paid more money than other sectors, especially academe. A Cohort III industrial interviewee said:

> After six years at_(a well known company), I was recruited by_(another well known company). I didn't take the position because I couldn't negotiate a salary that was commensurate with the cost of living there. For example, home replacement would run about $200,000. I didn't see that the salary was going to cover that and still provide a 5–10% increase to my base salary,

One Cohort III interviewee explained: "I left the_(a national lab) because the leadership changed . . . The financial situation was difficult . . . Funding was extremely tight."

Other interviewees described chemistry as a highly respected and well-paying field.

Financial considerations were not the only factor influencing job decisions. Some interviewees indicated that their job decisions were based on interpersonal relationships and the culture or climate of the employing organization. Sometimes academic advisors played key roles in these decisions. One Cohort III interviewee remarked: "My Ph.D. advisor was a good friend of the Research Director at_(a well known company)." One Cohort III interviewee commented: "After I decided to leave my first job, I decided to remain in the area because I still had colleagues at_(Ph.D.-granting department) and I was pretty close to my advisor and collaborated with him on several projects... It was basically where my ties were... At the time, I was also active in a local church."

A Cohort III interviewee had this to say about accepting a job offer: "I felt at home... When I walked into the lab, it was very much like the positive experience I had in graduate school. I really felt accepted." A Cohort III reported: "I chose_(a well known company) because it appeared to be a more humanistic company... It was less cutthroat than some other companies."

Some interviewees found the environment at some companies unwelcoming to African Americans. One Cohort III interviewee explained: "Although the management of my unit made a decision to hire black Ph.D. chemists, I'm not sure that the entire unit felt that way. I found out years later that some technicians said that they wouldn't work for blacks... Some of this (attitude) has changed over the course of time." Another Cohort III interviewee compares recruiting experiences: "When I took the interview at_(a well known company), the atmosphere did not look that inviting. However, I took the job because I felt that if I could survive in that environment, I believed that I could work anywhere." In sharp contrast, one Cohort III interviewee related this experience:

> ... a significant number of people in the Human Resources department were very welcoming... When I came for the interview, I was introduced to members of the black community with whom I could socialize... Some of these individuals invited me to attend a play... They (the company personnel) were very open and very friendly... I liked them... In contrast, in most of the other companies where I interviewed, I was never introduced to members of the local black community. In fact, at_(a well known company), I was introduced to alumni from my graduate school. But, I was never introduced to a black person... At_(another well known company), a young black woman was on my interview schedule. She was very bitter about the environment (racial insensitivity) that she found at the company... I had no question that my host was a bigot... He took me to places where he thought that I should live. I was insulted by that... I rejected the offer on the basis that if management didn't know that he was a bigot that was not the environment in which I would work.

The social impacts of relocation were important factors for some interviewees. One Cohort IV east coast interviewee explained: "I didn't want to move to the Midwest because I thought I would encounter prejudice."

PROMOTIONS

Well-educated and highly qualified African American professionals sometimes encounter attitudinal or organizational bias that prevents them from reaching their full potential. They have confronted what some researchers term the glass ceiling. In essence, they can see the higher tier positions in the organization but barriers block their promotion because of gender, racial status or both. Even before glass ceilings are encountered, African Americans may face concrete walls that block lateral movement.

This level of frustration was typical whether the chemists were on technical or non-technical tracks. However, chemists on the technical track expressed more frustration about the likelihood that they could climb to the top of the research and development (R&D) ladder. In fact, several interviewees reported that it was not uncommon for gifted but frustrated African American industrial chemists to leave the technical track for what was perceived as more financially rewarding positions in management in their companies. However, these interviewees pointed out that most of these jobs involved management of Equal Employment Opportunity, human resource and community outreach offices. This seems to have a basis in reality (see Quay, 1970). Unfortunately, these positions usually do not lead to high-level decision-making positions within the company.

Interviewees discussed careers in the technical management tracks, and making the transition from one track to another. One Cohort III interviewee commented:

> I know some very good black scientists whose career paths are almost identical to mine. (Moving from basic research to administration or out of science entirely.) . . . There is no guarantee that if I had remained in research that I would have been provided the opportunity to work in the frontier research that would have led to consideration for a Nobel Prize . . . I think this is a problem for many very capable black scientists.

According to a Cohort III interviewee:

> My experiences at the bench helped me understand what information I really needed to know. Having much more understanding helps one do a better job. How to communicate to those who had to make the decisions on what was worked on, and how many resources the company would put into the effort.

The same interviewee explains the reason for leaving the bench for management:

> I resisted it (management) . . . but after awhile I looked at the career paths . . . When I started out, I worked on a very interesting project and I thought a Nobel Prize was possible. Then after a while I knew I would not get a Nobel Prize. So, I set my sights on a Regional or ACS award . . . Then, I began shifting my sights even lower . . . I looked around and I realized that we had some of the top-notch scientists in the world . . . With that realization, I decided to go the management route . . . Plus, I was being encouraged to do so.

For some interviewees, promotions came as a matter of course, as indicated by one Cohort III interviewee's explanation for remaining in a second job: "I feel at home. I got promoted in a reasonable length of time . . . I had comparable (to whites) technical reports and high profile projects." For others, promotions came more slowly. One Cohort III industrial interviewee said: "It took 19 years to get my third promotion. I would say that this is typical for African American Ph.D.s but not for white ones." In the same vein, another Cohort III industrial interviewee asserted: "I think the administration is slower to recognize and to promote black Ph.D. scientists than they are to promote whites... They (management) don't prepare blacks for entry level management jobs... but whites get some mentoring." One Cohort II interviewee gave this description:

> I was asked to be group supervisor... then my boss got promoted to head the division. Everybody assumed that I would replace him because I had published several papers and performed well in my administrative role... But he 'gave' the position to a white colleague ... He called me over to his house to explain why he was not going to give the position to me. His explanation didn't make sense to me ... The fellow he 'gave' the position to was very nice but totally incompetent as an administrator... This guy was in my office every day asking for advice ... After this guy and his boss performed so poorly, both were removed from their positions. The new manager, promoted me immediately ... I continued to conduct some basic research while doing administrative work. ... Eventually, my administrative duties required that I give up my research ... Later, I got promoted to my current position ... No black had ever gotten to this level in the agency.

Several interviewees attempted to explain the slow rate of promotions for African Americans. One Cohort III interviewee suggested that it stems from attitudes of management: "I think the management team that came in last is less friendly to African Americans than the previous one."

Another Cohort III interviewee explained:

> The fact that I am the only African American at a senior rank is due to the way the company recruits. We go to, for example, Harvard and Cal Tech. We are in contact with faculty members there... I don't think we make an overt effort to develop networks which would identify African American Ph.D. chemists and recruit them.

TRANSITION FROM INDUSTRY TO ACADEME

Some interviewees viewed industrial careers as advantageous for subsequent careers in academe. One Cohort III interviewee said: "In the early 1970s, there weren't many African Americans in industrial laboratories. Therefore, I decided that I could probably be of greater service to black colleges if I went into industry then returned to teach." A Cohort V interviewee explained:

> I felt if I were to teach, I would only give students a two dimensional education ... If there was only one criticism that I have of (Ph.D.-granting department) it was that a lot of professors never got outside the department. They lacked networking experiences with chemists at other institutions, companies and government. They were more or less isolated. I would say that was probably one of the best chemists and didn't know any chemists outside of academe.

Realizing the positive impact mentors and role models have on students, and having committed himself to increasing the number of African Americans in the chemistry community, one Cohort III interviewee who left industry to take a position at an historically black college did so because "it was a chance to give back to black people something that I had – research skills and industrial experiences."

SALARY

Approximately 80% of the interviewees provided useable 12-month salary data for 1993–1994. The monthly salary ranged from $3,333 (academe) to more than $15,000 (industry). The median monthly salary was $7,583. The median years with the doctorate were 24 years. Two academic chemists earned the lowest salaries despite having their doctorates an average of 30 years. An industrial chemist reported the highest annual earnings but felt underpaid given the number of years and job responsibilities with the company. Not surprisingly, both the median monthly salary and median years with the doctorate varied considerably across employment sectors (see Table 4.6).

Around the same time of the current study, salaries of individual Ph.D. chemists were increasing at a higher rate than inflation (Heylin, 1995). In 1995, according to Heylin (1996), the median salary for Ph.D. chemists was approximately $66,000. A year later, this figure rose to $68,000. For Ph.D. chemists with 20–24 years beyond the receipt of the BS degree, the median salary was $74,100 (Heylin, 1996). Typically, the median salary tends to be higher in industry ($75,000), followed by government ($68,400) and academia ($52,000). The lower academic salaries are influenced by a variety of factors, especially in the early academic ranks. Academic institutions vary considerably in compensation when disaggregated by Carnegie classification. As has been shown, some of the salaries for African American Ph.D. chemists at some historically black colleges and universities are very low. Heylin

Table 4.6. Distribution of Median Monthly Salary by Sector and Median Years with the Doctorate [Interviewees].

Sector	Monthly Salary	Years With Doctorate
Historically Black College/University	$7,442	29.0
Historically White College/University	6,792	13.0
Industry	8,542	26.0
Government/Other	8,042	20.0

Table 4.7.   Percent Distribution by Level of Satisfaction with Salary by Race [Survey Respondents].

Level of Satisfaction	Race	
	White	Black
Very/Somewhat satisfied	83.0	85.0
Somewhat/Very dissatisfied	17.0	15.0
Total	100.0	100.0

Note: Percentages may not sum to 100 because of rounding.
Source: Survey of Doctorate Recipients.

(1995) points out that salaries for full professors at Ph.D.-granting institutions tend to be more competitive with those in industry and government. Regardless of professorial rank, salaries tend to be higher in Ph.D.-granting institutions (Heylin, 1996). These are precisely the institutions where African Americans are grossly underrepresented. He argues that the median salary of $92,000 for an 11 or 12 month contract fares well with salaries of senior Ph.D. chemists in the non-academic sectors. In industry, the salaries are higher in large companies (e.g. 25,000 and more employees). Finally, Heylin (1996) shows that salaries are generally higher in the East than other regions of the country.

Table 4.7 shows essentially no major racial differences among survey respondents in level of satisfaction with salary. In fact, the data reveal that slightly more than eight in 10 respondents of both racial groups are either very satisfied or somewhat satisfied with salary compensation.

Data in Table 4.8 show that African American and white survey respondents were similarly satisfied with their job responsibility. For example, approximately

Table 4.8.   Percent Distribution by Level of Satisfaction with Job Responsibility by Race [Survey Respondents].

Level of Satisfaction	Race	
	White	Black
Very/Somewhat satisfied	86.0	88.0
Somewhat/Very dissatisfied	14.0	12.0
Total	100.0	100.0

Note: Percentages may not sum to 100 because of rounding.
Source: Survey of Doctorate Recipients.

eight in 10 respondents of both racial groups are very satisfied or somewhat satisfied with currently job responsibilities.

JOB SATISFACTION

When asked about their level of satisfaction with their current or last job, a substantial majority (slightly more than 71%) of interviewees indicated some degree of satisfaction (see Table 4.9). Nevertheless, nearly 20% were unhappy with their jobs. For example, a Cohort III interviewee at an historically black college/university commented:

> We have no fax machine in this building ... We're getting wired for e-mail, but you have to have a computer for that and the department has not purchased any. We are supposed to be wired for it in a couple of months.

One Cohort III interviewee at an historically black college said:

> I got into administration by default. It was a way of having greater influence over the policies that would enhance the production of black scientists at the school. At this point in my career, I will say that I am only moderately satisfied with my position because it is such a challenge and such hard work. It doesn't give me the usual gratification you would get from working in a lab and when you are working with students.

Another interviewee working at an historically black college/university expressed dissatisfaction with some aspects of employment:

> We are not getting the same quality of black students that we got before the middle 1980s. They are not interested in doing the work. They don't know the basic math to keep up with the courses. We now have far more foreign students, especially in graduate programs.

A Cohort III interviewee at an historically black college said that: "There is no money for research ... The school can't even afford chemistry journals, so I had to purchase my own."

Table 4.9. Percent Distribution by Level of Satisfaction with Current or Last Job by Employment Sector [Interviewees].

Level of Satisfaction	Industry	Academe	Government/Other	Total
Very satisfied	62.0	73.0	100.0	71.0
Neutral	23.0	5.0	0.0	11.0
Very dissatisfied	15.0	23.0	0.0	18.0
Total	100.0	100.0	100.0	100.0

Note: Percentages may not sum to 100 because of rounding.

Another Cohort III interviewee summed up their work experience at an historically black college: "What is happening are the same things that happen at most HBCUs: they use you up and them they throw you away."

Despite the fact that this interviewee worked at that historically black college for more than 20 years, she reported that "Last year, my teaching load was heavier than it has ever been."

Interviewees working at historically white universities also expressed dissatisfaction with their working conditions, as did one Cohort IV interviewee:

> This is not a particularly supportive department for anyone. The chairman, in particular, is not very supportive. In fact, I have had several incidents where he has been just bitingly critical of my teaching. I thought he was excessive. He has also made some racially insensitive remarks to me over the years.

One Cohort III interviewee had this to say:

> My work still involves coming in on weekends, but there is no requirement for me to do that . . . It requires staying current with literature and with some of things not only that have an historic interest to me but a current interest as well.

One Cohort V interviewee said that "The company encourages its scientists to become involved in the community. I have judged science fairs and served as a volunteer for non-profit agencies."

Approximately 10% of interviewees were ambivalent about their level of job satisfaction. Specifically, industrial chemists were more likely than either academic or government and other chemists to express a neutral opinion. Nevertheless, most interviewees were either satisfied or very satisfied with their positions. In sharp contrast, academic chemists were less ambivalent. For example, 16 of the 22 were satisfied or very satisfied with their jobs, while five were very dissatisfied. Only one academic chemist indicated a neutral response. All government and other chemists were either satisfied or very satisfied with their jobs.

Except for interviewees employed at historically white colleges and universities, most interviewees were more satisfied with their influence on departmental rather than institutional policies. Industrial chemists expressed the lowest level of satisfaction in their ability to influence either institutional or departmental policies. One Cohort I interviewee from an historically black college explained that a simple departmental policy decision changed the dynamics of student/faculty interaction:

> We used to have computers in the science area . . . As they (computers) became more popular, the administration decided to establish computer labs in the buildings so that all students would have access to them . . . In our building the chemistry department was on the third floor and the computer lab was on the second floor . . . The students were always down in the lab using the

computers so you no longer had that one-on-one contact with students like you had when the computers were in the science area or in the office and you were in there with them.

SKILLS LEARNED IN GRADUATE SCHOOL THAT MOST HELPED IN CAREER SUCCESS

Interviewees reported that they learned a number of skills in graduate school that were invaluable in their careers. Some comments are illustrative. One interviewee said: "To think independently." Another pointed to the "ability to formulate the problem and formulate potential solutions." One interviewee commented: "Knowing when the problem is solved. Knowing the problem is not solvable with current resources or time limits." One interviewee pointed to: "Being tenacious, precise, and recognizing that if you are truly determined you will get the job done." One interview had this to say: "The ability to think logically and use scientific principles to order how to approach problems and develop solutions to problems. The rigors of the scientific training."

PERSON MOST INFLUENTIAL IN CAREER

When asked who had influenced them most in their careers, interviewees identified a variety of individuals (see Table 4.10). The most frequent responses were mentor and spouse (among those currently married). The mentor emerged as an inclusive category. For example, interviewees included former high school

Table 4.10. Percent Distribution by Individual Who Most Helped in Career [Interviewees].

Person	Percent
Spouse	21.0
Other relative	11.0
Friend	7.0
Dissertation advisor	15.0
Colleagues	4.0
Mentor	23.0
Other	6.0
No response	13.0
Total	100.0

Note: Percentages may not sum to 100 because of rounding.

teachers (including non-science and math teachers), college chemistry professors, graduate professors (including non-dissertation advisor), more senior graduate school classmates and job supervisors. The mentors were of various ethnic and racial backgrounds, although they were usually male. It was not uncommon for some interviewees with baccalaureate origins in historically black colleges and universities to share a common mentor (see Pearson & Pearson, 1985). One Cohort III interviewee said:

> I think they've all made some kind of contribution in small ways ... perhaps in key ways throughout the whole cycle. For example, _was instrumental in encouraging me to go back to graduate school. _and_(graduate faculty) who encouraged me that I had the skills to make it at_(a prestigious graduate program). My wife was supportive in the sense that she agreed to the life style and was willing to take risks.

Some interviewees did not have a positive experience, as one interviewee stressed: "My advisor has never helped me secure a job."

SECOND THOUGHTS ABOUT CHOOSING A CAREER IN CHEMISTRY

When asked if they had any second thoughts about having chosen a career in chemistry, 89% of interviewees answered that they did not, one took a neutral position, and only four indicated that they had second thoughts about their careers. Two of the four expressing doubts about having chosen a career in chemistry were women who admitted that they were not fully prepared to deal with the competitive nature of academic chemistry. Nevertheless, the vast majority of interviewees indicated that if they had to do it again, they would choose a career in chemistry because of their fascination with and love for the subject matter. In short, an overwhelming majority of interviewees were satisfied with their career choice.

Some interviewees, however, were ambivalent about their career choices, especially women:

> If I had known then what I know now, I might not have selected chemistry. I don't have any doubts in terms of my ability to do it or my love for it. But there have been some things that have been real problems for me – things that have prevented me from accomplishing what I was capable of in chemistry. If I were coming out of grad school now, I would be better off. I guess black females coming out now wouldn't have the kinds of problems I've had ... [D]uring the last five years or so, I have had real questions in my mind as to whether or not I could continue to talk up those needs to increase minority representation. I know I should be done, but I wonder sometimes if I should tell black females to go into chemistry. It won't be as bad as it has been from me but there still will be problems.

A Cohort II interviewee reflects:

> I have not done a good job of long range planning for my own career. I've not done any consulting to do those sort of things. I don't write down what I want to do when and when I want to do it. If I had an opportunity to do it over, would I do things differently? I'm not sure ... I don't do science for money ... My career has turned out alright. Would I want to be a vice president? Yes. But on my own terms and not someone else's.

One Cohort III interviewee believes that at his company "diversity is going to come with some people kicking and screaming." Another Cohort III interviewee explained:

> I honestly have to say yes that I have some doubts about having pursued a career in chemistry. In one way, I've always wondered if, in terms of job security, I should have gone to medical school. Like my father wanted me to. You can't help but think it would have been much easier to have been an M.D. .... And not worry about tenure. I didn't get tenure at_. In a sense, I sort of wonder if life would have been easier if I had gotten an M.D. In the end, I think that I would not have had as interesting a career, if I had simply practiced medicine. The thing that I love about research is that there is always a new challenge. And, it's always exciting.

A Cohort III interviewee chose to pursue a career in industry because "of the likelihood of more resources to support the type of research that I was interested in pursuing. My research required unusual and expensive instrumentation that was difficulty to obtain right a way in academe."

This excerpt from an interview with a Cohort II industrial chemist explains the reception of whites to his high level appointment:

> ... while there were perhaps doubts, or curiosity on the part of people working with and for me, I understood that they wanted to see if I could do the job. The managers who appointed me had similar doubts ... they saw it as a risk ... Finally, one manager told me in so many words that my appointment was an experiment. They (managers) were not certain whether the(white) customers would accept me. It was routine for whites with my profile to move from the bench to high level management positions. Although I performed well ... I dare say that there was probably much more discussion and scrutiny around me than my white male counterparts.

This excerpt reflects the experiences shared by many African American trailblazers:

> For any trailblazer, you are thinking about those blacks coming after you. You had to have the strength to deal with the racism and discrimination and still get the job done. I look back and think about that period of my career a lot! More than anything, I was extremely focused on succeeding. Failing was not an option. I always had the confidence that I could do the job ... I just needed the opportunity. Given the people I was working with or competing with for the kinds of assignments I was in were people who, in my view, certainly didn't have any greater insight than me in terms of what it took to succeed.

This also reflects the psychological cost of being the first or only African-American in a high-level decision-making position: "I was appointed to one position where

I had no mentor or sponsor. Fortunately, I was in the position less than one year before being promoted."

A Cohort I interviewee shared his experience:

> In some of the interviews they would offer me the job if I understood my place. I interviewed at_Company (in the Northeast). I was taken to the Research Director's office. He told me that I had an excellent record and I got along well with people. He said that we have a touchy situation which has nothing to do with you. He explained that there were no blacks on the professional staff and I would be the first one. He said the problem was that many of the (white) employees were prejudiced. Then, he explained that there was a black man who worked at the plant but not as a professional. He told me that every Christmas he would invite the employees over but the black guy and his wife would have to come at a separate time than the whites. I told him that I could not accept employment under those conditions.

The same interviewee related a similar experience:

> I took an interview at another company, _(in the Northeast) where my advisor knew the vice president. I was offered the job but the personnel director told me that he had to interview the research group (all white) to determine if they would be willing to work with a black man. One vote and I was out. About three of the 12 or 13 voted no, I was offered a research position in another department. However, this was not what I wanted. The chemist I was to work with was a screwball! He had this sign in the lab – "No Talking" – like grade school. I refused to be accepted on a second class basis. I said the hell with all of them. I wanted to be free of segregation. I refused to work at a black college because they were segregated and had poor research facilities. So, I went to work for myself where I am a first class citizen.

One Cohort I interviewee shared their experience

> While I was in town interviewing at a local company, I called a friend who was in graduate school with me at_. He had finished a year or two ahead of me. I called just to see how things were going with him. I told him that I was interviewing and said 'Why don't you come out here? We are looking for people.' As it turns out, he was working for another graduate of our Ph.D. program. So, I applied . . . and they liked what they saw. I was offered the job and accepted it. But the chemists had a general problem. We had to constantly fight to keep the work of our own choosing, and defining what the work should be rather than problem solving for the engineers.

A Cohort V interviewee related this experience about a job interview at a top ranked department:

> My initial indication with them was that they invited me solely because I was black and they were attempting to satisfy EEOC requirements on the interview process. Nothing was ever timely during and after the interview. I was called when I applied and then I met the representative at the ACS meeting. I considered his interest to be genuine. When I visited the university, I sensed that there were ulterior motives other than my research potential. The interview process just tended to drag out. I think the first contact was made in July . . . I went to the interview in November. I didn't hear anything from them until February of the following year. By the time they got back to me, I had accepted a job at_Company.

Another Cohort V interviewee related the following experience:

> When I was at (industry), I always had to play a psychological game with white folks. I was around a bunch of people who went to Ivy League schools and who were probably born with silver spoon in their mouths. I didn't come from that background. So, I always felt I had an advantage because they were under far more pressure to succeed.

Very negative experiences were discussed by a Cohort V interviewee: "Because of all of the negative experiences that I encountered at (a prestigious department), I wanted to get away from the United States scientific structure. And, I did."

RECRUITING MORE AFRICAN AMERICANS TO CHEMISTRY

While several recent reports have presented contradictory findings on the shortages (Atkinson, 2000; Jackson, 2003; National Science Board, 2004) vs. oversupply (Monastersky, 2004) debate, there is general consensus that the nation must recruit more talent from those demographic underparticipating in STEM fields (e.g. women, African Americans, American Indians, Latinos and persons with disabilities). Butz and his colleagues (2000) emphasize that regardless of the implications of a shortage of skills critical to U.S. growth, competitiveness, and security are significant, so are the implications of the continuing under-participation of female and minority students into many STEM fields. The criticality of drawing on this underutilized talent pool is expressed by a number of scholars.

When asked if there is a need to increase the representation of African Americans in chemistry, especially in the context of the supply and demand debate, 98% of the interviewees answered affirmatively. Most interviewees cited the following reasons: (1) untapped talent pool; (2) need for the acquisition of technical skills to be competitive in the twenty-first century workforce; (3) highly respected field; (4) future leaders for a global economy; (5) need for a critical mass to serve as more diversity; and (6) need for mentors and role models. Illustrative comments are presented below.

One interviewee said that there is a need to increase the number of African Americans: "I think that there are some good career opportunities and as the number increase then those career opportunities are going to be progressively better." Another interviewee pointed out that "there is no surplus of African American chemists." Yet another interviewee said that:

> I hope that no blacks buy into the notion of the surplus of scientists because it would inhibit the increase in black scientists. The workforce of tomorrow will, of necessity, reflect the

demographics of our society. If our young blacks are not pursuing studies that will lead to degrees and careers in chemistry, we will be underrepresented forever in important positions that will influence the direction and the quality of life for all our people. Until we reach some level of proportional representation in fields of science, we will not have full access and representation at the levels where decisions are made that influence the lives of people in general. There are going to be shortages and surpluses because that is the cyclical nature of the economy. Job opportunities always come back. Blacks are enormously underutilized potential talent pool to make contributions to research.

Another interviewee refuted the surplus argument:

If I had bought into the surplus of scientists' argument in high school, I would never have become a chemist. There is no surplus of African American chemists. We are looking for minorities but we can't find them . . . this is an excuse because they are not looking very hard. Don't let the over supply stop you! If there is a pool of black Ph.D.s without jobs, they should be encouraged to start their own companies. We do not have to follow the paths of others. We can forge new paths. This is precisely what is happening to Indians in IT industry.

According to another interviewee:

I think the surpluses are in someway analogous to that in medicine where there have been a lot of imported foreign medical graduates. I think that these surpluses have been artificially generated by professors in graduate schools who have been importing Asians because they believe that these individuals can help them publish more papers and at a more frequent pace than can domestic students, especially blacks. I have very strongly opposed to this practice.

Still another interviewee noted that:

There is a tendency to import people, non-U.S. citizens, who are beginning to dominate our graduate schools in the U.S. The number of people on visas in graduate programs is beginning to rival that of the domestic population. This means lost opportunities for a lot of people especially young blacks. I've heard it called the Asian solution to the U.S. shortage of domestic manpower in science . . .

According to economist Richard B. Freeman (2004), there is no shortage of scientists and engineers in the U.S. because the U.S. imports large numbers of the best and brightest students, researchers, and science and engineering workers from foreign countries. This has allowed U.S. science and engineering to stave off a virtual human resource crisis. He points out that in 2000 nearly two-fifths of Ph.D.s working in science and engineering occupations were foreign-born (compared around one-fourth only ten years earlier) and slightly more than half (52%) of all employed Ph.D. scientists and engineers in the age bracket 24–45 were foreign-born. Foreign-born scientists and engineers accounted for an even higher proportion of postdocs – nearly six in 10. Freeman believes that the influx of foreign-born students and immigrant scientists and engineers is a mixed blessing. On the one hand, foreign scientists and engineers strengthen the nation's competitive advantage in science and high-tech fields. On the other hand, the presence of large numbers of foreign students and workers is believed to suppress wages and employment opportunities which to serve to discourage U.S. citizens from investing in STEM careers. Thus, setting into motion a cycle of increased dependence on foreign-born talent (Freeman, 2004: see also *The Journal of Blacks in Higher Education*, 1993/1994).

This practice has its inherent risks to the U.S. economy (i.e. standard of living) and security. The pursuit of STEM degrees needs to be more attractive and affordable for students. There must be jobs with competitive salaries available at the end of the training period (Field, 2004; see also, Tietlebaum, 2001). In more recent reports, Heylin (2004, 2003a, b) reports that the deterioration of the economy has been largely responsible for the record high unemployment rates in the chemical industry and slow salary growth. According to Heylin, the ACS member survey of salaries and employment revealed an unemployment rate of 3.6%. This rate represents the highest reported in the 30-year history of the survey. Members of the ACS continue to report unemployment rates below that of the general population. For example, in March 2003, the overall jobless rate was 5.8 or 2.3% above that of chemists who were members of the ACS. Furthermore, in 2004, ACS members reported a median base salary ($82,000) that was 2.5% higher than the previous year.

Overall, the proportion of full-time instructional faculty with tenure has remained relatively stable-around 64%. Jones believes that the employment outlook for college faculty is expected to be good but competitive, particularly for tenure-track positions at research institutions (Jones, 2003). As in any job market, some doctorate recipients have difficulty finding suitable employment even when employment conditions are good. However, as one interviewee points out:

> Everything that I see suggests that there are opportunities for black people who are good and who really have a talent for chemistry. In my specialty, if you are average, you are going to have a harder time finding a job. But if you are good, you will have multiple offers. Although the market does tend to get tight at times, students who are good have opportunities.

The distribution of funds for academic research by field has shifted as well. In 2000, the largest research and development expenditures in science and engineering were in the medical sciences, biological sciences, and engineering (Jones, 2003). Funding was such an important issue for one interviewee that they were ambivalent about recruiting students to careers in chemistry:

> I am not going out on a bandwagon to recruit more African Americans to chemistry. It is hard to get funding these days. It is hard to attract students. Although I believe that there is a need for more African Americans in chemistry, I am not certain that a person should go into a high risk venture like chemistry.

For years, the Ph.D. job market has been characterized by fluctuations which are caused by imbalances in the supply and demand in the labor force. Among the reasons for the imbalances are: the length of time required to earn a Ph.D. degree makes it difficult for the supply of workers with doctorates to respond quickly to changes in the demand for them; and inaccurate projections about labor market demand. For example, in the 1980s, the predictions of a shortage of STEM doctorates were based on the fact that large numbers of retirements would occur. But those mass departures from academia failed to materialize. Jones attributes the oversupply problem to the fact that universities have no incentive to discontinue producing doctoral students, even if the labor market is unable to absorb them upon graduation. Doctoral students often provide their department and university with benefits that include assistance with research and teaching of undergraduate students.

Until now, the United States has been able to rely on foreign-born workers to fill the gap. But with global competition for top talent increasing coupled with fewer foreign students applying to study at American colleges, the country can no longer depend on foreign labor to augment its work force. The pursuit of STEM degrees needs to be more attractive and affordable for students. There must be jobs with competitive salaries available at the end of the training period (Field, 2004). This resonates with one interviewee's remarks: "There is a need to produce more African American chemists if for no other reason than to have enough of them at the table where key decisions are being made. More must graduate from the top departments but they must also have access equal to that of Whites to achieve."

One interviewee had this to say:

> I believe that there is a need to increase the representation of blacks in chemistry . . . but I am bit cautious of going out actively recruiting because of some of the racism and sexism that I have experienced. I do think that some things have changed since I got my Ph.D., but not enough has changed in the racial attitudes of white male chemists. The profession will not wake up to embracing blacks until the number of white chemists begins to dwindle.

Although one Cohort III female interviewee agreed that there was a need to increase the number of African Americans in chemistry, she felt uneasy recruiting African American women because of the sex discrimination that she encountered in her scientific career. The interviewee believes that having access to such information may better prepare young African American women to develop more critical coping strategies.

A Cohort III industrial chemist who expressed frustration about overt and covert discriminatory practices in his unit believed that African Americans should not be recruited to chemistry. However, even this dissenter acknowledged his affection for the discipline. Most interviewees emphasized that it was the racial barriers that they encountered in the pursuit of their scientific careers and not the practice of their science that disturbed them. These experiences prompted most interviewees to argue that a critical mass or a substantially increased participation of African Americans in chemistry is required to breakdown racial barriers. It is important to note that such critical mass may be necessary but not sufficient to dismantle racial and gender discrimination. Stronger enforcement of anti-discrimination laws remains at issue.

PARTICIPATION IN PROFESSIONAL ACTIVITIES

Chemists, like other professional scientists and engineers, engage in a variety of professional activities. Among these activities are attending scientific conferences, engaging in the conduct of research, writing proposal to support research, and participating in scientific societies. In this chapter, the focus is primarily on the interviewees' engagement in the activities of scientific societies, research activities and recognition.

SCIENTIFIC SOCIETIES

Although interviewees participate in variety of scientific associations (e.g. subspecialty and general) in terms of meetings, committees and member services, the value of belonging to these organizations emerged as a significant topic. This seems to be the case for a variety reasons, including costs in time, money, and utility. Nearly all interviewees hold membership in the ACS, while a small fraction were members only of National Organization of Black Chemists and Chemical Engineers (NOBCChE). Although two-thirds of the interviewees reported membership in some predominantly black scientific organizations, only a third indicated active participation. The value of being a member of and attending meetings of both ACS and NOBCChE generated the most emotion in the interviews.

One Cohort IV interviewee asserted: "The ACS meetings are just so huge that I don't find them useful. There aren't many people in my field who speak at those meetings...I find the organization kind of paternalistic towards African Americans and people of color in general."

A Cohort III interviewee exclaimed: "NOBCChE is absolutely necessary. Because of the small numbers of Afro-Americans in the area of chemistry sort of get overlooked by the larger organizations. It provides African Americans with an opportunity to present their work and be recognized. Also, it permits them to network with each other." A Cohort IV interviewee recalled:

> One of the predominantly white organizations had a program for minority students, and no minorities showed up. This was because they hadn't really advertised it. They didn't know how to reach out to the minority community. I find a lot of this sort of ignorance and it's a turn off.

Regarding NOBCChE, one Cohort I interviewee provided this lengthy explanation:

> I don't attend the NOBCChE meetings just because of what it is. Others may elect to segregate me and I can't do anything about that. But, I don't intend to segregate myself, not in the 1990s! I think NOBCChE is an historical and philosophical mistake. When we look back on it, we will see that it is the wrong thing to do. Imagine the reaction by blacks if the American Chemical Society would change its name to the Society of white Chemists. Why would I then want to organize a society of black chemists? I am a chemist and I resent the label of black chemist. For a group of people who have suffered so much from deprivation and isolation to turn right around and segregate themselves is next to stupid. I don't understand why they would want to do that. The physicists and engineers are doing it, too! I would not institutionalize segregation on any basis . . . That is utopian . . . It is idealism. That is where I stand but they (officers of NOBCChE) don't know it. This makes me feel like a hypocrite because I can't bring myself to say this publicly. I think that the people who suffered most from segregation are the very people who should take the lead and move away from it. Scroll the standards wherever you want. But, whatever the standards are, I consider myself a chemist. If I don't qualify by what you consider the minimum standards to be a chemist, then for you I am not a chemist. If you are a chemist, you ought to be a member of ACS

Similar sentiments were expressed by another Cohort I interviewee:

> I have a problem with some parts of with NOBCChe. I can agree with them helping young blacks go into science. I can't go along with segregated part – having a separate, black organization. One should be active in ACS in terms of professional development and direction. However, there is also a dimension of sharing, understanding, and appreciating one another in what one is dealing with. And, if you utilized NOBCChE appropriately you get something you don't get from ACS, until such time that race doesn't matter. We have people who achieved high status in chemistry who remain active in NOBCChE because it touched them in their heart early in their careers.

It should be pointed out that interviewees who grew up in involuntary racially segregated environments were particularly critical of voluntary racially segregated organizations. A Cohort II interviewee from industry asserted: "When I've been to NOBCChE, I have been disappointed in the quality of what I have seen. I've seen more rhetoric in most things than I have seen action. I've been very disappointed in the kinds of critical analyses that I've seen occurring in some of the research activities."

A majority of interviewees, however, did not express this level of criticism towards NOBCChE. In fact, most interviewees viewed NOBCChe's role as sharply different from that of the ACS. NOBCChe's mission statement emphasizes its commitment to build a community of eminent scientists and engineers by increasing the number of minorities in these fields. To this end, NOBCChE designed several programs to foster professional development and encourage students to pursue careers in science and technical fields. Educational partnerships with school districts, municipalities, businesses, industries, other institutions and organizations provide networking opportunities for its members. Some comments are illustrative. One Cohort II interviewee makes these points:

> For me, NOBCChe's role is to (1) assist in the career advancement of black chemists and chemical engineers; (2) serve as a clearinghouse of information for black chemists and chemical engineers; (3) serve as a bridge from one laboratory to another where blacks might be isolated and unaware of what is going on; and (4) serve as a mentoring organization to a generation of kids who are going to follow us . . . I don't buy the notion that NOBCChE should integrate with the ACS. Historically, when blacks have integrated, there has been virtually no change in terms of our plight. We get shoved to the side. If it had a national office that worked on a full-time basis, NOBCChE could have a greater influence and impact on the science policies of this country. The downside of NOBCChE right now is that it is going into twenty-plus years as a volunteer organization.[1] You can't run a major enterprise like that. In terms of its mission, I think the role it can play is clear. There is still a great need for the NOBCChE!

Another Cohort II interviewee explains:

> I see NOBCChE as an outlet for some minority scientist to publish papers or to do presentations. And use it almost as a screening first and then submitting it to a major journal. That's one thing that I see as one role it could play. When dealing with the majority community (ACS), unless you are exceptional, you may not get a chance to take part in affecting change. You may get that opportunity more so with NOBCChE.

One Cohort III interviewee explained:

> I would support being a member of both ACS and NOBCChE because they are not in competition with each other. NOBCChE as never created to replace ACS. It was established more as a networking organization . . . and a way to reach out to minority communities to heighten awareness of career opportunities in chemistry and chemical engineering. ACS is the most recognized rofessional entity for chemists. So, you don't give up ACS for NOBCChE.

Several interviewees saw the two professional organization as complimentary. One Cohort III interviewee said: "I think there is a need for both ACS and NOBCChE. I don't think membership in one should exclude the other. I wouldn't say that ACS is that conservative because it has elected a black president . . . That speaks for itself . . . There are no racial barriers in ACS." To date, Hill (1975–1977) is the only known African American to serve as a president of ACS. In November 2004, an African American, Isaiah Warner, Vice Chancellor for Strategic Initiatives at Louisiana State University, Baton Rouge, was a contender for the president-elect. He was opposed by F. Sherwood Rowland, Bren Research Professor of Chemistry and Earth System Science at the University of California, Irvine and petition candidate, E. Ann Nalley, professor of chemistry at Cameron University (Mehta, 2004). Nalley won the election (Raber, 2004).

One Cohort II interviewee alleged that a young African American chemist did not receive tenure in the department because the young chemist's publications were concentrated in NOBCChe's proceedings. This interviewee explains: "I advised_rather than publishing papers in NOBCChe's literature, publish them in some reputable refereed journals_didn't listen to me, and_didn't get tenure. NOBCChe's publications are not considered refereed by our tenure review committee." Nevertheless, the interviewee adds: "I believe that NOBCChE does good in some areas."

According to one Cohort V interviewee, ACS and NOBCChE are equally important to the chemistry community. The interviewee explains:

> I think it is important to belong to both ACS and NOBCChE . . . I have had my moments of doubt about ACS . . . I don't think there will ever be a time when we don't need NOBCChE . . . I see NOBCChE as an opportunity for minorities in industrial settings to network and support each other . . . I think it serves that purpose very well . . . ACS will never do anything like that . . . I've always thought it was important to belong to both . . . I see absolutely no conflict whatsoever in belonging to both . . . Each serves an unique purpose.

A Cohort III interviewee agreed:

> One should be active in ACS, in terms of professional development and direction . . . It is the professional organization that chemists should belong to and be actively involved with. However, there is also a dimension of sharing, understanding, and appreciating one another in what one is dealing with . . . I believe that if you are going to serve our community, being active in NOBCChE can add value to you and others. You can assist young people, you can talk about things, you can meet people . . . If you utilize NOBCChE appropriately, you get something you don't get from ACS, until such time that race doesn't matter.

One Cohort III interviewee succinctly explained why he does not attend professional meetings: "I am not into meetings. Plus, I don't like most of those people."

RESEARCH ACTIVITIES

Variations in the rate of productivity and recognition among scientists in general and chemists in particular have long been the subject of extensive research. In his study of chemists, Hagstrom (1971) found a high correlation between time required to complete the Ph.D. and productivity. Several studies report a positive correlation between the quality of the doctorate-granting department and productivity. In her study of chemists, Reskin (1977) reported that graduates of prestigious doctoral departments were more productive than those with doctorate origins in lesser-ranked departments. She argues that scholars at the top departments are usually better researchers and consequently provide their protégés with better research training. Long (1978), however, asserts that initial academic appointment is typically independent of earlier productivity and concludes that it has a significant impact on subsequent productivity. In their study of male biochemists, Long and McGinnis (1981) conclude that the stratification system in science is not universalistic. They believe that the initial advantages accumulate and actually play a role in inequality among scientists in levels of productivity. These studies provide no or limited insight into the performance of African American chemists because either they do not include African Americans or data are not disaggregated by race.

As late as 1974, Clemente noted that race received minimal attention in studies of scientific productivity. In a study of sociologists, Clemente reported that non-blacks tend to be more productive than blacks. In fact, he reports that non-blacks published nearly twice as many articles as blacks. However, he concluded that race actually did not exert any statistically significant impact on scholarly productivity. Pearson's (1985) examination of the effects of race on scholarly productivity yields considerable insight into the problem. He found that regardless of scientific discipline, white respondents held a slight advantage over their African American peers in terms of the average number of articles published prior to receipt of the Ph.D. Pearson's data for chemists were aggregated under the category of physical scientists. He reported that among African American respondents, 40% listed predoctoral publications, compared to 48% of white respondents. In terms of career articles, whites averaged nearly 28 articles compared to 15 for African Americans. Using multivariate analysis, Pearson concluded that race was negatively associated with mean number of career articles among physical scientists. On average, white respondents were more likely than African American respondents to have their work cited by peers in the scientific community (9 citations vs. 4 citations). There were no racial variations regarding the average number of grants received.

Because there are so few studies of doctoral scientists in general and chemistry in particular that include African Americans, little is known about their research activities. There a number of explanations for the lack of inclusion or disaggregation by race. The most common explanation involves the low participation of African Americans at the doctorate level. Consequently, this presents methodological and ethical challenges, especially in multivariate statistical analyses and confidentiality. However, African American science doctorates seldom make the qualitative studies as well. Further, government data are often presented in aggregated form for physical sciences, lack performance variables, focus primarily on academics and linear career patterns, and do not oversample certain small groups. Sometimes these challenges are related to cost.

Nevertheless, these and other data limitations severely restrict our understanding of the experiences of African Americans in the chemistry community. For example, much of the most insightful and interesting data requested from NORC could not be provided or, if provided was of little or no used because of suppressed counts to protect confidentiality. The survey that was provided was for presentations and articles over the past three years. These results show that the median numbers of papers presented by white respondents was two compared to one for black respondents at professional meetings. Each group published a median of one article. An interview questioned the fairness of the so-called peer review journal process. The Cohort III interviewee asserts that: "Science is political. I saw a lot of it at because some of my colleagues were journal editors. I saw firsthand why certain articles got published and certain ones didn't. Some got published with scant reviews, while others were scrutinized reviews."

GRANTS PEER REVIEW SYSTEM

Not surprisingly a discussion of the grants peer review process bring out considerable emotion regardless of the scientific community under study. The case of African American doctoral chemists is no exception. Some of the most talented researchers questioned the fairness of the peer review system. What may be surprising to many is the interviews discussion of the role of "race" in the process. Below are some of the highlights from the interviews. One Cohort III interviewee commented:

> Blacks are going to have problems getting research grants. When reviewing grants many of the white chemists know or have been in contact with the proposer. I call it the "I'm on the review board for this one and you may not be on the review board but you may know someone on the review board when I'm submitting my paper. If I review yours favorably and then let you know after the fact that I have done so, then, you know what I have done and return the favor.'

One Cohort IV interviewee commented: "I have seen the research at major research universities . . . A lot of the faculty is on legacy and not substance. If you are not at one of these places, you must have advocates." A Cohort IV interviewee at a predominantly white university expressed this concern: "My inability to network with white chemists continues to be a major problem in developing collaborations and getting my research funded.

One interviewee, a graduate of a prestigious Ph.D.-granting department, employed at an historically black college expressed this concern:

> My biggest problem has been my inability to get my research supported. You wouldn't have a person at Duke or any other predominantly white university with my credentials (doctoral

origins) who couldn't get a research grant. I haven't had a grant in 15 years! Early in my career, I submitted a proposal to_(federal agency) which I was commended for support through a mainstream program. But it was funded. So, they kept it for a year and took the money out of the 'minority pool' and gave me a mainstream grant. What that effectively did was to eliminate any possibility of my getting money from' minority pool. 'Since I had a mainstream grant. After a year and a half, _(federal agency) wouldn't renew the award. I was told by someone in the know that some reviewers made negative comments about my progress on the grant and my institutional affiliation. I have trying to get another grant but without success.

Although research productivity differs somewhat from one employment sector to another, it is important in all. Regardless of employment sector, interviewees seemed to be acutely aware of the requirement to be productive. Pressure to produce is reflected in one academic interviewee's story about a research assistant:

She was extremely hard working ... almost pathological ... I should have known something was wrong because she always carried her lab notebooks home ... I think she felt that she owned the data ... When my funding ended, she took half of the data with her ... I spent an enormous amount of time trying to get her to return the data. We (interviewee and Department Chair) tried to explain to her that the data were university property and that I had to keep records to demonstrate that the work was actually done ... She was the type of person who wrote down every detail about the experiment. She would write down notes like, "I turned the cylinder upside down." She was very thorough, so I knew when data were missing on the design of a particular experiment that she had it. I really needed those notebooks to write-up the research ... Finally, I got some of the data back ... But, I had to spend a lot of time reconstructing the missing notes ... This was an unbelievable experience, especially since the university administration didn't take any strong action ...

The intensity of research and the burden of production did not appear to affect the interviewees' desire to make new discoveries. One Cohort V interviewee remarked: "The thing I love about research is that there is always something new and challenging ... It is always exciting." Most interviewees' desire to conduct research remained high throughout their careers.

Time and money, as in most undertakings, are precious commodities and greatly impacted the interviewees' ability to conduct quality research. One Cohort IV interviewee, with Ph.D. origins in a prestigious department, explains how the pressure to secure funding and publish influenced the first job decision: "I didn't think the position at_(a branch campus of a major research university) was good for the type of research that I wanted to do ... I didn't want to go to_(a top-rated research university) because they expected you to get out of the blocks at a sprinter's pace ... I wasn't prepared to do that." One Cohort V interviewee expressed this concern: "As an Assistant Professor, you are always working ... Now that funding is getting harder, it makes it difficult. I see so many people unhappy in the field."

Reflecting on a long career in one historically black college, a Cohort III graduate of a prestigious Ph.D. department said:

> Looking back, I am very annoyed that I don't have a long string of publications when I could have. I could have published more. Had I realized_[an historically black college] was incapable of providing the kind of support necessary to be successful, I probably wouldn't have stayed as long. Now, I'm stuck. I stayed here too long. Because I don't have publications, I can't go to a lot of places. Given my love for research, I could have been more productive in a different environment.

In some companies, the criteria for promotion are similar to those of the university. For example, several interviewees reported that in order to move from the entry level to the next level required "demonstrable research independence . . ." The next major promotion required a national reputation and successful contributions to projects in progress. For the highest rank, the individual had to have an international reputation and be identified with some high-profile products. Publications also played a major role. Moreover, some companies had distinguished ranks for its most prolific scientists. A number of chemists pointed out that their companies had promotion review committees.

Regarding the reward system of chemistry, one Cohort III interviewee said: "Good work gets funded and published." A Cohort IV agrees:

> If is good work, it will be published and funded. If you are really good, it will happen (recognition in chemistry). If you are marginal, there are going to be problems . . . The realty is what you bring to the table. What can you deliver. At a certain point, it doesn't matter where you went to school. High-quality research can overcome a strong but less prestigious Ph.D.

However, several interviewees believe that good work does not always get published or receive the credit, as the following anecdote illustrates:

> My postdoc supervisor and I developed an assay using a colleague's equipment. When it came time to write-up the results, the colleague thought that he should be first author on the paper. My supervisor at the time didn't have enough backbone to fight him. So, he was first author. Later, I discovered that the assay was sold without my knowledge. They are making lots of money on my idea. I didn't get first authorship. Plus, I didn't get any financial benefits from it.

A Cohort IV interviewee said bluntly: "An awful lot of 'bad' research is funded, too."

Most interviewees believe that African American chemists are at a disadvantage when competing for so-called peer-reviewed grants because of race or institutional affiliation. The following excerpts are illustrative. One interviewee said:

> I am not one who elevates race as an issue at the drop of a hat. I remained in research during my entire career in the federal government. I was part of the review process when the proposals came in to_(a federal agency). I certainly saw some proposals that were not well written, didn't even have any significant detail, but yet were funded. I also saw proposals from historically black colleges and universities that were well written, well thought out, but yet they were not funded unless someone like me would argue the merits of the proposal. This is either racism or

a miseducation on the part of the folks who control the resources . . . I'm not naive enough to think that the people controlling the resources don't know this already. I say it is racism.

A Cohort II interviewee relates a case involving a talented young African American chemist:

> One of our young black professors applied for a grant at_(federal agency) audit and it went through the review process . . . The Committee Chair wrote back to_saying that he was very impressed with his background and his ability . . . but, the reason the proposal was turned down because he was not at a research institution . . . He was advised to leave and go somewhere else . . . So, even though 'race' was not a directly mentioned, it was being at a black institution.

One Cohort IV interviewee provides this description: "If I were proposing the same research at_(Ph.D.-granting department), my proposal would have received higher marks. No matter how good I am, as long as I am at_(an historically black college), my research proposal will not be reviewed as favorable as the same one from a major predominantly white university." Another Cohort III interviewee said:

> Its not just good work that gets supported. At_(federal agency), the program directors have a lot more influence on who is actually going to get funded. If they want to push women, they can. If they want to push a particular area of research, they can. I think the scientific rating you get is certainly going to be influenced by the institution where you are . . . It's going to be harder to get a really good rating at_(historically black colleges and universities), especially when you get bad publicity about how there isn't any research atmosphere here. It could be that program directors want their programs to be successful. They don't want to take a risk. There is no question that the evaluation is not based on merit alone. From my own experience with the peer review system, people who have already made a name for themselves, their proposals are not reviewed as stringently as the young person who is coming in with the very same idea. They are going to give them the benefit of the doubt.

A Cohort IV interviewee made this comment: "I don't think that race is a determining factor. It is more determined by location and what institution you are affiliated with . . . In a lot of review processes, environment is part of the review. If you are at Harvard, Berkeley, or Yale, then the idea is your proposal will be better because you are among brighter people and among the cutting edge."

One Cohort III interviewee at an historically black college believes that industry's review process is more objective: "I would say that industry more so than_(federal agency) administers funds on an equitable basis without regard to race because of the bottom line. We got money mostly from industry because it was just opening up to hire blacks . . . But there was a limited talent pool." One Cohort III interviewed made this plea: "$10,000 grant would help me a lot in my research but I can't get that from_(federal agency)."

A Cohort II interviewee believes that some black chemists at historically black colleges and universities use heavy course load as an excuse for lack scholarly productivity. The interviewee explains:

Having a heavy teaching load is no excuse for not publishing and getting grants . . . You are going to do the work if you are going to or you are not going to do it. You make up any excuse. I love doing research. I just like taking the data and understanding what is going on. Understanding how systems work. Finding new things. I really enjoy it. I enjoy the whole process.

However, a Cohort V interviewee counters:

I just need time to be creative. I have a lot of publishing opportunities which are generated from how I work . . . If I am this productive with all the responsibilities that I have . . . imagine what I could do with more time . . . In addition to a heavy teaching load, one year I was on 13 of 15 departmental committees. This doesn't include university committees. This is ridiculous!

Zuckerman (1977, p. 59) asserts that rank in science is primarily achieved, and that like other merit-oriented systems, "even when upward mobility is based on meritocratic principles, it involves a process of accumulative advantage that helps to shape, maintain, and modify the structure of stratification in science."

Over the course of their careers, interviewees' level of motivation (based on a ten-point scale, ten being the highest) to do research changed considerably. For example, 86% of interviewees indicated that their level of motivation to do research was extremely high (9 and 10) at the time they completed the Ph.D. degree. By the current or last job, the comparable figure was 59%.

ELUSIVE NOBEL PRIZE

When asked about why no African American has received a Nobel Prize in chemistry, interviewees provided a variety of responses. Many cited insufficient support at the graduate and postdoc levels, and difficulties attracting research funding. Other factors concerned aspects of their careers: that proprietary research is largely unpublishable; and that their career focused on increasing the talent pool rather than on research. Still others cited the lack of cumulative advantages, such as being a protégé of a previous winner, prestigious employing institution, and the fact that the prize has both an objective and subjective side. Some comments are illustrative. One Cohort III interviewee explained:

When you think in terms of the level of scientific achievement required to merit consideration for the Nobel Prize, it is not something accomplished in the lab today. It may be something that a chemist did twenty-five or thirty years ago. Only recently have blacks produced leading-edge research. You aren't going to get a Nobel Prize for research produced in an academic setting unless you are at a prestigious research university. Blacks don't have a history of employment at these types of universities . . . I don't know of any black chemists producing Nobel Prize-level research.

Several interviewee asserted that increasing the pool of African American doctorates in chemistry will simultaneously increase the chances of producing a Nobel laureate, if they are able to accumulate advantages. This point is re-enforced by a Cohort I interviewee explains:

> I don't think there have been enough black research chemists. Most of the blacks in the past have been at black institutions where there was not an opportunity to do frontier research. They haven't had the opportunity to really contribute. I don't think blacks have had the time to devote to research. Take someone like Percy Julian, who did not become a prolific publisher until he left Howard University. I think that is true with most of the well-published blacks. If they have done a lot of publishing, it has been in an industrial setting or at a major research university.

One Cohort III interviewee explains:

> I know so many very good black scientists whose (career) paths are almost identical to mine. I don't know of too many who work in the frontier research . . . that could lead to a Nobel Prize. I don't think that the system is set up to do that because of so many outside influences. For example, looking back on my own career in terms of moving out from strictly research to an administrator, there is no guarantee that if I had stayed a researcher, and they chose someone to run the operation besides me, there is no fact that I would be allowed to do the kinds of things that could probably lead to some national recognition. I think that is the problem.

According to one prominent Cohort I interviewee, racism is major factor in limiting the highest performance of African Americans:

> I think the major shortcoming that any black scientist will have in any organization is having to divert so much of their energy overcoming racism as opposed to being able to devote their full energies to the kind of work and acceptance of that work that they may be engaged in. All too frequently, African American scientists are given full credit for what they are doing. The lab used to have some of the scientists teach the apprentices in math and science because the apprentices had to go through certain courses in order to get their journeyman status. I was in a section many years when I found out that one a Caucasian Ph.D., who joined the company after I did, was teaching math. I said to him, "how did this happen?" He said the section head asked him. I went to the section head and I said that is teaching math, how did that happen? He said we asked some staff members. I said you didn't ask me. He said, "Oh, I didn't think that you would be interested. It turned out that he did not ask any black to teach a course.

Interviewees identified a number of U.S.-born African Americans whom they considered the most productive chemists and the strongest candidates for the Nobel prize. Individuals who were most frequently mentioned by interviewees were: Percy L. Julian, William Lester, William Jackson, Joseph Francisco and Isaiah Warner. The vast majority of interviewees felt that the late Percy L. Julian was the strongest candidate for a Nobel Prize to date.

Interviewees suggesting these names pointed out that the academic chemists were employed at major research institutions with excellent resources, e.g. graduate students, postdocs, staff and facilities: Joseph Francisco (*Purdue University*), William Jackson (*University of California, Davis*), William Lester (*University of California, Berkeley*), and Isaiah Warner (*Louisiana State University, Baton Rouge*).

Nevertheless, most interviewees admitted that these candidates were long shots for the Nobel Prize. Zuckerman's (1977) study of Nobel Laureates supports some of the speculation offered by interviewees. She found that Laureates have their social origins disproportionately in middle and upper occupational strata families where the fathers are generally employed in science or science related occupations. Although Nobelists are more likely than the general populace to have origins in Protestant and Jewish families, they tend to describe themselves as agnostics or non-affiliates. They are usually graduates of elite undergraduate and graduate schools. If employed in academe, Nobelists tend to be on the faculties of elite colleges and universities. Zuckerman reports that more than half of Nobelists have studied under the tutelage of Nobel laureates. Compared to other scientists, future Nobelists tend to earn their doctorates much earlier and begin publishing earlier and more frequently. Early in their careers, they establish reputations as rising stars by making significant contributions to the advancement of science.

Few African Americans have been in a position to accumulate such advantages that will lead to the Nobel Prize or imminence as a member of the National Academy of Sciences. The comments of some interviewees are illustrative:

A Cohort III interviewee asserts: "You have to be a protégé of someone who has done world class research. You have to have experiences in labs conducting leading research . . . When African Americans have these opportunities, a Nobel laureate will eventually be produced."

Finally, another Cohort III interviewee expressed these reservations:

> I still believe that it is going to be extremely difficult for any black chemist to get the Nobel Prize because one of the requirements is to have very good students do all of the work. The black chemists that I know in top research places don't get the best students. Even the best black students don't go to work with them because they want to prove that they are so good that they can go work for a Nobel Prize winner at Harvard. The case in point is who is excellent but he has managed to attract mostly foreign-born students who speak very little English. But, these students are serious about their education . . . In order to do Nobel Prize level work, one needs a very smart, very motivated and large staff. People are just dying to go to work for Nobel Prize winners. Even when they have money, the top Black researchers have a hard time attracting top students. It is the system that is a problem.

NOTE

1. Based on correspondence with NOBCChE, the National Office was established in 1988 at Howard University. The office was housed in Howard's Chemistry Department and staffed by a secretary charged to answer the telephone, prepare correspondence, and file information. An office manager was appointed, but received no salary.

RACIAL ATTITUDES

In a review of the literature on racial attitudes, Schaefer (2000) drew two major conclusions: (1) not only are attitudes subject to change, but dramatic shifts in attitudes can occur within a single generation and (2) the rate and intensity of the progress made in the 1950s and 1960s was not realized in subsequent periods. In fact, he argues that now whites may be practicing a more sophisticated or symbolic form of racism by expressing opposition to policies related to eradicating poverty, crime, or immigration. Schaefer sees these as smoke screens carefully designed to hide socially unacceptable racist attitudes.

National surveys have consistently shown growing support by whites for integration. In 1942, only 30% of white respondents supported school integration; in 1970, the figure was 74%; and by 1991, 93% of white respondents expressed support. History has shown that just as changes in attitude can mobilize public support to rectify racial inequality, the process can also work in the opposite direction. Consider, for example, the case of affirmative action: nationwide surveys conducted in the mid-1990s showed increasing resistance by whites (Schaefer, 2000).

Traditionally, affirmative action has been viewed as an important tool for reducing institutional discrimination. Today, affirmative action has become a polarizing and pejorative term associated with racial-preference programs and goals. It has also become a lightning rod for opposition to any programs that suggest special consideration for racial minorities. National polls also reveal the U.S. is divided sharply by race. In 1995, for example, 46% of whites and only 8% of African Americans indicated that affirmative action had gone too far (Schaefer, 2000, p. 93). To illustrate, the journalist Ellis Cose (1993, pp. 111–112) describes a personal social drama:

> The scene takes place with a well-educated white male confronting an African American professional regarding the unfairness of affirmative action and its attendant preferential treatment of unqualified minorities. The young white male demands an explanation as to why minorities should not be required to compete on equal footing with white males like him. He demands to know why hardworking white men like him should be passed over for

second-rate affirmative action hires. After the young white male pauses, the African American male suggests to the white male that he is being hypocritical because he has benefited from preferential treatment. The African American describes the white male as a person of modest intellect, whose family connections were responsible for him getting into Harvard, landing his first summer internship at the White House, and a second internship at the World Bank. The African American male surmises that the accumulation of these experiences (advantages) with his Harvard degree, led to his selection to a major corporation's executive training program.

Cose concludes that the young white man would not view his experience as preferential treatment, nor will his white colleagues look down on him as an undeserving hire who kept better qualified individuals out of the work.

Cose argues further that even if evidence were presented demonstrating that minorities filling quotas were well-qualified, it would do little to eliminate racial hostility toward affirmative action. Moreover, he notes that programs that set aside slots for children of alumni tend not to have the same outrage as affirmative action. Therefore, Cose concludes that the issue is not solely about qualifications. Rather, he believes that the primary issue is "race." He argues that Americans continue to be in denial about the issue of race.

There is strong evidence that institutional discrimination may be more significant than individual discrimination. Despite the rhetoric, few whites have filed claims of reverse discrimination. From 1990 to 1994, more than 3,000 discrimination opinions were filed in federal courts. Fewer than 100 pertained to reverse discrimination. Furthermore, in only six cases were findings of reverse discrimination actually established (Schaefer, 2000).

Evidence suggests that wealth does not end prejudice and discrimination. As Steinhorn and Diggs-Brown (1999) have shown, affluent African Americans routinely report being victimized in public places. Professional achievement and wealth do not provide shelter for racial indignities. Many are constantly on guard because they never know when the next racial insult will be leveled at them. Cose (1993) identifies racial insults as a major factor underlying the causes of the rage of the African American privileged class. African Americans entering nontraditional areas of employment become *marginalized* and are made to feel uncomfortable. For some organizations, one African American in a visible position is enough proof of enlightenment or progressiveness. Consequently, the next potential African-American candidate may incur difficulties as he/she attempts to move up through the management ranks. Decision makers may perceive that their clientele (e.g. donors and alumni) will be reluctant to do business with them if they have too many people of color in the organization.

Proponents of the contact hypothesis contend that inter-group contact between people of equal status in harmonious circumstances will cause them to become less prejudiced and to abandon previously held racial stereotypes. They point to evidence indicating that such contact also improves the attitude of racial minority group members. While there is considerable research support for this hypothesis, critics out that in the highly segregated U.S., contact between African Americans and whites – even those of equal status – is usually brief and superficial (Schaefer, 2000). Furthermore, what is the relevance of this contact hypothesis for the scientific community, where the Ph.D. degree is the ultimate credential and performance is to be based on merit not on a functionally irrelevant status such as "race." According to Merton (1973, p. 272), "universalism finds its basic expression in the notion that scientific careers be open to talent. Restricting scientific careers in any fashion other than lack of competence is an impediment to the extension of knowledge. Free unrestricted access to scientific pursuits is an institutionalized goal in science. Merton acknowledges that these will be occasions when the ethos of science may collide with that of the larger society. He explains: in short, universalism may be affirmed in theory, but suppressed in practice.

Many of the relevant issues to the discussion above are reflected in the responses of interviewees in this study. To begin, nearly 70% of interviewees believed that racial status is a limiting factor in the full participation of African Americans in the American chemistry community. Most of these explanations fell into five categories: (1) stereotypes that African Americans are incapable of doing science; (2) African American chemists are not promoted at a rate commensurate with performance; (3) exclusion of African American chemists from the "*Old White Boy's Network*"; (4) difficulty in securing federal grant money even with a proven track record of producing high quality research; and (5) reluctant recognition – always having to prove themselves.

Pearson (1985) supports many of these claims in his study of African American doctoral scientists. Most of his respondents believed that their career mobility had been limited by their racial status. This finding varied across cohorts. For example, 74% of those earning doctorates before 1955 believe their career were restricted by race. By the last cohort, doctorates earned between 1965 and 1974, 60% reported that their career mobility had been restricted. Further, at least half of the females respondents reported that race and gender played significant roles in limited their careers. Some 59% of respondents who earned doctorates at the most prestigious department also reported the negatives effects that race exerted on the careers. Most respondents attributed these limiting factors to discrimination (especially exclusion from the communications network). Many respondents report that open communication between African American and white scientists is impeded by the perception that many white scientists fail to accept African American scientists as intellectual peers.

Moreover, approximately 80% of Pearson's respondents believed that race played a significant role in the awarding of federal research grants. One Cohort III respondent perceived NIH to have made more progress than the NSF in addressing historical funding inequities along racial lines. One Cohort III interviewee said that "The biomedical field has made more progress (than chemistry) in addressing historical funding inequities along racial lines." In one Cohort IV interviewee's opinion: ". . . chemistry is one of the more conservative scientific areas. There is still a high level of racism. Chemistry is still very clannish and white-oriented." This assessment was supported by a Cohort V interviewee who said "seldom do you see a black as chair or as a presenter of a session at the national meetings."

One Cohort I interviewee described how racism impacted the graduate school experience:

> _(interviewee's Ph.D.-granting department) was like a religion to me . . . You have to understand that in those days not many places that offered Ph.D. degrees in chemistry would take black people. One of my best friends earned his bachelor's degree at_(Northeast university). He went to graduate school at_(Midwest university). After a year of dealing with racism, he transferred to_(interviewee's Ph.D.-granting department). He told me that in one lecture, a professor told the only Jewish student in the class that he should be out opening up a grocery store somewhere. Neither blacks nor Jews were welcome at that university. Although there were some universities that accepted blacks into their graduate programs, many of them had a double standard. They would give a black person a Ph.D. without a publication. I won't identify the departments. _(interviewee's Ph.D.-granting department) was more inclusive and had one standard.

In the words of one Cohort III interviewee, "being Black has exerted an enormous negative influence on my professional mobility."

A Cohort III interviewee described racism in the context of recruiting:

> . . . based on some of the recruiting trips that I've gone on with a white colleague . . . If the black student shows up with this big afro (hairstyle) and is huge and the white recruiter is small in stature, then, the white recruiter is intimidated. So, the black student doesn't get the same response that I would give him. A female is not going to be nearly as intimidating to the white male recruiter – all things being equal. So, there are going to some preferences . . . If an African comes in with an English accent and is fair complexioned, The white male recruiter is going to be receptive.

One Cohort II interviewee had this to say about his career:

> I think that I could have contributed a hell of a lot more to this organization than I have been able to contribute by virtue of not having to deal with that baggage (racism). And baggage in the sense that I have to manage structural racism that continues to exist in the organization. Having to be on stage all the time in an organization where I am asked to make major contributions but in a context of how others define the way it ought to be done.

This is reflected in a Cohort III interviewee's experience:

> Some whites who have the same title as I do but they are given more responsibility. Management trusts them more and they are not micromanaged . . . Even though my track record is better. I am convinced, given my performance, if I had been a white male I would be a vice president.

I have had to fight all the way and all of the time to get to where I am in the organization. If I didn't have this ball and chain around me I would have been in the upper echelon of the organization. I am underutilized because I am black.

One Cohort IV interviewee responded: "Blacks were denied appointments and resources that would have placed them in competitive positions . . . One has to acknowledge that racism limited blacks' opportunities in chemistry." A Cohort V interviewee argues: "There is a tendency for contributions made by African Americans to be downplayed simply because they are African American or that an African American is involved. I think it is still true that if African Americans want to get the recognition deserved, they have to be much better than a white."

A Cohort V interviewee from industry said:

Anything that is a high priority type of project, I hear about it after they have been given to someone else. Nine out ten times, if I make suggestions it is much harder to get those suggestions approved for research projects. It is almost impossible to get some type of support that is needed to carry out those projects in many cases.

Another Cohort V interviewee related a negative experience:

There was one other person in the country at the time who identified the_, too. My research was at the point that I wanted it to fly. So, I wrote to this guy and told him that I would like collaborate with him . . . He never responded to my letter!

A Cohort III interviewee asserts: "There is no doubt in my mind that I would be a_scientist (highest position on the R&D side), if I was not black." Another Cohort III interviewee had this to say: "Some (white) students told me that they were thwarted somewhat in choosing to work with me because of pressures from the chairman. Then you get a reputation because students tell other students and you don't get grad students."

A Cohort II respondent had this to say about his white colleagues:

Even though I joined my organization prior to affirmative action in higher education, I am still looked upon by whites as suspect. I went to one of the top departments, made good grades but I still hear this stuff about qualifications. Despite this, I have been very successful in the organization. Now, I have hit the glass ceiling despite having glowing performance evaluations . . . but the raises stopped.

On the other hand, a Cohort III interviewee who did not believe that "race" *per se* hamper African Americans' participation in chemistry, made this clarifying comment:

I don't think that African Americans are hampered in their participation in chemistry . . . I do believe that they are hampered in their growth and development and progress. If they don't end up looking like, talking like, being like the average or traditional chemist, then they tend not to be as greatly accepted or appreciated.

This sentiment was echoed by other respondents. For example, one said that "If you don't look like me, or sound like me or talk like me, then there is something wrong with what you are doing. It is rare that blacks are fully accepted into academe on equal footing with whites. However, another Cohort III interviewee thought blacks were hampered because:

> ...too much energy is expended in working through the issues of racism and getting the appropriate attention and recognition of what they do. African American scientists and their work are seen as suspect because of the notion of inferiority. They are typically given assignments to test their capabilities as opposed to being viewed as competent as their white peers...People of color should be given the same opportunities as whites to fail.

A Cohort IV interviewee reported that "I was concerned about being comfortable. And, I was not comfortable with some of the behavior displayed towards me by some of the workers of the company."

On the other hand, other interviewees reported that, in their career experience, race was not a negative factor: One interviewee notes that "Personally, I have not found race to be a negative factor in my career...Sometimes, I feel I have led a sheltered life when I do hear black people complain of mistreatment."

Generally, one major impediment to professional growth is a lack of mentoring, as one Cohort III interviewee explains: "blacks are not mentored or supported to the same extent as whites in their career trajectory. As a result, blacks don't achieve as much as they could. If blacks can be given a modicum of support, their achievement would be far greater." Another interviewee shared their experience with an adviser at a predominantly white southern institution: "You were assigned an advisor and this person was supposed to first ask questions to find out what you interests were and then advise you. Well, my first time showing up to meet with my adviser, his first question was 'are you the work study student?' Before I could answer, he goes over to show me where to wash the glasses. That situation sat the tone with me and the level and nature of interaction for the rest of the year."

Regarding racial stereotypes, one interviewee related this summer experience at a large company:

> During the summer, I worked in the biochemistry unit...The experience really didn't prepare me for doing chemistry because the work environment was very, very conservative. I think the expectations were that black chemists would be working under white chemists. I really didn't like it and I thought that they had not fully planned out what to do with black chemists...I am convinced that they didn't want to allow blacks the freedom to be equal with their white counterparts.

A Cohort II interviewee explained why a racial incident led to his decision to leave the research track:

I had an immediate supervisor who didn't like the fact that he had a black Ph.D. who told him that he didn't know what he was doing. He was trying to get rid of me. If it wasn't for the color of my skin, I would have been gone! Fortunately, I had a department head who was very enlightened. He told me that I had good ability and that I should get out of this situation... get out of the lab and into another situation which in the long run would be better. At the time, that was a very hard decision because I had done a lot of work in one technical area. Moving over to management turned out to be the right decision.

One interviewee said this about his career at a well-known company: "While I worked on some important research... I was aware that despite having a Ph.D. from an Ivy League university, it was automatically assumed that I was inferior to them (white males)." Another interviewee recounted a similar experience:

I was the only black Ph.D. in the company... I recall one guy who got his degree from (a Southern historically white university) always challenged my work... But, he was the only one who did so out of the 15–20 people in the Division.

A Cohort III interviewee at a historically black college provided this account of a summer experience at a cross-town historically white university:

When I went to (a major research university), the fellow I was assigned to work with said to me, "Oh, you're that analyst. I'm trying to get into your area..." I spent half of the summer trying to explain to him that his project wasn't going to work... He just brushed my advice aside... Eventually, I came across some old publications that supported what I was telling him... I wrote it up and put it on his desk... He said, "You better explain it to me because I don't read journals." When I finished explaining it to him, he said, "You know that was beautiful." I didn't take it as a compliment because earlier he had questioned my ability although I had a Ph.D. from one of the most prestigious chemistry departments in the country and he didn't... He took my dissertation and used it as a guide to write his... Although he did sloppy research, they hired him in a tenure-track position the next year. But they didn't offer me a job.

Describing the process for promotions in the company, one interviewee explains:

I would characterize it as subtle discrimination. I think there are people who are recognized as being on fast track because I think... they mirror the image of their supervisors (white males). Those are the ones who get preferences. Two of the people who joined the company about the time that I did are now vice presidents. I think that they were targeted early for administrative growth. I could recognize the kinds of patterns that were occurring. For example, they were given opportunities for program areas that had high visibility. I don't think that this is a frequent occurrence but it happens. But, I still think that the more one mirrors the supervisors in terms of race and gender there is an advantage in promotion.

One Cohort II interviewee explained how he dealt with racism and discrimination in his career by having to be more than equal:

I am able to handle racism with ease. I think it is because I was raised in a segregated system before going to a predominantly white university for graduate studies. In the segregated schools, I learned that I had to be twice as good as the white guy. Those kinds of things stick with you. I believe that once you are accomplished, you can't just try to get by and say I didn't get appointed because of my race. People use that. That is not always true when a black person is not promoted. But I also believe that blacks have to have the edge in terms of qualifications.

One of Benjamin's (1991, p. 126) African American interviewees provides a similar account: "I am never surprised by racism. I never assume there is a minimum of racism among white colleagues . . . so I don't get angry when it comes up." Benjamin concludes that while this individual has learned to negotiate the political and racial tightrope in academe, others have dealt with the issue by being apolitical and aracial. She argues that the latter tend to enjoy their status as a token in the university. Benjamin points out the various personal reactions to racism. She suggests that some persons incorporate racism as a major impediment in their lives but accept some responsibility for overcoming it. Others blame themselves or the system. For example, a competent individual who is denied a promotion may blame himself or herself instead of the discriminatory system. At the other extreme, are individuals who view racism as the sole cause of any negative stress they experience.

SEXISM AND RACISM

Some interviewees discussed discrimination based on both race and sex (see Koelewijn-Strattner, 1990; Marasco, 1994). One Cohort III female interviewee said: "A lot of white people believe that African Americans cannot do science . . . being a woman makes it worse." A Cohort V female interviewee adds: "I think men believe that there are acceptable career fields for females. Chemistry is not one of them." According to one Cohort IV female interviewee:

> Women don't get the same level of support as other people. Men are privy, especially white men, to a lot more information and they are not as scrutinized. I think the old white guys don't respect women in science very much . . . I think black men have a little bit better chance of being respected for their work. But, I don't think that it is a huge difference.

One Cohort V female interviewee related this experience: "We were assigned to subgroups. However, I was not expected to be able to contribute much because no one expected me to be able to do chemistry. The low expectations on the part of my colleagues were negated when my work turned out to be more high powered and successful. One of the white women became visibly upset over my success."

This graduate school experiences were recounted by a Cohort III male interviewee:

Those guys didn't know how to treat their black female classmates. The women felt completely isolated . . . no one would study with them . . . and they always sat in class with me . . . Eventually, they dropped out of the program.

One Cohort V female interviewee reported this formal attempt to sensitize men to sexism:

At one meeting, we had a scholar to give a presentation on women in science. She discussed how sexism impacted women. The audience was about 70% male. Unfortunately, the men did not take the presentation seriously. We need to establish a 'girl's network' to combat the sexism in science. But, we need to sensitize males because they continue to make light of sexist acts.

These sentiments are reflected in the comments of one Cohort V female interviewee:

I was giving a talk at a national meeting where I was also a co-organizer. We invited this well-known chemist to speak. He tried to cut me down. I recognized what he was trying to do and I answered all of his questions. It became apparent to everyone that he was trying to badger me. After the session, folks came to me to say that they were impressed at the way I handled his badgering.

Regarding sexism in the chemistry network, one Cohort II female interviewee recalled:

When I graduated, opportunities for employment in industry and major research universities were not very open to women in general and black women in particular. Even today, black females are essentially on the bottom of the pole . . . When people talk about recruiting more minorities to science, they mean black males and when they say women, they mean white women.

Some female interviewees pointed out gender differences in how African Americans were treated. The collective sentiment is expressed by this Cohort V female interviewee:

African American males got more mentoring than African American females. However, the disparity between African American males and white females was somewhat noticeable. White males got the most mentoring followed by white females, African American males and African American females.

Based on interviews with chemists in historically black colleges and universities, sexism is not limited to predominantly white campuses. Sexism is an issue for predominantly black institutions, even among the faculty, as reflected in the comments of a Cohort III female interviewee:

There is sexism at black colleges, too . . . it may not be as prevalent as in white institutions, but there is no question that it is present . . . I guess it [how women are treated] depends on who are the top administrators . . . My experience has been that black males impose upon Black females the same restrictions that whites impose on blacks in general.

A Cohort V female interviewee lends support:

> I think that male dominance continues regardless of the racial composition of the institution...When I was a graduate student at (a prestigious university. I thought the discrimination was because I was female and black. When I came to (an historically black college) and I was discriminated against, I realized that it was not race, but gender. One of the most disheartening experiences was the realization of being discriminated against by people of my same race based on my gender. Now, I know it [discrimination] is both race and gender.

Experiences of both racism and sexism were so bad for one Cohort III female interviewee that she made this assertion:

> If I had known then, what I know now, I might not have selected chemistry. I don't have any doubts about my decision in terms of ability or my love for it. I wonder sometimes if I should tell black females to go into chemistry. Some of the Black females coming out now, probably don't have some of the challenges that I did. But they will face racism and sexism.

Strategies for coping with sexism were shared by one Cohort V female interviewee:

> One thing that has helped me deal with sexism is not being afraid of being a woman. Like some women in science I had down played this side of me. So, I began to wear bright colors, perfume of my choosing...just being feminine! I carry myself as a lady. I keep the professionalism and social things totally separate. Also, I do my work. I have confidence in my ability and the courage to say no to unreasonable assignments.

During the interviews, the painful recollections of growing up in a racist environment came flooding back. Although more southerners related these kinds of experience, interviewees from other regions also recounted personal experiences with discrimination. For those who have been victimized by racism, the story is timeless. There remains a sense of outrage at injustice and inequality. These experiences transcend cohorts (Cose, 1993). Given some of the personal experiences related by these interviewees, it not surprising the most believe that the chemistry, like the general society, is not free racism. Many of the interviewee expressed concern that the scientific community continues to be in denial or at least dismissive about presence of racism, sexism, and discrimination. The feelings of most interviewees are captured in the following quote by Steinhorn and Diggs-Brown (1999, p. 139): "Especially irritating for blacks is how whites criticize them for dwelling on race but never acknowledging how they themselves make so many judgments based on race."

SUMMARY AND IMPLICATIONS

In this final chapter, I summarize some of the substantive findings from each chapter as well as discuss some implications for research, policy and practice. Chapter 1 presented an overview of the historical relationship between race and science and the presence of African Americans in chemistry. Historian Kenneth R. Manning points to the possible conflict or tension resulting from being African American and scientist, especially during periods of pervasive scientific racism. He also describes the damning effects of science on African American in general and those in science in particular. The awarding of the first chemistry doctorate to an African American – St. Elmo Brady – in 1916 occurred at a time when the nation's scientific elite was steeped in the development and perpetuation of scientific racism. As Percy Julian points out, Brady was unprepared for the challenges that lay ahead for him as an African American in the practice of chemistry. Despite the fervent nature of scientific racism with its doctrines of black inferiority and unsuitable for science, a few African Americans did pursue scientific careers. Eminent scientists, such as biologist E. E. Just and chemist Percy Julian, were publishing and presenting papers at scientific meetings, while some of the scientific elite were developing racial hierarchies associated with mental capacity (Gould, 1981). As we have seen, despite barriers, African Americans have, albeit in *small* numbers, a rather long tradition of pursing careers in chemistry – even under the most trying conditions. Although most of the blatant aspects of scientific racism began to fade following World War I, the scientific community was not a welcoming one for African Americans. According to Rossiter and others, both the civilian and defense scientific and technical workforces had a bountiful crop of white, Christian men to fill its labor force needs. As a result, other demographic groups, especially African Americans, were not recruited to science.

The turn of the twentieth century ushered in a period in which a well-educated cohort of African American scientists began conducting research and publishing in peer reviewed journals. Most of the doctoral chemists' careers were confined to historically black colleges and universities. However, conditions both in and out of the scientific community were slowly changing. Between World War I and just prior to World War II, a few African Americans were trickling in and out of some of the nation's top Ph.D. chemistry departments. Although most would find their career opportunities confined to fledgling historically black colleges and universities, many still managed to conduct viable research that resulted in publications in the most prestigious chemistry journals. One such chemist, Percy L. Julian, would change the course of employment for African American Ph.D. chemists. Julian broke the industrial Research and Development (R&D) color barrier for doctoral recipients when he became Chief Chemist of the Soya Products Division at the Glidden Company in 1936. This watershed moment broadened, to some extent, the limited career options of African American doctoral chemists. In short, Julian's appointment represented an opportunity for African American doctoral chemists to practice their science in a variety of sectors. Of course, these opportunities were slow to evolve and continued to be located largely at historically black colleges and universities. With the advent of World War II, a major transformation occurred when the demand for scientists outstripped the supply primarily because of the participation of white males in the military. This window of opportunity, fueled in part by federal pressure against racial discrimination in the labor force, facilitated the employment of African American chemists in the industrial and government jobs. A number of African American doctoral chemists made the most of this situation by working on the Manhattan Project and other defense-related projects and activities. Because of historical circumstances, many of these scientists had their baccalaureate origins in historically black colleges and universities. Similarly, the federal government played a role in increasing the participation of African Americans in the U.S. scientific workforce during the 1960s. During this period, punctuated by federal legislation and the introduction of affirmative action programs, the participation of African Americans increased in science in general and in chemistry in particular. The fact that so many African American chemists took advantage of the opportunity speaks to the desires of the group to practice its science in settings commensurate with their education and skills. Despite these changes, however, a substantial number of African American scientists perceived the scientific community to be tainted by the particularistic practices of racism and sexism.

Chapter 2 presented a demographic portrait of the study's interviewees. Most of the interviewees were born and educated in the South (followed by the Midwest and Northeast), and grew up in two-parent households with two or more siblings. Although most of the interviewees' parents possessed at least a high school education, fathers were more likely than mothers to hold a college and graduate degree. Most interviewees' parents, however, were not professionals, and a few of the parents were in fact sharecroppers. For a minority of the interviewees, at least one parent did not value academic achievement; but in such cases, teachers or another member of the professional community encouraged, rewarded and reinforced academic achievement. Having well educated teachers who believe that children can learn and achieve is critical.

At the time of the study, approximately half of the interviewees were married, and one in five was divorced. Women were more likely than men to have never married. On average, for those who had children, the first child was born when the chemist was age 31 and most tended to have a second child. Although 80% cited some religious affiliation, mostly Protestant, a number reported no religious affiliation.

Chapter 3 focused on the educational background of the interviewees. Overall, interviewees had fond memories of their (mostly racially segregated) K-12 education, especially in science and mathematics. A majority recalled a special teacher or principal who encouraged and recognized their scholarly achievements. Many interviewees were greatly influenced by teachers, and a few were influenced by biographical sketches of African American scientists and by scientific magazines geared to secondary school students. Generally, interviewees reported developing an interest in mathematics before developing one in science. Yet, many did not have a rigorous mathematical background because so many of their teachers were not certified in the subject area. This is a reflection of the era of racially segregated schools. Despite the interviewees' individual and collective achievement in high those educated in segregated schools indicated that there were deficiencies in their math and science curricula. These curricular deficiencies were exacerbated by poor equipment and underprepared teachers who were themselves the products of underfinanced colleges. Although many of the teachers were unevenly prepared, they encouraged high achievement. The cumulative effect of the deficiencies restricted some interviewees' research specialty choice to less quantitative areas.

This study confirms previous findings on the contributions of historically black colleges and universities to chemistry. Despite their significant contributions to the development of scientific talent, many of the historically black colleges and universities continue to be underfinanced; the graduates of these institutions acknowledged the limitations of some of the course offerings and equipment. Previous studies have shown that a majority of black doctoral students earn their degrees from institutions with high-quality ratings. Thus, it appears that many academically gifted African American students who chose the nurturing environment of an historically black college or university for undergraduate studies are opting for graduate programs in which academic strength and reputation are the prime considerations. Nevertheless, historically black colleges and universities continue to contribute disproportionately to the science and engineering doctoral talent pool. Perhaps even more alarming is that compared to the past decade or so, few top administrators at historically black colleges and universities have science or technical backgrounds. Also, interviewees having their baccalaureate origins in historically black colleges and universities were far less likely than their peers at predominantly white colleges and universities to be engaged as undergraduates in ACS meetings. This may be a reflection of the connectedness-of lack thereof-of their professors to so-called "mainstream" chemistry. Although most interviewees indicate that their interest in a scientific career emerged around the junior year of high school, a few indicated that their interests surfaced as early as middle school or as late as post baccalaureate education. Like scientists in general, these interviewees were high academic achievers. Parents and teachers played critical roles in influencing the interviewees to continue their education beyond high school. However, financial aid was a critical factor in college attendance. Few interviewees had any idea of the occupational roles of chemists, other than teaching.

Although most entered college, (usually an historically black college) intending to major in chemistry, a substantial minority planned pre-med majors. While in colleges, interviewees attending historically black college and universities were more likely than their peers attending predominantly white colleges and universities to have attended a scientific meeting. Interviewees attending predominantly white colleges and universities, however, were far more likely than their peers at historically black colleges and universities to attend ACS regional or national meetings. Graduates of historically black colleges and universities reported higher levels of satisfaction with their undergraduates experience than did those having their origins in predominantly white colleges and universities.

While in college, most interviewees decided to attend graduate school. Although most interviewees were self-motivated to attend graduate school, mentors from high school and college also played a significant role. Across the cohorts, more interviewees reported an African American classmate in graduate school; however, it was rare for any respondent to encounter an African American faculty member. Despite African American faculty members' underrepresentation, a few predominantly white colleges and universities seem to find ways to foster a nurturing environment for all of its students. One respondent indicated that although there were no African Americans on the faculty, at his graduate institution, the faculty was welcoming and nurturing to all students. In short, the departmental climate was extremely supportive of all students and was influential in that individual's academic success. Generally, the vast majority of interviewees expressed high levels of satisfaction with the quality of their graduate education. The level of satisfaction was highly correlated with having a positive relationship with one or more mentor(s). Postdoctoral study became more prevalent over the cohorts, usually as a way to increasing publications and further specialization.

The median age at receipt of the Ph.D. was 29 years, with a range of 25–39 years. While the early cohorts (I and II) earned their doctorates in highly selective institutions, this was not true for subsequent cohorts. The exception, of course, was at an historically black college. Regardless of doctoral origin, a vast majority of interviewees reported attending a scientific meeting, usually ACS and/or NOBCChE. There was considerable debate regarding the advantages and disadvantages of attending one or the other of these professional meetings.

In retrospect, some baccalaureate recipients from historically black colleges and universities reported that laboratory facilities and equipment at their alma mater were inadequate. Many of the interviewees indicated that labs at their graduate departments at predominantly white colleges and universities underscored this observation. It was also pointed out that many of their white peers in graduate school had significantly more extensive chemistry course offerings at their undergraduate institutions. There is considerable evidence that many of the historically black colleges and universities are underfinanced and lack funds to upgrade their science facilities. To improve these facilities and instrumentation, increasing state, federal and private funding is essential.

Chapter 4 discussed career patterns. Historically, the career patterns of African American chemists closely parallel those of their African American peers in the non-scientific and technical workforce; this is due primarily to *racial discrimination*. The interviews revealed that the employment opportunities were bound by what Cohort I and II interviewees described as a caste system. Virtually all job opportunities were limited to teaching at historically black colleges and universities. Institutionalized discriminatory employment practices were gradually dismantled, however, due primarily to effective civil rights campaigns by African Americans and white supporters. Consequently, some African American Ph.D. chemists were able to find employment commensurate with their skills. However, interviewees indicated that government and industry opened their doors well before major predominantly white colleges and universities. Several interviewees described selective research universities as places where they were good enough to be educated but not hired. Improvement in the scientific opportunity structure for African American chemists and other scientists appears to be closely tied to general societal improvement for African Americans resulting from federal intervention. African Americans' general pattern of concentrating in academe mirrors' that of whites in the first two cohorts, except that African Americans' employment opportunities were restricted to historically black colleges and universities. Interviewees working academe were more likely to take their first position in an academic institution with a student body that mirrored the racial composition of their undergraduate alma mater; this pattern largely held when interviewees moved to a second academic position. Approximately, two-thirds of those in academe were employed in public institutions. Of those employed in predominantly white colleges and universities, slightly less than two-thirds were in research universities; while a similar proportion of those employed in historically black colleges and universities were working comprehensive universities. Interviewees employed in historically black colleges and universities reported higher student evaluations than those employed in predominantly white colleges and universities.

Some interviewees in both historically black colleges and universities and predominantly white colleges and universities reported felling isolated; however, a greater proportion of those in predominantly white colleges and universities reported feeling like tokes. Overall, those with undergraduate origins in historically black colleges and universities were somewhat more likely to pursue careers in industry primarily due both to higher salaries and the importance of a company's racial climate. In industry, promotions tended to be uneven-some interviewees reported being in the same rank for most of their careers. Others within the same company, but in different units, reported remarkably different career experiences and upward mobility. A number of the interviewees cited instances of African American colleagues leaving the line R&D track for positions on the staff track in Equal Opportunity Employment, community outreach, human resources and educational outreach.

In academe, more interviewees at predominantly white colleges and universities cited tenure difficulties and problems of promotion beyond the associate professor level. Women tended to cite additional challenges associated with gender regardless of the sector and its racial composition. The women indicated that they were unprepared for the competitiveness that they encountered in the chemistry community. As a result, they said that they would do a better job of communicating to the next generation of women of the "reality" of being a woman in science in general and in chemistry in particular. Nevertheless, most interviewees indicated that they were satisfied with their current or last position. The vast majority of interviewees reported that they were very satisfied with their choice of a career in chemistry. Regardless of gender, most interviewees cited mentors as the major influence in their careers. For married interviewees, spouses were also cited as a major influence.

Chapter 5 focused on professional activities. A majority of interviewees held memberships in professional scientific associations mostly ACS and NOBCChE. Although interviewees were divided with respect to the value of belonging only to ACS or NOBCChE or both, several industrial chemists believed that NOBCChE was a vital networking and support mechanism that allowed them to overcome their employment isolation.

Whether employed in academe or industry, most interviewees reported that research productivity was critical in performance reviews for promotional opportunities. Although most interviewees questioned the fairness of the peer review system in science, a small minority believe that good scientific work will always be recognized and rewarded. However, even those individuals reported racist and sexist incidents in their careers. In fact, approximately seven in 10 interviewees believed that race limits the full participation of African Americans in chemistry.

When asked if there is a need to increase the representation of African Americans in chemistry, 98% of interviewees answered affirmatively and cited the following reasons: untapped talent; need for technical skills to be competitive in the workplace; highly respected field; future leaders for a global economy; the need for diversity in chemistry; and increased numbers will provide the visibility to attract others. Although one female respondent agreed that there was a need to increase the number of African Americans in chemistry, she felt uneasy recruiting African American women because of the sex discrimination that she encountered in her scientific career. The respondent believes that having access to such information may better prepare young African American women to develop more critical coping strategies. One industrial chemist who expressed frustration about overt and covert discriminatory practices in his unit believed that African Americans should not be recruited to chemistry; even this dissenter acknowledged his affection for the discipline. Most interviewees emphasized that it was the barriers that they encountered in the pursuit of their scientific careers and not the practice of science that disturbed them. These experiences prompted most interviewees to argue that a critical mass or a substantially increased participation of African Americans in chemistry is required to break down racial barriers. It is important to note that this critical mass is necessary but not sufficient to dismantle racial and gender discrimination.

The findings of this study indicate that there is much more to learn about the family, education, employment, and professional experiences of African American doctoral chemists. There is a need for more comprehensive, systematic studies of these scientists and other underrepresented racial/ethnic minority scientists and engineers. Below, I summarize some of the key findings and their implications for policy, practice and research.

PRIMARY AND SECONDARY EDUCATION

Findings #1: Mathematics as a Catalyst to Interest in Science. Most interviewees reported developing an interest in mathematics before developing one in science.

Implications for Practice. Early interest in mathematics must be sustained with high quality instruction and materials throughout the educational pathway.

Exposure to science can and should occur much earlier than it does now in many schools attended by large numbers of African American students.

Findings #2: Stimulating and Sustaining Interest in Science and Mathematics. Hands-on science and math experiences (in classrooms and/or in the field) are powerful catalysts for piquing the curiosity of young minds. Regardless of gender, interviewees reported that participation in science fairs was critical in developing the confidence that they could excel in science and math courses. A number of interviewees also cited the role of science and technology magazines and chemistry sets in stimulating and sustaining their interest and competency in science and mathematics.

Implications for Research. Historians and sociologists of science need to address the contributions and experiences of African American chemists in particular and African American scientists in general. Far too many textbooks ignore the contributions of African Americans to science and society. While there are book-length biographies of George Washington Carver, Ernest E. Just, and Charles Drew, comprehensive accounts of the lives and careers of other eminent African American scientists are yet to be written. For example, despite Percy L. Julian's significant scientific achievements, he remains invisible in the scholarly and public literatures. African American women scientists are virtually invisible in the literature.

Implications for Practice. School curricula need to broaden the base of contributors to sciences and develop curricula materials that reflect the contributions of the racial and gender diversity of scientists, especially chemists. All students need to know that scientific talents resides in all groups.

Findings #3: Impact of High School Teachers and Counselors. The impact of teachers on the interviewees is underscored by the fact that they were second only to parents in influencing interviewees to attend college. Several graduates of predominantly white high schools reported that counselors often discouraged them from taking advanced mathematics and science courses (including AP courses when available) and pursuing science, technology, engineering and mathematics (STEM) majors because of the difficulty of the courses.

Implications for Research. Determine the extent to which this allegation or claim is true. Examine, on a larger scale, the extent to which counselors direct African American students away from advanced mathematics and science courses.

Implication for Practice. If substantiated in a larger study, this represents an opportunity for professional counseling organizations, teacher organizations and other relevant stakeholders to develop intervention strategies. Moreover, counselors and teachers should make special efforts to assist African American students in understanding the relationship between their education and anticipated careers. This also represents an opportunity for chemists and other scientists to serve as volunteers in both formal (schools) and informal STEM educational settings (museums, youth centers). This is where role models and mentors are instrumental in sharing their knowledge of the profession.

CAREER CHOICE

Findings #1. Several of the interviewees admitted that they chose a career in chemistry without any knowledge of the role of a chemist, other than teaching. In addition to standard hiring issues (salary, advancement), a welcoming and supportive environment was a deciding factors in their career decisions. This stems partially from the lack of visibility of scientists.

Implications for Research. Counselors and teachers should make special efforts to assist African American and other students in understanding the relationship between their education preparation and anticipated careers.

Implications for Practice. Stakeholders should do a better job communicating both the attractiveness of careers in chemistry, and the diverse sectors in which they can practice (including self-employment).

Findings #2: Reading the biographies or biographical sketches (typically published in minority focused magazines or reference books) of eminent African American scientists influenced a number of the interviewees to pursue science careers.

Implications for Research. To date, European American historians and sociologists of science have largely ignored African American scientists in general and chemists in particular. Recently, some magazines geared towards African Americans have focused on African American scientists. Moreover, a few websites focusing on African Americans in science have emerged; unfortunately, some contain factual errors. One of the higher quality websites is *Just/Garcia/Hill* which remains underfunded. Unfortunately, these activities are not well know, especially to the public.

If the culture of science is responsible for the loss of many students, including curricular materials from the social studies of science actually may help students recognize, understand, and overcome their estrangement. Scientists can no longer afford to ignore the fact that science is a social activity, with norms, attitudes, and practices shaped by history, institutions, beliefs, and values (see Lederman, 2004).

Implications for Practice. Efforts to increase the participation of African Americans in science should be informed and driven by research on African Americans and other underrepresented racial/ethnic minorities in the history and sociology of science. The cycle of teaching just the facts should be broken by including science-and-technology studies in teacher education, so that K-12 students will be exposed to the principles of the field (see Lederman, 2004).

UNDERGRADUATE EDUCATION

Findings #1: Racial composition of undergraduate institution. Many graduates of historically white colleges and universities reported that isolation and little or no mentoring negatively affected their self-confidence to do chemistry. The survey findings reveal that most African American doctoral recipients now have their baccalaureate origins in historically white colleges and universities. However, some interviewees who had their origins in historically white colleges and universities reported very positive experiences because a faculty member had engaged them in an undergraduate research experience. Interestingly, this was the case across the cohorts-prior to the more common federally-supported programs for research experiences for undergraduates. In short, a nurturing, welcoming environment or climate that holds high standards and provides opportunities for all students to experience chemistry seems to be the key to increasing participation in STEM fields. This seems to be especially the case in the absence of African Americans on the faculty.

Implications for Research. Further systematic research is needed to identify those characteristics of the environment and climate of historically black colleges and institutions that sustain and nurture African American students' interest in careers in STEM fields. Additional research should explore ways in which historically white colleges and universities can adapt those characteristics to sustain and nurture African Americans' interest in STEM fields.

Implications for Practice. The research suggested above should inform policies and practices to increase the representation of African Americans in STEM fields at historically white colleges and universities. These institutions can avoid "reinventing the wheel" by drawing on the experience of historically black colleges and universities in sustaining and enhancing African Americans' interest in STEM fields, especially for those students who may not be well prepared.

Findings #2: Undergraduate research experience. Undergraduate research experiences were cited as enriching experiences that solidified the interviewees' decision to pursue science careers. Many of these opportunities resulted from programs supported various federal agencies and private foundations.

Implications for Research. Systematic research is needed on the effect of undergraduate research experience for African American students; this should include assessing the impact of multiple undergraduate research experiences.

Implications for Practice. Research on undergraduate research experiences should inform funding institutions that support such experiences. This research could provide information on which to base an undergraduate research experience program as well as feedback to enable existing programs to enhance the effectiveness and efficiency of their operation.

GRADUATE EDUATION

Finding #1: Inadequate preparation for graduate school. When they enter science or engineering programs in college or graduate school, women and member of minority groups have had little experience with the norms and attitudes they encounter such as, for example, unnecessarily harsh grading standards or being told point-blank that they cannot succeed in those fields. Some female and underrepresented minority students do not know what to make of the new culture that they find themselves in, or how to respond to it; they feel alienated and lose self-confidence. Graduates of small colleges (especially historically black colleges and universities) reported more difficulty than graduates of larger schools in adjusting to graduate school, especially at large research universities. In general, the former characterized their undergraduate experiences as extremely rewarding because of the nurturing they received from professors who were not only outstanding teachers and mentors but who also took a personal interest in them. This was in sharp contrast to what they characterized as the impersonal nature (and in a few cases, antagonism) of the professors in their doctoral programs. Interviewees described these professors as gifted researchers but poor teachers. For the most part, these interviewees were not prepared for taking major responsibility for this own learning. They decried what they called the "sink or swim" teaching techniques at major research universities, especially in the top rated programs. In a sense, the interviewees experienced "culture shock."

Many graduates of historically black colleges and universities reported that only when they began their doctoral studies did it become apparent that their undergraduate curricula were limited in the scope of advanced course offerings, laboratory facilities and equipment, pedagogical approach and preparation of professors. Several interviewees voiced disappointment that they had not been taught to critically read and analyze scientific readings. They reported facing stiff competition from white classmates who were graduates of major research universities and elite liberal arts college, because these white classmates had taken more courses in chemistry and knew how to read and critically assess journal articles and other scientific material. In graduate school, many interviewees cited a lack of strong mathematical skills as a reason for choosing their research specialities. However, the interviewees expressed considerable gratitude for the motivation and mentoring received at institutions clearly underfinanced in a racially segregated and unequal system.

Implications for Practice. Professors in doctoral programs working in close collaboration with faculties at small undergraduate institutions can and should define the necessary intellectual competencies that are crucial to effective performance at the graduate level. Additionally, it represents an opportunity for collaboration between faculty in research institutions and teaching institutions to develop high quality undergraduate research experiences and faculty exchanges.

Finding #2: Absence of African American faculty. African Americans were virtually absent from the graduate faculties at historically white universities, especially in highly ranked departments. This is reflected in the fact that for those interviewees providing the ethnicity of their dissertation advisor, none from historically white universities reported an African American (or female) dissertation advisor. Overall, more than one-third reported their advisor's ethnicity as Jewish, and two as Asian.

Currently, African Americans are severely underrepresented on the chemistry faculties of historically white colleges and universities. This is especially the case at highly selective research universities. Some critics argue that this situation may play a major role in the under production of doctoral chemistry degrees awarded to African Americans, especially at highly selective universities.

The focus should not be on historically white colleges and universities alone. Efforts should be made to increase the numbers of African American faculty in STEM fields in historically black colleges and universities. This is a critical factor in increasing the numbers of African American women pursuing doctorates and careers in STEM fields.

Implications for Research. There is a need for research that systematically tracks and collects longitudinal data on African Americans aspiring to careers in academe. A good starting point would be existing programs designed to increase African Americans' participation in academic careers.

Implications for Practice. Policies and practices to increase the numbers of African American faculty-at all types of institutions-should be informed by a systematic body of research. The existing programs pursuing this goal should communicate strategies, successes, and failures so that each can learn from the others.

Finding #3: Funding: and time-to-degree. Both funds and time are critical factors in career choice. Research indicates that there is a substantial disparity between the educational opportunities and achievements of African American and white students. The longer it takes to earn the requisite credentials, the more funding is required. Time-to-degree has been increasing in STEM graduate programs. Many see this increase as arbitrary and a mechanism for professors to retain a cheap source of high-quality labor. As the time-to-degree for STEM fields has increased, the time-to-degree for MD, DD, DVM, JD and MBA degrees has remained relatively constant for decades, and the prospects for successful completion, remain high (Butz et al., 2000). This makes careers in medicine, law, and business more attractive than careers in STEM fields. Unless all students, regardless of race or economic status, have equal opportunities to meet standards, the gap will continue to widen.

Implications for Practice. Time-to-degree in STEM fields must be shortened. The U.S. can make STEM career prospects more attractive to its citizens by increasing the number and size of stipends available from the National Science Foundation, the National Institutes of Health, and other government agencies. Since these awards are limited to U.S. citizens, they represent a strategic tool for differentiating U.S. citizens from non-citizens (Freeman, 2004). If the gap is to be eliminated, the disparities in educational opportunities associated with social class and race, will have to be eliminated beginning at preschool. This is critical to increase the representation of African American STEM careers.

RACISM AND SEXISM

Finding #1: Racism as a barrier to professional achievement. Approximately seven in 10 interviewees believed that race limits the full participation of African Americans in chemistry. Some interviewees reported the existence of double standards in their graduate programs. For example, many interviewees (especially Cohorts I, II, and III) reported that advisors had low expectations that African Americans could contribute to leading edge science. As a consequence, some interviewees complained that they did not always get the most rigorous critique of their work or high-quality research experiences (e.g. proposal writing). The advisors saw African Americans as being no competition for their white male students who planned academic careers, because higher education institutions were still largely segregated. In short, most African Americans pursued their academic careers outside of so-called mainstream research departments. Several interviewees cited personal experiences or experiences of other African American academics at major research departments in terms of recruiting top graduate students to their labs even when they had grant support. Some interviewees, however, reported instances in which graduate students were actively discouraged by some white faculty members from working with them. Ironically, rampant racism was the catalyst for many of the interviewees to develop diverse and multiple skill sets. Because they were often prevented from fully utilizing their knowledge, skills, and expertise in all sectors, many of the interviewees developed creative solutions to the problem of racism. For example, one interviewee started his own business when racism prevented him from working as a chemist in industry.

Implications for Practice. Established chemists should share their experience with their junior colleagues or students. Not only will this alert the junior chemists to potential pitfalls in the field, it will also inculcate in them the need to be flexible and adaptable.

Finding #2: Regardless of both cohort and racial composition of their employing institution, women reported having experienced rampant and virulent sexism. Many of the female interviewees indicated that they were unprepared for the competitiveness and harshness that they encountered from their male colleagues in the chemistry community. As a result, they said that they would do a better job of communicating to the next generation of women the "reality" of being a woman in science in general and in chemistry in particular.

Across cohorts, women reported problems of balancing family and work lives. Women tended to cite additional challenges associated with *gender-regardless of the employment sector and racial composition of employing institution*. In fact, some women believed that they, shouldered a disproportionate share of service courses and committee work in their departments.

Implications for Research. More research must be conducted on African American women in STEM fields in general, and chemistry in particular. Some extant research indicates that the profile for African American women in science careers is similar to that of non-Hispanic white women. For example, both African American and non-Hispanic white women in STEM careers attended an historically white college as an undergraduate. Future research should systematically examine the similarities and differences between African American women's STEM education and career pathways and those of African American males and non-Hispanic white women.

Implications for Practice. Research on African American women in chemistry should inform both policy and practice at all points along the education and career pathways.

Finding #3: There is a need to recruit more African Americans-female and male – to careers in chemistry. African Americans are virtually invisible in science and technology policy. Moreover, only a few are in the ranks of the scientific elite-Nobel laureates, and members of the National Academy of Science. When asked if there is a need to increase the representation of African Americans in chemistry, 98% of interviewees answered affirmatively and cited the following reasons: untapped talent; need for technical skills to be competitive in the workplace; highly respected field; future leaders for a global economy; the need for diversity in chemistry; and increased numbers will provide the visibility to attract others.

When they enter science or engineering programs in college or graduate school, women and members of minority groups have had little experience with the norms and attitudes they encounter such as, for example, unnecessarily harsh grading standards or being told point-blank that they cannot succeed in those fields.

Incorporating discussions of the social dimensions of science into science courses broadens students' understanding of current theory, tools, analytical techniques, and how different disciplines investigate and interpret the natural world. Exposure to science-and-technology studies would give non-scientists the perspective they need to participate in such debates. Instead of indoctrinating more students into the current scientific culture, scientists should work with social scientists and scholars of education to make science more welcoming to those who were formerly excluded from STEM fields.

Implications for Research. A new pedagogy should include science-and-technology studies, in which researchers look at science as a social enterprise. The subject matter of a reformed science education would include the interaction of science and the society in which it is practiced-for example, how society influences scientists in choosing problems to investigate (see Lederman, 2004).

Implications for Practice. One benefit of new science pedagogy might be to encourage women and members of minority groups to study science in college and graduate school, by making its culture easier to understand and thus less forbidding. At the college level, we should provide support, information, and institutional recognition and rewards for scientists who teach the social aspects of their disciplines (see Lederman, 2004).

SUGGESTIONS FOR FUTURE RESEARCH

Institutional Climate. More research should focus on institutional climate issues. For example, several interviewees pointed out that their advisor was supportive on a social level, but often held low expectations of them on academic and intellectual levels. This underscores the need for comparative studies that include interviews with advisors.

This study confirms findings from other studies that historically black colleges and universities consistently produce more than their proportional share of African American scientists, especially those earning the Ph.D. (see Constantine, 1994; Hill, 1996; Russell, 1994; Trent & Hill, 1994). In a recent *New York Times* column, Arenson (2002) reports that the overall graduation rate for African Americans is 46%. The gap between African Americans and whites, however, averages 10 percentage points. Furthermore, graduation rates tend to vary across institutions – even those with similar student profiles. This suggests that institutional policies and climate play a significant role in retention.

Effects of Critical Mass of African Americans. Future studies should examine the effects of critical mass-and the lack thereof – on African Americans in certain departments. At present, we have minimal empirically-based understanding of these situations. For example, many of the interviewees who pursued their doctoral studies in departments with three or more African Americans or departments with a history of sustained African American graduate student presence were not aware of this history. In some cases, the African Americans arrived at the graduate program because an undergraduate mentor was an alumnus or the department had a reputation for openness to African Americans.

Career Satisfaction. A majority of interviewees indicated that they were satisfied with their current or last position. Overall, most interviewees reported that they were very satisfied with their choice of a career in chemistry. Regardless of gender and cohort, most interviewees cited mentors as the major influence in their careers. For married interviewees, spouses were also cited as a major influence.

Industry. The findings of high levels of dissatisfaction among industrial chemists suggest the need for more systematic research to better understand the roots of the problem. Overall, the interviewees with undergraduate origins in historically black colleges and universities were somewhat more likely to pursue careers in industry – mostly due to higher salaries. However, this pattern also holds for chemists in general. The trend to industry for African American doctoral chemists lagged behind that of whites largely because of racial barriers, especially prior to the Civil Rights Act of 1964. In industry, promotions tended to be uneven at best – some Cohort I and II interviewees reported minimal advancement in their careers. Interviewees working within the same company, but in different units, reported remarkably different career experiences. A number of the interviewees, especially in Cohorts II and III, cited instances of African American colleagues leaving the line R&D track for managerial positions in Equal Opportunity Employment, community and educational outreach, and human resources. The primary reason seems to be frustration with advancement in the R&D track.

Academe. In academe, more interviewees at historically white colleges and universities cited difficulties associated with tenure, and promotion beyond the associate professor level. Indeed, many interviewees who took non-academic appointments expressed concern about pursuing an academic career because of the subjectivity of the tenure process and the lower salary levels relative to those in industry. Several chemists at research universities said that they were unable to recruit top graduate students in their department – even when they had funded projects. In fact, some interviewees claimed to have knowledge of well-trained chemists leaving academic chemistry out of frustration because their research was stymied without students. These claims require further investigation.

Professional Association Membership. A majority of interviewees held memberships in professional scientific associations-primarily ACS and NOBCChE. Although interviewees were divided about the value of belonging only to ACS or NOBCChE or both, several industrial chemists believed that NOBCChE was a vital networking and support mechanism that allowed them to overcome their employment isolation. Some interviewees in both historically black colleges and universities and historically white colleges and universities reported feeling isolated; however, a greater proportion of those in the latter reported feeling like tokens. More systematic studies are needed of the impact of professional scientific associations on the careers of their minority members.

REFERENCES

A Monthly Summary of Events and Trends in Race Relations (1945). *3*, 4–8, 53–55.

Abir-Am, P. (1993). Women in research schools: Approaching an analytical lacuna in the history of chemistry and allied sciences. In: S. H. Mauskopf (Ed.), *Chemical Sciences in the Modern World* (pp. 375–391). Philadelphia: University of Pennsylvania Press.

Aguirre, A., Jr., & Turner, J. H. (2001). *American ethnicity: The dynamics and consequences of discrimination* (3rd ed.). New York: McGraw-Hill.

Allen, W. R., & Wallace, J. (2001). Black college students: Achievement, social integration, and aspirations. In: J. O. B. Ura & L. Morris (Eds), *One-Third of a Nation: African American Perspectives* (pp. 363–379). Washington, DC: Howard University Press.

Anderson, J. D. (1988). *The education of blacks in the South, 1860–1935*. Chapel Hill, NC: University of North Carolina Press.

Arenson, K. W. (2004). Study faults colleges on graduation rates. *The New York Times* (Thursday, May 27), A16.

Astin, A. W. (1963). Undergraduate institutions and the production of scientists. *Science, 141*, 334–338.

Astin, A. W. (1982). *Minorities in American higher education*. San Francisco: Jossey-Bass.

Atkins, C. F. (1949). The Negro scientist comes of age. *Industrial Trends, 6*, 10–11.

Atkinson, R. C. (1990). Supply and demand of scientists and engineers: A national crisis in the making. *Science, 248*, 425–432.

Babbie, E. (2001). *The practice of social research* (9th ed.). Belmont, CA: Wadsworth/Thomson Learning.

Bechtel, H. K. (1989). Introduction. In: W. Pearson, Jr. & H. K. Bechtel (Eds), *African Americans, Science and American Education* (pp. 1–20). New Brunswick: Rutgers University Press.

Benjamin, L. (1991). *The black elite: Facing The color line in the twilight of the twentieth century*. Chicago: Nelson-Hall.

Bennett, P. R., & Xie, Y. (2003). Revisiting racial differences in college attendance: The role of historically Black colleges and universities. *American Sociological Review, 68*, 567–580.

Berelson, B. (1960). *Graduate education in the United States*. New York: McGraw-Hill.

Bhattacharjee, Y. (2003). People. *Science, 301*(July 11), 164.

Black Issues in Higher Education (2000). Newspaper report confirms black children more likely to be in inferior schools. Retrieved May 2004.

Blackwell, J. E. (1981). *Mainstreaming outsiders: The production of black professionals* (2nd ed.). Dix Hills, NY: General Hall.

Blalock, H. M. (1967). *Toward a theory of minority-group relations*. New York: Wiley.

Blanchard, W. (1946). Cited in Paul de Kruif. The man who wouldn't give up. *The Readers Digest* (August), 113–118.

Bordieri, C. (1991, May). A manly profession: Women in chemistry. *Workforce Report.* Washington, DC: American Chemical Society.

Borman, S. (1993). Black chemist Percy Julian commemorated on postage stamp. *Chemical & Engineering News* (February 1), 9–12.

Bowen, W. G., & Bok, D. C. (1998). *The shape of the river: Long-term consequences of considering race in college and university admissions.* New Jersey: Princeton University Press.

Branson, H. (1952). The Negro and scientific research. *The Negro History Bulletin, 15,* 131–136, 151.

Branson, H. (1955). The Negro scientist. In: J. H. Taylor, D. Dillard & N. K. Proctor (Eds), *The Negro in Science* (pp. 1–9). Baltimore: Morgan State College Press.

Building Engineering and Science Talent (BEST) (2004, February). *A bridge for all: Higher education design principles to broaden participation in science, technology, engineering and mathematics.* San Diego: BEST.

Burris, V. (2004). The academic caste system: Prestige hierarchies in Ph.D. exchange network. *American Sociological Review, 69,* 239–264.

Butz, W. P., Bloom, G. A., Gross, M. E., Kelly, T. K., Kofner, A., & Rippen, H. E. (2003). Is there a shortage of scientists and engineers? *RAND Issue Paper* (Science and Technology), 1–7.

Cattell, J. M. (1914). Science, education and democracy. *Science, 39*(996), 155–159.

Cherlin, A. J. (1981). *Marriage, divorce, remarriage.* Cambridge, MA: Harvard University Press.

Clement, R. E. (1939). Legal provisions for graduate and professional instruction for Negroes in states operating separate school systems. *The Journal of Negro Education, 8,* 142–149.

Clemente, F. (1974). Race and research productivity. *Journal of Black Studies, 5,* 157–166.

Clinton, W. J. (1997). Call to action for American education in the 21st century (February 4). State of the Union Address.

Cole, J. R. (1987). *Fair science: Women in the scientific community* (2nd ed.). New York: Columbia University Press.

Cole, J., & Cole, S. (1973). *Social stratification in science.* Chicago: University of Chicago Press.

Commission on Professionals in Science and Technology (July, 2002). *Professional women and minorities* (14th ed.). Washington, DC: CPST.

Committee on Equal Opportunities in Science and Engineering (CEOSE) (2002). *2002 Biennial report to congress.* Arlington, VA: National Science Foundation.

Condron, D. J., & Roscigno, V. J. (2003). Disparities within: Unequal spending and achievement in an urban school district. *Sociology of Education, 76,* 18–36.

Conyers, J. E., & Kennedy, T. H. (1963). Negro passing: To pass or not to pass. *Phylon, 24,* 215–223.

Cose, E. (1993). *The rage of a privileged class.* New York: HarperCollins.

Crane, D. (1965). Scientists at major and minor universities: A study of productivity and recognition. *American Sociological Review, 30,* 699–714.

Crisis Staff (1916). Men of the month. *Crisis, 12,* 190–191.

Cross, T. (1998, Spring). The Black faculty count at the nation's most prestigious universities. *The Journal of Blacks in Higher Education* (19), 109–115.

Crowder, K. D., & Tolnay, S. E. (2000, August). A new marriage squeeze for Black women: The role of racial intermarriage by black men. *Journal of Marriage and the Family, 62,* 792–807.

Dartmouth College (2003). *Race matters in the university of the 21st century.* Report of the Conference at Dartmouth College (October 4–5, 2002).

de Kruif, P. (1946). The man who wouldn't give up. *The Readers Digest* (August), 113–118.

de Solla Price, D. (1986). *Little science, big science and beyond.* New York: Columbia University Press.

Downing, L. K. (1939). Contributions of Negro scientists. *Crisis, 46,* 167–189.

Drewry, H. N., & Doermann, H. (2003). *Stand and prosper: Private black colleges and their students.* Princeton: Princeton University Press.

DuBois, W. E. B. (1977). *The souls of black folk.* Mineola, NY: Dover.

Ellis, E. (2000). Race, gender and the graduate student experience: recent research. *Diversity Digest, 5,* 10–11. Association of American Colleges and Universities.

Ellis, S., & Pearson, W., Jr. (1988). Race, science, and religious affiliation. *Journal of the Association of Social and Behavioral Scientists, 34,* 305–317.

Embree, E. R. (1935). In order of their eminence. *Atlantic Monthly, 155,* 652–664.

Eshleman, J. R. (2003). *The family* (10th ed.). Boston: Allyn & Bacon.

Esterberg, K. G. (2002). *Qualitative methods in social research.* New York: McGraw-Hill.

Ferguson, L. N. (1949). Negroes in chemistry. *Industrial Trends, 6,* 17–19.

Field, K. (2004). U.S. is said to produce too few scientists. *The Chronicle of Higher Education* (May 14), A28.

Fleming, J. (1984). *Blacks in college: A comparative study of students success in Black and White institutions.* San Francisco, CA: Jossey-Bass.

Fortune (1950). *The chemical century* (March), 69–76, 114, 116, 121–122.

Franklin, J. H., & Moss, J. A. A. (1994). *From slavery to freedom: A history of African Americans* (7th ed.). New York: McGraw-Hill.

Frazier, E. F. (1975). *Black bourgeoisie.* New York: Collier.

Freedman, S. G. (2004, May 16). Still separate, still unequal. *The New York Times Book Review,* 8–9.

Freeman, R. B. (1976). *Black elite: The new market for highly educated Black Americans.* New York: McGraw-Hill.

Freeman, R. B. (2004). Stimulating careers in science and engineering. *Science Next Wave* (Retrieved May 7).

Gaines, K. K. (1996). *Uplifting the race: Black leadership, politics, and culture in the twentieth century.* Chapel Hill, NC: University of North Carolina.

Gavins, R., & Hill, I. T. (2004). Behind the veil. *OAH Magazine of History,* 3–5, 36.

Geiser, S. W. (1935). The Negro in American chemistry. *Opportunity, 13,* 43–45.

Ginzberg, E. (1956). *The Negro potential.* New York: Columbia University Press.

Glenn, D. (2004). Minority students fair better at selective colleges, sociologists find. *The Chronicle of Higher Education* (Retrieved August 16).

Glock, C. Y. (1962). On the study of religious commitment. *Religious Education, 62,* 98–110.

Goldsmith, P. A. (2004, April). Schools' racial mix, students' optimism, and the Black-White and Latino-White achievements gaps. *Sociology of Education, 77,* 121–147.

Goodrich, H. B., Knapp, R. H., & Boehm, G. A. W. (1962). The origins of U.S. scientists. In: B. Barber & W. Hirsch (Eds), *The Sociology of Science.* New York: Free Press.

Goodwin, P. Y. (2003). African American and European American women's marital well-being. *Journal of Marriage and Family, 65,* 550–560.

Gorden, R. (1987). *Interviewing: Strategy, techniques, and tactics* (4th ed.). Chicago: Dorsey.

Gould, S. J. (1981). *The mismeasure of man.* New York: W. W. Norton.

Greely, A. W. (1965). The religious behavior of graduate students. *Journal for the Scientific Study of Religion, 5,* 34–40.

Greenberg, M. (2004, June 18). How the GI bill changed higher education. *The Chronicle of Higher Education,* B9–B11.

Greene, H. W. (1946). *Holders of doctorates among American Negroes: An educational and social study of Negroes who have earned doctoral degrees in course, 1876–1943.* Boston: Meador.

Gurin, P., & Epps, E. G. (1975). *Black consciousness, identity and achievement: A study of students in historically Black colleges.* New York: Wiley.

Gutman, H. G. (1976). *The black family in slavery and freedom, 1750–1925.* New York: Pantheon.

Haber, L. (1970). *Black pioneers of science and invention.* New York: Harcourt, Brace & World.

Hagstrom, W. O. (1971). Inputs, outputs and the prestige of American university science departments. *Sociology of Education, 44*(Fall), 375–397.

Hall, A. E. (1984). Baccalaureate origins of doctorate recipients in chemistry. *Change, 16,* 47–49.

Hardy, K. R. (1974). Social origins of American scientists and scholars. *Science, 185,* 497–505.

Harmon, L. R., & Soldz, H. (1963). *Doctorate production in the United States' universities, 1920–1962.* Washington, DC: National Academy of Sciences, National Research Council.

Hawkins, W. L. (1982). Cited in Barry Meier, Why are there so few black chemists? *Industrial Chemical News, 3,* 1–6.

Healey, J. F. (2005). *Statistics: A tool for social research* (7th ed.). Belmont, CA: Thomson/Wadsworth.

Heylin, M. (1995). Chemists' job market still weak but those employed post solid pay gains. *Chemical & Engineering News* (May 29).

Heylin, M. (1996). Chemists' employment situation continues to worsen, salaries weak. *Chemical & Engineering News* (July 29).

Heylin, M. (2003a). Salary survey. *Chemical and Engineering News, 81*(31), 37–44.

Heylin, M. (2003b). Unemployment at record high. *Chemical and Engineering News, 81*(25), 12.

Heylin, M. (2004). Employment and salary survey. *82*(33), 26–34.

Higginbotham, A. L., Jr. (1998). Breaking Thurgood Marshall's promise. *The New York Times Magazine* (January 18), 28–29.

Hill, S. T. (1996). *Undergraduate origins of recent (1991–1995) science and engineering doctorate recipients.* Special Report. Arlington, VA: NSF 96–334.

Jackson, S. A. (2003). *Quiet crisis.* San Diego: BEST.

Jacobs, D. (1999). Ascription or productivity? The determinants of departmental success in the NRC quality ratings. *Social Science Research, 28,* 228–239.

Jacobs, M. (2001). Reasons sought for lack of diversity. *Chemical & Engineering News, 79*(40), 100, 102–103.

Jacobs, M. (2002). Focus on diversity. *Chemical and Engineering News, 80*(26), 35–39.

Jacobs, M., & Storck, W. (2000). *Chemical and Engineering News, 78*(19), 36.

Jay, J. M. (1971). *Negroes in science: Natural science doctorates, 1876–1969.* Detroit: Balcamp.

Jaynes, G. D., & Williams, R. M. (1989). *A common destiny: Blacks and American society.* Washington, DC: National Academy Press.

Jenkins, E. (1984). Impact of social conditions: A study of the works of American black scientists and inventors. *Journal of Black Studies, 14*(4), 477–491.

Jones, E. (2003). Beyond supply and demand: Assessing the Ph.D. job market. *Occupational Outlook Quarterly* (Winter 2002/2003), 22–23.

Julian, P. L. (1969). On being scientist, humanist, and Negro. In: S. L. Wormley & L. H. Fenderson (Eds), *Many Shades of Black* (pp. 147–157). New York: Morrow.

Karon, B. P. (1975). *Black scars.* New York: Springer.

Klein, A. E. (1971). *The hidden contributors: Black scientists and inventors in America.* Garden City, NY: Doubleday.

Kluger, R. (1975). *Simple justice: The history of Brown v. Board of Education and Black America's struggle for equality.* New York: Vintage Books.

Knapp, R. H., & Goodrich, H. B. (1952). *Origins of American scientists.* Chicago: University of Chicago Press.

Koelewijn-Strattner, G. J. (1990). *Race, gender and the scientific professions: Double negative or double jeopardy*. Master's Thesis. University of Maryland, College Park.

Krislov, S. (1967). *The Negro in federal employment: The quest for equal opportunity*. Minneapolis: University of Minnesota Press.

Langford, G. (2003). Introductory remarks. Workforce Workshop, National Science Board (August 12).

Langford, G. (2004). The science and engineering workforce: The long-term. *Science Next Wave* (Retrieved May 7).

Lederman, M. (2004). Science is a social enterprise. *The Chronicle of Higher Education* (May 14), B16.

Leggon, C. B. (1993). Changing baccalaureate origins of African American doctoral scientists 1975–1992. A paper presented at the Conference on Race and Science. Washington University, St. Louis, MO.

Leggon, C. B., & Malcom, S. M. (1989). Human resources in science and engineering: Policy implications. In: W. Pearson, Jr. & A. Fechter (Eds), *Who Will Do Science? Educating the Next Generation* (pp. 141–151). Baltimore: Johns Hopkins University Press.

Leggon, C. B., & Pearson, W., Jr. (1997). The baccalaureate origins of African American female Ph.D. scientists. *Journal of Women and Minorities in Science and Engineering, 3*, 213–224.

Lehman, E. C., Jr. (1974). Academic discipline and faculty religiosity in secular and church-related colleges. *Journal for the Scientific Study of Religion, 13*, 205–220.

Leuba, J. H. (1934). Religious beliefs of American scientists. *Harper's Monthly Magazine, 169*, 291–300.

Lincoln, C. E., & Mamiya, L. H. (1990). *The Black church in the African American experience*. Durham: Duke University Press.

Lipset, S. M., & Ladd, E. C. (1971). Jewish academics in the United States: Their achievements, culture and politics. *American Jewish Yearbook*. Cited in H. Zuckerman (1977). *Scientific elite: Nobel laureates in the United States*. New York: Free Press.

Litwack, L. F. (2004). Jim Crow blues. *OAH Magazine of History*, 7–11, 58.

Locke, M. (2004). African Americans at Berkeley drop 30%. *The Atlanta Journal-Constitution*, A9 (Friday, June 4).

Logan, R. W. (1969). *Howard university: The first one hundred years, 1867–1967*. New York: New York University Press.

Long, J. R. (2000). Women chemists still rare in academia. *Chemical and Engineering News, 78*(39), 56.

Long, J. S. (1978). Productivity and academic position in the scientific career. *American Sociological Review, 43*, 889–906.

Long, J. S. (2001). *From scarcity to visibility: Gender differences in the careers of doctoral scientists and engineers*. Washington, DC: National Academy Press.

Long, J. S., Allison, P. D., & McGinnis, R. (1979). Entrance into the academic career. *American Sociological Review, 44*, 816–830.

Long, J. S., & McGinnis, R. (1981). Organizational context and scientific productivity. *American Sociological Review, 46*, 422–442.

Mackintosh, B. (1978). George Washington Carver. The making of a myth. *The Journal of Southern History* (42), 507–528.

Majors, R. G., & Gordon, J. U. (Eds) (1994). *The American black male: His present status and his future*. Chicago: Nelson-Hall.

Malcom, S. M., George, Y. S., & Van Horne, V. V. (Eds) (1996). *The effects of the changing policy climate on science, mathematics, and engineering (SME) diversity*. Washington, DC: American Association for the Advancement of Science.

Manning, K. R. (1983). *Black apollo of science: The life of Ernest Everett Just.* New York: Oxford University Press.

Manning, K. R. (1993). Race, science, and identity. In: G. Early (Ed.), *Lure and Loathing: Essays on Race, Identity, and the Ambivalence of Assimilation* (pp. 317–336). New York: Allen Lane, Penguin Press.

Manning, K. R. (1994). Henry C. McBay: Reflections of a chemist. In: W. M. Jackson & B. J. Evans (Eds), *Henry C. McBay. A Chemical Festschrift* (pp. 1–41). Proceedings of a Symposium in Honor of the First Martin L. King, Jr. Scholar at the Massachusetts Institute of Technology. Cambridge, MA: MIT Press.

Manning, K. R. (1999). Can history predict the future? In: R. E. Mickens (Ed.), *The African American Presence in Physics: A Compilation of Materials Related To An Exhibit* (pp. 8–10). Atlanta: National Society of Black Physicists.

Marasco, C. (1994, April). Harassment and discrimination in the workplace. *Workforce Report.* Washington, DC: American Chemical Society.

Massie, S. (1982). Cited in Barry Meier, Why are there so few Black chemists? *Industrial Chemical News, 3,* 1–6.

McWilliams, C. (1948). *A mask for privilege: Anti-semitism in America.* Boston: Little, Brown & Company.

Mehta, A. (2004). Slate finalized for fall elections. *Chemical & Engineering News, 82*(30), 15.

Meier, B. (1982). Why are there so few Black chemists? *Industrial Chemical News, 3,* 1–6.

Merton, R. K. (1973). *The sociology of science: Theoretical and empirical investigations.* Chicago: University of Chicago Press.

Mervis, J. (2004a). Down for the count. *Science, 300,* 1070–1074.

Mervis, J. (2004b). Perceptions and realities of the workplace. *Science, 304,* 1285–1286.

Monastersky, R. (2004). Is there a science crisis? Maybe not. *The Chronicle of Higher Education, 50,* A10–A14.

Murry, V. M., Brown, P., Adama, B., Gene, H., Cutrona, C. E., & Simons, R. L. (November, 2001). Racial discrimination as a moderator of the links among stress, maternal psychological functioning, and family relationships. *Journal of Marriage and the Family, 63,* 915–926.

Myrdal, G. (1944). *An American dilemma: The Negro problem and modern democracy.* New York: Harper.

National Research Council (2003). *Minorities in the chemical workforce: Diversity models the work.* A Workshop Report to the Chemical Sciences Roundtable. Washington, DC: National Academy Press.

National Science Board (2004). *Science and engineering indicators 2004.* Volumes 1 and 2. Arlington, VA: National Science Foundation (Volume 1, NSB04–1; Volume 2, NSB04–1A).

National Science Foundation (1997). *Division of science resources statistics.* Unpublished tabulations.

National Science Foundation (2002). *Women, minorities, and persons with disabilities in science and engineering.* Arlington, VA: Division of Science Resources Statistics, NSF.

National Science Foundation (2003a). *Characteristics of doctoral scientists and engineers in the United States: 2001.* Arlington, VA (NSF 03–310).

National Science Foundation (2003b). *Science and engineering doctorate awards: 2002.* Arlington, VA (NSF 04–303).

Nelson, D., Wendt, A., Ea, L., LaMothe, R., & Brammer, C. N. (2001). Survey of race/ethnicity of the "Top 50" chemistry department faculties. Paper presented at the 222nd ACS Meeting, Chicago, IL.

Nye, M. J. (1996). *Before big science: The pursuit of modern chemistry and physics 1800–1940*. New York: Twayne Publishers.

Oakes, J., Ormseth, T. H., Bell, R. M., & Camp, P. (1990). *Multiplying inequities: The effects of race, social class, and tracking on opportunities to learn mathematics and science*. Santa Monica, CA: RAND. (ERIC ED329615).

Orfield, G., & Yun, J. T. (1999). *Resegregation in American schools*. Cambridge, MA: Civil Rights Project, Harvard University.

Orr, A. J. (2003). Black-White differences in achievement: The importance of wealth. *Sociology of Education, 76*, 281–304.

Parks, C. (2004). Diversity in the workforce: Industry vs. academia. *Science Next Wave* (Retrieved May 21).

Parrillo, V. N. (2005). *Contemporary social problems* (6th ed.). Boston: Allyn & Bacon.

Pascarella, E. T. (1984). College environmental influences on students, educational aspirations. *Journal of Higher Education, 55*, 571–751.

Pearson, W., Jr. (1985). *Black scientists, White society and colorless science: A study of universalism in American science*. Millwood, NY: Associated Faculty Press.

Pearson, W., Jr. (1986). Race, religious apostasy and scientific productivity. A paper presented at the Southwestern Sociological Association Meeting (March 19–22). San Antonio, TX.

Pearson, W., Jr., & Earle, J. R. (1984). Race and gender differences in the social characteristics of American doctoral scientists. *Sociological Spectrum, 4*, 229–248.

Pearson, W., Jr., & Ellis, S. C. (1988). Race, science and religious affiliation. *Journal of Social and Behavioral Sciences, 34*, 305–317.

Pearson, W., Jr., Ness, C., & Hoban, E. (1999). Race, gender and the baccalaureate origins of Ph.D. chemists. *Journal of Women and Minorities in Science and Engineering, 5*.

Pearson, W., Jr., & Pearson, L. C. (1985). The baccalaureate origins of black American scientists: A cohort analysis. *Journal of Negro Education, 54*, 24–34.

Pearson, W., Jr., & Pearson, L. C. (1986). Race and the baccalaureate origins of American Ph.D. scientists. *Journal of Social and Behavioral Sciences, 32*, 149–164.

Pearson, W., Jr., & Warner, I. (1998). Mentoring experiences of African American Ph.D. chemists. In: H. T. Frierson (Ed.), *Examining Mentoring-Protégé Experiences. Diversity in Higher Education: Volume II* (pp. 41–57). Greenwich, CT: JAI Press.

Pinkney, A. (2000). *Black Americans* (5th ed.). Upper Saddler River, NJ: Prentice-Hall.

Poe, J. (2002). Black colleges under pressure to change, close. *The Atlanta Journal-Constitution* (Thursday, November 14), A1, A8.

Quarles, B. (1988). *Black mosaic: Essays in African–American history and historiography*. Amherst, MA: University of Massachusetts Press.

Quay, W. H., Jr. (1970). The Negro in the chemical industry. In: H. R. Northrup (Ed.), *Negro Employment in Basic Industry: A Study of Racial Policies in Six Industries*. Philadelphia: University of Pennsylvania Press.

Raber, L. (2004). Ann Nalley is 2005 ACS President-Elect. *Chemical and Engineering News* (November 16). Retrieved November 17.

Rawls, R. L. (1991). Minorities in science. *Chemical and Engineering News* (Special Report) (April 15), 20–35.

Reskin, B. F. (1977). Scientific productivity and the reward structure of science. *American Sociological Review, 42*, 491–504.

Reskin, B. F. (1979). Academic sponsorship and scientist careers. *Sociology of Education, 52*, 129–146.

Roe, A. (1953). *The making of a scientist*. New York: Dodd, Mead.

Rossiter, M. W. (1982). *Women scientists in America: Struggles and strategies to 1940*. Baltimore: Johns Hopkins University Press.

Sanders, W. L., & Rivers, J. C. (1996). *Cumulative and residual effects of teachers on future student academic achievement*. Knoxville: University of Tennessee.

Sapiro, V. (1986). *Women in American society*. Palo Alto, CA: Mayfield Publishing Company.

Schaefer, R. T. (2000). *Race and ethnic groups* (8th ed.). Upper Saddle River, NJ: Prentice-Hall.

Schexnider, A. J. (2003, Summer). Will private black colleges survive in the 21st century? *The Journal of Blacks in Higher Education*, 128–130.

Schomburg Center for Research in Black Culture (1999). *African American desk reference*. New York: Stonesong Press.

Selingo, J. (1997). A self-published college guide goes big-time, and educators cry foul. *The Chronicle of Higher Education, 44*(11), A45–A46.

Skolnik, H., & Reese, K. M. (Eds) (1976). *A century of chemistry: The role of chemists and the American chemical society*. Washington, DC: American Chemical Society.

Slater, R. B. (1994, Summer). The blacks who first entered the world of White higher education. *The Journal of Blacks in Higher Education* (4), 47–56.

Slater, R. B. (1998/1999, Winter). The first black faculty members at the nation's most highest-ranked universities. *The Journal of Blacks in Higher Education* (22), 97–106.

Smith, M. (1994). The national education reform movement. Paper presented at the Sigma Xi Forum Program: Scientists, Educators and National Standards: Action at the Local Level, Atlanta, GA.

Sonnert, G., & Holton, G. (1995). *Gender differences in science careers*. New Brunswick, NJ: Rutgers University Press.

Spanier, G., & Glick, P. (1980). The life cycle of American families: An expanded analysis. *Journal of Family History, V*, 98–112.

Staples, R. (1999). *The black family: Essays and studies* (6th ed.). Belmont, CA: Wadsworth.

Stark, R. (1963). On the incompatibility of religion and science. *Journal for the Scientific Study of Religion, 3*, 3–20.

Steinberg, S. (1974). *The academic melting pot*. New York: McGraw-Hill.

Stephenson, F. W. (1997). Jack Gourman's preposterous survey [Letter]. *Chronicle of Higher Education* (December 19).

Stoecker, J. L., & Pascarella, E. T. (1991). Women's colleges and women's career attainments revisited. *Journal of Higher Education, 62*, 394–406.

Strauss, A. L., & Rainwater, L. (1962). *The professional scientist: A study of American chemists*. Chicago: Aldine.

Suggs, E. (2004). Witness to history. *The Atlanta Journal-Constitution* (Monday, May 24), D1 and D3.

Taeuber, K., & Taeuber, A. F. (1965). *Negroes in cities: Residential segregation and neighborhood change*. Chicago: Aldine.

Thackray, A. Y., Sturchio, J. L., Carroll, P. T., & Bud, R. (1985). *Chemistry in America 1876–1976*. Dordrecht, Holland: D. Reidel Publishing Company.

The Journal of Blacks in Higher Education (Winter 1993/1994). Are nonresident Asian students displacing black Ph.D.s in science and engineering? (2), 15.

The Journal of Blacks in Higher Education (1995). The National Research Council assigns low ratings to doctoral programs at black universities. (9), 12–13.

The Journal of Blacks in Higher Education (1996). National Academy of Sciences: Nearly as white as a posh country club in Alabama. (12), 8–9.

The Journal of Blacks in Higher Education (1996/1997, Winter). The mounting financial burden of a college education for middle-class black families. (14), 30–31.

The Journal of Blacks in Higher Education (1999, Autumn). African-American college graduation rates: Blacks do best at the nation's most selective colleges and universities. (25), 122–127.

The Journal of Blacks in Higher Education (2000, Spring). JBHE's report card on the progress of black faculty at the nation's leading liberal arts colleges. *27*, 6–8.

The Morehouse Journal of Science (1928). 2.

The New York Times (2004). Editorial. The college aid crisis (Tuesday, May 25), A26.

Tidball, M. E. (1986). Baccalaureate origins of recent natural science doctorates. *Journal of Higher Education, 57*, 606–620.

Tidball, M. E., & Kistiakowski, V. (1976). Baccalaureate origins of American scientists and scholars. *Science, 193*, 646–652.

Tietlebaum, M. (2001). How we (unintentionally) make scientific careers unattractive. In: D. Chubin & W. Pearson, Jr. (Eds), *Who Will Do Science in the New Millennium* (pp. 71–79). Washington, DC: Commission on Professionals in Science and Technology.

Trent, W., & Hill, J. (1994). The contributions of historically black colleges and universities to the production of African scientists and engineers. In: W. Pearson, Jr. & A. Fechter (Eds), *Who Will Do Science? Educating The Next Generation* (pp. 68–80). Baltimore: Johns Hopkins University Press.

Tucker, M. B., & Mitchell-Kernan, C. (Eds) (1995). *The decline in marriage among African Americans: Causes, consequences, and policy implications*. New York: Russell Sage.

U.S. Department of Education (1991). Historically black colleges and universities and higher education desegregation. Washington, DC: U.S. Department of Education, Office for Civil Rights.

Watson, J. D. (1968). *The double helix: A personal account of the discovery of the structure of DNA*. New York: Atheneum.

West, C. (1994). *Race matters*. New York: Vintage.

Wideman, J. (1978). Publish and still perish: The dilemma of black educators on white campuses. *Black Enterprise, 9*, 44–49.

Williams, L. (1981). Educational opportunities for African Americans in the sciences, 1955–1980: An assessment of the impact of the 1954 Supreme Court decision. *The Negro Educational Review, 32*, 101–105.

Wilson, R. (1995). In political science: Interpreting the ranking shuffle. *The Chronicle of Higher Education* (September 22), A31–A33.

Wilson, R. (1996). Affirmative action: Yesterday, today and beyond. Reprinted in S. Malcom, Y. George & V. V. Van Horne (Eds), *The Effect of the Changing Policy Climate on Science, Mathematics, and Engineering (SME) Diversity*. Washington, DC: American Association for the Advancement of Science.

Wilson, W. J. (1978). *The declining significance of race: African Americans and changing American institutions*. Chicago: University of Chicago Press.

Winston, M. R. (1971). Through the back door: Academic racism and the Negro scholar in historical perspective. *Daedalus, 100*, 678–719.

Wodsedalek, J. E. (1916). Causes of sterility in the mule. *Biological Bulletin, 30*(1), 1–56.

Woodard, C. V. (1957). *The strange career of Jim Crow*. New York: Oxford.

Woodson, C. G. (1939). Negroes distinguished in science. *The Negro History Bulletin, 8*, 67–70.

Wuthnow, R. (1985). Science and the sacred. In: P. E. Hammond (Ed.), *The Sacred in a Secular Age*. Berkeley: University of California.

Xie, Y., & Shauman, K. (2003). *Women in science: Career processes and outcomes*. Cambridge, MA: Harvard University Press.

Young, H. A., & Young, B. A. (1974). *Scientists in the black perspective.* Louisville: Lincoln Foundation.

Young, H. A., & Young, B. A. (1976). Black doctorates: Myth and reality. *Chemical Technology, 6,* 296–299.

Zuckerman, H. (1977). *Scientific elite: Nobel laureates in the United States.* New York: Free Press.

Zuckerman, H. (1987). Persistence and change in the careers of men and women scientists and engineers: A review of current research. In: L. Dix (Ed.), *Women: Their Underrepresentation and Career Differentials in Science and Engineering: Proceedings of a Conference* (pp. 127–156). Washington, DC: National Academy Press.

APPENDIX: DATA AND METHODS

A mixed methods approach was used to gather data for the book. These methods included both qualitative and quantitative data gathering techniques. The qualitative data were primarily derived from personal interviews conducted by the authors between 1994 and 1995, of a national sample of African American Ph.D. chemists. To clarify responses follow up interviews were conducted in 1996. The semi-structured interviews were tape-recorded (except where informants spoke off the record), transcribed verbatim, checked for accuracy by the interviewees, and edited for identifying information. The author identified categories, themes, and recurring processes. Both the population and sample are comprised of United States citizens who completed their K-12 education in the U.S. The sample was randomly selected from a list of African American Ph.D. chemists compiled from several sources. The names and addresses of approximately 366 Ph.D. chemists were identified from lists maintained by individuals who keep personal files (including the author), published biographical sketches/biographies, newspaper and magazine articles. Additional names were ascertained through a snowball procedure whereby letters were sent to African American and other Ph.D. scientists (especially chemists) requesting names and addresses of African American chemists. Once a list was compiled and authenticated, 46 subjects were randomly selected and sent up to three waves of letters requesting participation in the study. All subjects initially agreed to participate in the study. However, two chemists who initially agreed to be interviewed did not respond to scheduling requests. As a result, these methods resulted in 44 chemists being interviewed in person (one by telephone because of scheduling problems). Because females were over sampled, they comprised 7 (16%) of the 44 interviewees (see Table A.1).

Interviewees ranged in age from 31 to 86 years. The median age was 56 years (see also Table A.2). The length of interviews ranged from 1.5 to 4 hours; the average interview was approximately two hours long. An interview protocol was developed and pretested. It was then revised and adapted for interviews according to employment sector and stage in the career. All interviewees were asked: about their family background; what attracted them to chemistry; educational backgrounds

171

Table A.1. Percent Distribution by Sex and Cohort [Interviewees].

Sex	Cohort					
	I	II	III	IV	V	Total
Males	100.0	88.0	89.0	80.0	57.0	84.0
Females	0.0	13.0	11.0	20.0	43.0	16.0
Total	100.0	100.0	100.0	100.0	100.0	100.0

Note: Percentages may not sum to 100 because of rounding.

and experiences; career patterns and experiences; level of satisfaction with work, advancement and career choice; professional activities and their perceptions of the impact of race on African American participation in science. The author conducted all interviews. The published quotes have been edited for readability (see also Sonnert & Holton, 1995).

Some data are not presented in detail in order to protect the anonymity of informants. However, where possible and appropriate, cohort data are presented. These cohorts are as follows: (I) before 1955; (II) 1955–1964; (III) 1965–1974; (IV) 1975–1984; and (V) 1985–1994. For analytical purposes, the cohorts are grouped to generally correspond to the introduction and enactment of various federal laws, executive orders and court decisions that affected civil rights in the U.S. For example, in Cohort I, the 1954 *Brown v. Board of Education* decision legally ended segregation in public schools and Roosevelt's Executive Order 8802 targeted race discrimination in defense plants. In Cohort II, executive orders by Kennedy (10925) and Johnson (11246) laid the groundwork for affirmative action programs and the 1964 Civil Rights Act prohibited hiring discrimination in the public and private sectors. During the third cohort, the 1964 Civil Rights Act was applied to higher education faculty, and the *Adams v. Richardson* decision ended segregation in higher education, where there were two separate and unequal systems. The fourth cohort witnessed Nixon's Revised Order No. 4 and the *Bakke*

Table A.2. Percent Distribution by Age [Interviewees].

Age	Percent
Under 35	5.0
35–44	18.0
45–54	23.0
55–64	32.0
Over 64	23.0
Total	100.0

Table A.3. Percent Distribution by Cohort and Race [Survey Respondents].

Cohort	Race	
	White	Black
Before 1985 (I)	58.0	42.0
1985–2002 (II)	42.0	58.0
Total	100.0	100.0

Note: Percentages may not sum to 100 because of rounding.
Source: Survey of Doctorate Recipients.

v. Regents of the University of California decision. The final cohort begins a period of dramatic shift from some of the earlier support for affirmative action (see, for example, *Wards Cove Packing v. Atonio, Martin v. Wilks, and Hopwood v. Texas*) (Higginbotham, 1998; Wilson, 1996).

The quantitative data are derived from special data tabulations of U.S.-born African American and white males and females who earned the doctorate in chemistry before 2003 (see Table A.3). These data were provided under contract with the National Opinion Research Center (NORC). Because of small cell sizes for African American Ph.D. chemists for certain years and variables, confidentiality rules do not allow the data to be disaggregated by cohorts that align with the interviews. Therefore, survey data are aggregated into two cohorts: (1) before 1985 and (2) 1985–2002. More specifically, some of the potential more informative data would be derived from the sample. Most of these data had to be suppressed and could not used. These conditions to the low participation of African Americans at the doctoral level in chemistry. Nevertheless, the availability of these data provide some analytical insight into race and gender measures. The quantitative data are derived from two surveys contracted by NORC under contract with the National Science Foundation and other federal agencies: (1) Study of Doctorate Recipients (SDR) and (2) Study of Earned Doctorates (SED). SED is an annual survey designed to obtain data on the number and characteristics of persons earning research doctorates from U.S. institutions. Information includes individual's educational histories, funding sources, and post-doctoral plans. The graduate schools are responsible for submitting completed forms to be added to a larger historical record of doctorate-degree graduates – the Doctorate records File (DRF). The DRF began in 1920. The DRF contains data used to track the numbers of graduates in a particular field, educational and career paths, etc.

SDR is a biennial survey of science and engineering doctorate recipients who earned their doctorates from U.S. institutions. The sample is selected from the DRF.

This is the only source of national data on the careers of science and engineering doctorate holders. When appropriate and available, survey data are presented.

LIMITATIONS OF THE STUDY

Budget constraints did not allow for inclusion of a comparative sample of white interviewees earning their doctorates during the same period as the African Americans. The parameters of the population from which the interview sample was selected are unknown because the exact number of African American recipients of doctorates in chemistry is unknown for a variety of reasons. Specifically, data on U.S.-born African American Ph.D. chemists are not always available due to the inconsistencies in data collection, low response rates, and lack of disaggregation of data by race, gender and nativity. Further, anecdotal information is suggestive that some African American Ph.D. recipients may have chosen to assume a different ethnic identity (see Aguirre & Turner, 2001; Conyers & Kennedy, 1963), the number choosing to do so is likely remain unknown. Although the findings are not statistically generalizeable, they are more representative of the experiences of African American chemists than has been reported heretofore in the literature.